MW00810371

FIREARMS IN THE AMERICAN WEST 1700–1900

MARTIN PEGLER

The Crowood Press

First published in 2002 by
The Crowood Press Ltd
Ramsbury, Marlborough
Wiltshire SN8 2HR

British Library Cataloguing-in-Publication Data
A catalogue record for this book is available from the British Library.

ISBN 1 86126 488 7

Dedication
To Katie, for her patience and for being acting unpaid editor.

Acknowledgements
A book like this can only be written with the assistance and generosity of others, so I would like to thank the following people: my friend Roy Jinks for access to his extraordinary Smith and Wesson archives and for permission to reproduce some of his photographs. The Royal Armouries Museum, Leeds, for unlimited access to archive photographs of their extraordinary firearms collection, and Rod Joyce for his help. Also the following, in no particular order, who have all assisted with information or photographs of their collections: J. 'Jim' Lewis, Russ Young, Gary Williams, Barry Lees, Chris Scott and Nichole Herbert, and others who generously provided photographs at short notice. Also Tony Barton and Ginger for their interludes of very welcome silliness.

Wherever possible, acknowledgement has been given to the copyright holders of the photographs used but despite diligent research, in a few instances the original copyright holder has proved impossible to trace. The author will be happy to rectify any omissions if he is notified.

Typeface used: Times.

Typeset and designed by D & N Publishing
Baydon, Marlborough, Wiltshire.

Printed and bound in Great Britain by Bookcraft, Midsomer Norton.

Origination by Black Cat Graphics Ltd, Bristol, England.

Contents

Major A. Meyer, pictured with his Colt Revolving rifle in about 1858. There is little about him to indicate he is a serving member of the US Army. Photo courtesy of the US Signal Corps.

Introduction

America has always attracted adventurers, from the first Vikings through to the mass migrations of the nineteenth century. These early settlers were a hungry breed for many reasons, personal and religious freedom, land, work, opportunity or simply for the chance to succeed. From the time that the Pilgrim Fathers arrived on the East coast in the early seventeenth century, the opening of the continent was to see an era of the most extraordinary inventiveness, optimism and energy. However, it was the colonization of the Frontier, the land west of the Mississippi, that was to ultimately shape the destiny of the United States. The images of plodding lines of pioneer wagons, bearded prospectors, saloon girls, cowboys, Indians, gunfighters and lawmen have become a fundamental part of the American psyche, and have been successfully exported round the world.

Yet despite 200 years of American history, it is this brief frontier era which lasted only from the early 1860s to the late 1880s that has become America's most idealized myth. While it was certainly a pivotal period, both politically and socially, many modern firearms' collectors and historians have a tendency to ignore the earlier years and talk in terms of American firearms' as beginning and ending with Samuel Colt and Oliver Winchester. Of course, this is nowhere near the truth, for the basis on which were laid the successful mass-production techniques of the nineteenth century had evolved from the development of rural gunmaking from the early eighteenth century. To ignore this fruitful period is to tell only a part of the story of a firearms' manufacturing industry that was to become the biggest and most efficient in the world, challenging even the English gun trade. It would enable America to become the most powerful nation in the world by the twentieth century. The men who set out on the monumental Lewis and Clark expedition in 1804 were to see a land virtually untouched by mankind, except for largely nomadic bands of stone-age native Indians. Yet from the time of the first movement west by organized parties of pioneers two decades later, the destruction of this untouched landscape was already in sight and it was to take a frighteningly short period of time, about an average lifetime. Most of this change was accomplished by one specific tool – the firearm. By the 1880s, the 'Wild West' had almost been civilized out of existence. The buffalo had gone and with them had also gone the way of life of the native Indian tribes, aided in no small part by political duplicity, double-dealing and sheer military brute force. The vast expanses of the West had been conquered by railways, telegraphy and cattle ranches, and the Mid-West was dotted with homesteads and clapboard towns. Even law and order, of a sort, was being exercised and criminals were finding it increasingly difficult simply to vanish into the vastness of the prairies and mountains. The firearms used went from primitive musket to sophisticated high-velocity breech-loading repeating rifles using smokeless powder in about the same period of time. By the late 1890s, the last Indian resistance had been crushed and the modern automatic pistols had begun to appear, appropriately signalling the death knell of the traditional six-shooter and, prophetically, the end of both an era and a way of life.

The history of these years spanning the settlement of the last truly wild region in the North American continent also charts the history of the development of the firearm, both as a military weapon and a working tool. There is no doubt that the sheer inventive genius of American manufacturers contributed materially to this explosion of technology but it should be remembered that most Americans were immigrants, who had brought their skills from Europe. Certainly much of the technology that enabled the American firearm to develop was adopted, adapted and improved from European firearms. Firearms' development in America owed a great debt to Europe, a fact that is often forgotten, particularly by Hollywood. Huge numbers of firearms were imported into America from England and the Continent and they formed a crucial part of the American armoury throughout the two centuries of colonization. That said, the subsequent inventive genius of manufacturers such as Creamer, Deringer, Hall, Sharps, Whitney, Colt, Winchester and literally hundreds of others cannot be underestimated.

It would take several volumes to cover in detail every manufacturer who sold or produced firearms in America during this period – to give some idea of the scale of production, in the 1860s there were over 300 manufacturers in the Connecticut Valley alone. Out of practicality, I have concentrated on the firearms that were the most interesting and important technically, although not necessarily always the most successful, and the manufacturers behind them. In addition, I have used as many contemporary accounts as possible to give glimpses of the lives of the men and women for whom the musket, revolver or rifle were as necessary a part of their lives as the clothes they wore. I hope the end result is as interesting as the lives they led.

1 Smoothbores: Muskets and Shotguns

The importance of the smoothbore musket in American history has been much undervalued, so completely has it been overshadowed by the rifle. However, these early longarms provided the main means of hunting and defence for generations of settlers, hunters, farmers and adventurers. The musket was a simple weapon, easily mastered with the minimum of instruction. It was not particularly accurate, having an aimed effective range of about 80yd (75m), but it was adaptable, capable of being loaded with solid ball, shot or a popular combination of both that was to become known as 'buck and ball'. Even in the hands of an inexperienced shot, such a loading was devastating at close range and for over 100 years more muskets were to be found in homesteads, sod cabins, farms and hunting lodges than any other form of firearm. And despite its limitations of range and accuracy there was no denying that the musket, for all its faults, was a very useful firearm to have.

The earliest settlers on the East coast of America in the seventeenth century had arrived bringing heavy, European matchlock muskets with them. These large-calibre, muzzle-loading smoothbore muskets, typically with a bore of .75in or larger, were little different from the military muskets of the period, and had hardly changed in form since the sixteenth century. They were little more sophisticated than a hollow iron tube, mounted on a simple wooden stock and ignited by a smouldering match. Many were very heavy-barrelled, and required a forked rest to take the weight of the barrel for firing but they were effective enough, particularly against native tribes who had never before encountered firearms. Samuel de Champlain, a French adventurer who set out on a punitive expedition into Indian territory in 1609, was armed with a light matchlock which he sensibly opted to load with buckshot. It proved very efficient when his party were attacked by Iroquois.

> I marched on until I was within thirty yards of the enemy … when I saw them make a move to draw their bows upon us, I took aim with my arquebus and shot straight at one of their chiefs, and with this shot two fell to the ground and one of their companions was wounded, who died thereof a little later. I had put four bullets into my arquebus. The Iroquois were much astonished that two men should have been killed so quickly, although they were provided with shields made of cotton thread woven together, and wood, which were proof against arrows.[1]

While the matchlock was effective enough, it had its limitations, the main one being the match itself, which was awkward to use, unreliable in bad weather and more crucially, almost impossible to substitute for anything else when it ran out. So it was fortuitous that, in the mid-seventeenth century a new and radical improvement occurred in the field of firearms' design in Europe. It took the form of the invention of a perfected flintlock mechanism, most likely by a French gunmaking family from Lisieux, named le Bourgeoys. Some time between 1610 and 1620, they perfected a mechanism not unlike that of a tinder lighter, that was able to strike sparks using flint and steel. It was a vast improvement over the old matchlock system and by the 1650s it was becoming commonplace for both sporting and military use. Small numbers had begun to arrive in America in the hands of Dutch settlers and Russian and French fur trappers and some East coast gunmakers had begun to copy them. Initially, these muskets took the form of the typical military weapon of the early eighteenth century. They were fully stocked to the muzzle, with long barrels retained by steel bands, but they were not ideal for use in dense woodland and poor accuracy limited their use. Spanish adventurers had, of course, penetrated many decades before the *Mayflower* reached the East coast and as a result many Spanish muskets with their uniquely styled miquelet locks had found their way into Spanish Colonial America, although their use was mainly limited to the South and South-Western United

Davy Crockett, wearing early frontier garb of buckskins and moccasins. He has a shoulder bag containing bullets and patches and a horn powder flask. He carries a fully stocked octagonal barrelled musket.

States. They were mostly well-constructed arms and some saw use during the Mexican War of 1836, whilst others were occasionally to be found in the hands of warring Apaches and other southern tribes.

By the early years of the eighteenth century, a more practical American form of musket was appearing that mimicked the style of some of the popular German guns. These muskets were shorter with heavy octagonal or half-octagonal barrels and with both fore and rear sights. When firing a carefully patched bullet they could give tolerable accuracy out to 100yd or even 150yd (90–140m). This gave them some capability as hunting guns while still retaining their useful ability to fire any mix of ball or shot that the shooter desired. There was a serious drawback with the smoothbore, however, and it was one that had tested the ingenuity of inventors and gunsmiths since the introduction of the musket. The use of an undersized ball meant that on firing, a large proportion of the propellant gas escaped past the ill-fitting bullet and simply vanished into the air. This was known as windage and it drastically affected the ability of any smoothbore to fire a projectile at any reasonable velocity, which in turn severely limited its range. The poor fit between bore and bullet also meant that the bullet bounced down the barrel like a golfball being fired down a large drainpipe. When it left the muzzle it could be heading off at almost any conceivable angle, which was why aimed range of the musket was limited to a poor 80yd (75m) or so. It was a problem that was not satisfactorily resolved until the mid-1840s, but it could be partially alleviated by using patches. These were a small piece of cloth onto which the ball was placed before being rammed down the barrel. This acted as a crude but fairly effective gas seal, improving range and accuracy. Contemporary accounts talk of friendly shooting matches using small iron skillets as targets at a range of 150yd (137m), which is an impressive distance for accurate shooting with a smoothbore musket. Flintlock muskets were purchased in large numbers from Europe, and the British gun trade supplied thousands to America.

Many of these guns found their way into the hands of native tribes, who had very quickly learned to use the white men's firearms and trade muskets became a common currency. A good musket could be exchanged for almost anything that the Indians had and the European men wanted – furs, gold, land, even on occasions, women. The Indians became adept at telling the difference between poor quality European muskets, and good quality British or French ones. A British trade musket by Tatham could be worth $6 in trade, a Belgian copy half of that. But it was not only muskets that found their way to the new continent, for the blunderbuss was not uncommon. The muzzle size of the blunderbuss actually made little or no difference to the shot pattern, being designed simply to facilitate easy loading. Although generally regarded by many as something of a joke, facing the gaping muzzle of one at close range was anything but a laughing matter. Their usefulness was certainly not lost on some explorers who made a point of carrying them, such as Manuel Lisa, who explored the upper reaches of the Missouri in 1811 and noted that he carried 'two brass blunderbusses

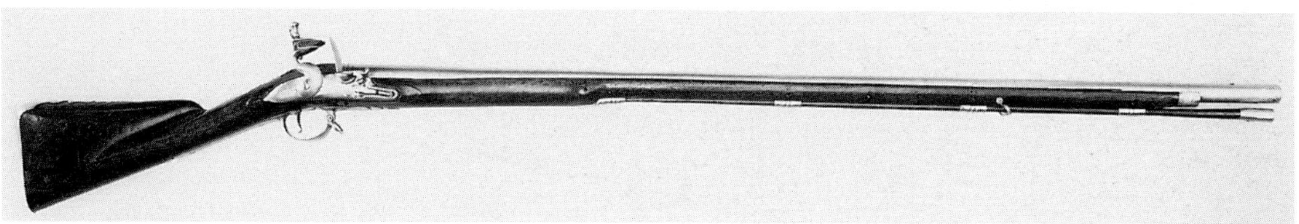

An English-made sporting gun, based on the military Land Pattern Musket in .75 calibre, circa *1790. Private collection.*

in the cabin [which] are absolutely necessary from the hostility of the Sioux'.[2] The situation had not changed very much fifty years later.

By the 1820s, the percussion or cap-lock had begun to appear in increasing numbers. Its development is looked at in greater detail in a later chapter, but it was a pivotal technical advancement, which enabled many old flintlock muskets to be cheaply and effectively converted to percussion, giving them a new lease of life. Smoothbore flintlock muskets had been the mainstay of most European armies but by the 1830s were gradually becoming surplus to military needs. As a result, large numbers were sold out of service for export to what would now be termed 'third world' countries, and this included the United States. Late in the nineteenth century many American gun dealers held large stocks of surplus muskets – in New Orleans in 1850, at least one dealer was advertising for sale '2,500 muskets in splendid order' and Horace Dimick, one of the foremost gunmakers, was listing as late as 1854 '400 *surplus muskets'* for sale. The demand certainly existed for firearms, as the tendrils of civilization began to creep inexorably west across the Missouri, and naturally English gunmakers took full advantage of this trade, producing a very wide variety of military-pattern and sporting muskets as well as fowling guns for the burgeoning American market. Generally, though, the long-barrelled fowling pieces with their lighter construction did not prove as popular, for their purpose was too specific. If the demand for smoothbores in Europe was dwindling, America was certainly proving a very lucrative market for them and many otherwise obsolete firearms were shipped across the Atlantic.

A considerable quantity of these were destined to be used as trade guns in the profitable business of trading with the native Indians. Having learned very quickly the power of firearms, the eastern Indian tribes had taken to them with, what appeared to the settlers, indecent haste. For centuries, Indians had had little option but to close to within bow range of their quarry, be it bear, deer, bison or human. This was fraught with danger and they appreciated, possibly more so than the white men, the possibilities

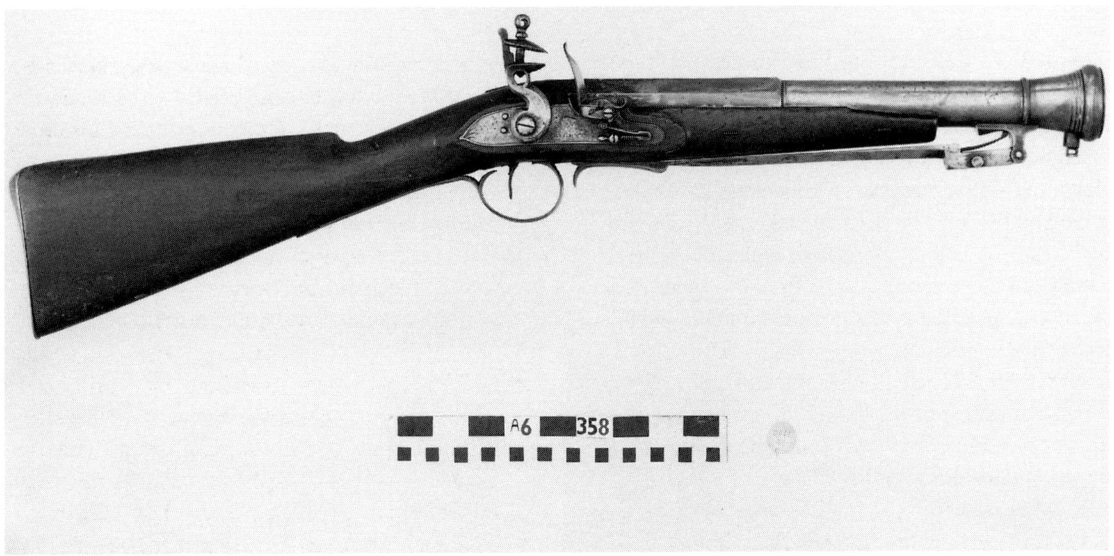

A flintlock blunderbuss of 1820 by Rigby, with spring bayonet underneath the barrel. Courtesy of the Trustees of the Royal Armouries.

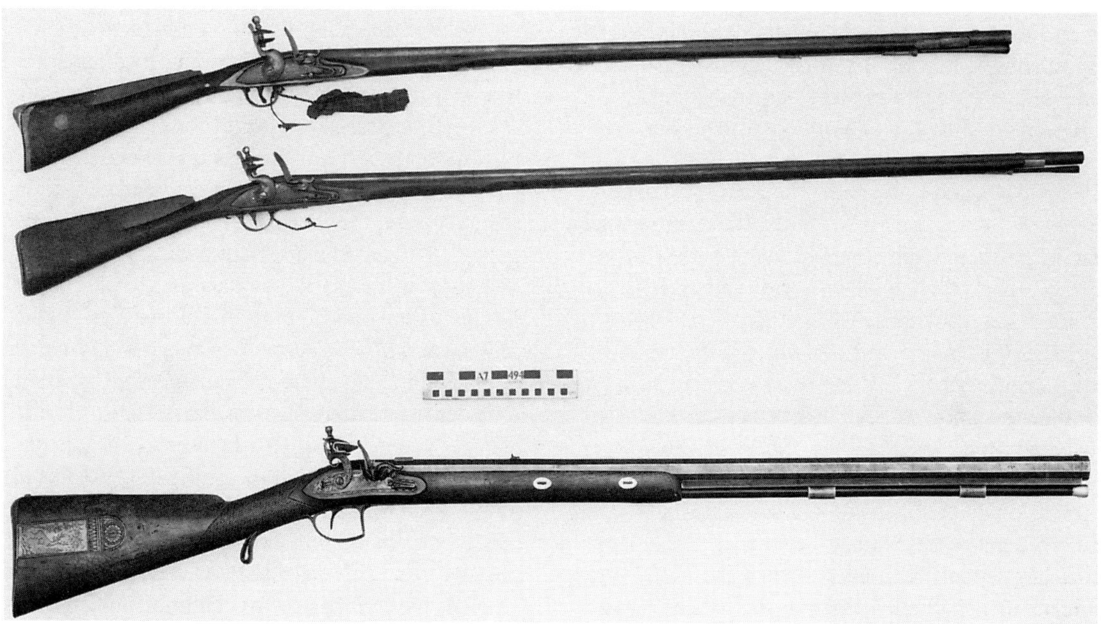

(Top) Two flintlock trade guns. The top example is a typical musket manufactured for the East India Company about 1796. The lower musket is an unmarked English gun of the type commonly traded with Indians. It has a 49in barrel and is in .65 calibre. Private collection.
(Above) A trade rifle by Tatham. This was one of a number of rifles specially made as presentation pieces. They are of above average quality. Courtesy of the Trustees of the Royal Armouries.

presented of being able to kill from up to 100yd (90m) away. By the time Lewis and Clark headed up the Missouri in 1804 there was already a well-established gun trade with tribes such as the Gros Ventre, Mandans, Sioux, Pawnee, Wichita and Comanches. In the South-West, the Apache had traded guns with the Spanish and Americans. Indeed, so well acquainted were they with the firearm that in 1795 a visitor to an Omaha village noted that the Indians preferred English guns to French, because they knew the French ones 'burst in their hands'. Many of these guns had been traded with French or Russian trappers but considerable numbers came from the British in Hudson's Bay. Many of these muskets were what was to become known as 'Northwest' guns. They were a distinctive style, with octagonal breech, fully stocked to the muzzle and retained by pins in the manner of military muskets. They had flat brass buttplates, often removed by the Indians as they made a quite excellent hide scraper, and large brass trigger-guards that did not cause hindrance to a gloved hand. Most importantly from a selling point of view, they had a serpent-shaped sideplate on the left of the stock, opposite the lock. Some had been fitted to British military muskets that had been sent to the colonies at the very end of the seventeenth century, and the serpent was considered a vital sign of quality by the Indians. This inevitably led to much fakery in the trade; several hundred muskets were imported from Belgium bearing fake English 'Barnett' lockmarks with brass serpent sideplates. In the late 1880s, an Indian on a Canadian reservation was photographed wearing a treasured family heirloom, a necklace made of brass serpents taken from trade muskets. These trade smoothbores were long-barrelled, between 42 and 46in and of between .42 and .50 calibre. Sad to relate, there appears to be no truth at all in the old tale that a gun could be exchanged for a stack of pelts high enough to reach the muzzle. If it were, gunmakers would undoubtedly have been manufacturing 70in barrels. As was so often the case, English guns were preferred, particularly those by Ketland, Tatham, Barnett and others. The English guns were, for the most part, very strongly built and in the 1830s at the very twilight of the flintlock period, these trade muskets were being sold for about $10 to $15 each to the government by the gunmakers. Many Indians were injured or killed as a result of being traded substandard muskets but they had long memories, often wreaking fatal revenge on traders who returned. In the early trading years, the flintlock smoothbore guns were initially all that were available to them as trade or stolen guns, but they understood very well the difference in accuracy between a smoothbore and a rifle. When the American Fur Company were offered smoothbores as trade guns, the local agent replied that:

> The smoothbored 'rifles' will not suit us. The more we reflect upon it the more we are satisfied that they will not answer at all for our Indian trade. When the Indians use a rifle, it must be a real one, and they will not carry a smooth bore of such weight.[3]

It is interesting to note that the Indians were not always enamoured of the smoothbores, generally expressing a preference for the rifle. In some respects it was a curious anomaly that the Indians preferred the more modern technology of the rifled barrel over the smoothbore. For the very specific purpose that they required a gun, predominantly killing for survival, the rifle actually offered few advantages as Indians rarely fought at long range, preferring to close with their quarry. Nevertheless, although any firearm was better than none, Indians would replace a musket with a rifle if the opportunity presented itself, but they did not express the same preference for the new percussion mechanism. As late as 1853 one Indian trader sent a note to a gunmaker stating that 'no percussion locks [were] wanted this year'.[4]

Even when the percussion mechanism was in common use, Indians still preferred the flintlock for its ease of maintenance and ready availability of flints. Percussion caps may have been more efficient, but the musket was useless if caps could not be obtained. Not all American gun dealers were entirely honest in their dealings with the American public. Edward Meade of St Louis, having received a consignment of sporting muskets from the Birmingham gun trade, proudly advertised in 1849 a number of 'Fowling pieces … with fine stub, Damascus wire and plain twist double and single barrel guns, made in England expressly to my order.' These were stock sales items, purchased from a British trade manufacturer called Turner, but this did not deter Meade from being a little economical with the truth, although this was common practice at the time. Aside from Indian trade, there were of course other uses for the smoothbore musket on the early frontier, one of which was hunting buffalo. Although they did not have the range of the rifle, these large calibre muskets produced terrific muzzle energy at close range and hunters soon learned from the Indians the trick of hunting buffalo from horseback using muskets. In a journal written in the 1850s, traveller Rudolph Kurtz described the process in detail:

> … the hunters do not use rifle-patches but take along several balls in their mouths; the projectile thus moistened then sticks to the powder when put into the gun. They do not carry rifles, for the reason that … the care required in loading them takes too much time … and anyway they find the rifle balls too small. The hunter chases the buffalo at full gallop discharges his gun, and reloads without slackening speed. To accomplish this he holds the weapon close within the bend of his left arm and, taking the powder horn, in his right hand, draws out with his teeth the stopper, which is fastened to the horn to prevent its being lost, shakes the prerequisite amount of powder into his left palm, and … closes the powder horn. Then he grasps the gun with his right hand, holding it in the vertical position, pours the powder down the barrel and gives

> the gun a sidelong thrust with his left hand, in order to shake the powder well [down] to the priming hole into the touchpan. Now he takes a bullet from his mouth and with his left hand puts it into the barrel, where, having been moistened by spittle, it adheres to the powder … Hunters approach the buffaloes so closely that they do not take aim, but lifting the gun lightly with both hands, point in the direction of the animal's heart, and fire.[5]

Although some hunters and trappers may have been content to rely on the old smoothbores, elsewhere on the frontier interest was increasingly turning to the rifle as a more practical firearm. It should be stressed though that in the years leading up to the Civil War, flintlock muskets still comprised the majority of longarms on hunting parties. Indeed, on the outbreak of the war in 1861, a number of backwoodsmen arrived at their regimental depots carrying their flintlock muskets, many of which were family heirlooms that had been bequeathed to them by their fathers or even grandfathers. At least one venerable farmer, named John Burns, turned out to fight at Gettysburg armed with a long-barrelled smoothbore flintlock sporting gun that dated back a century. He fought in the ranks, loading and firing his musket until wounded, and he subsequently became something of a national hero.

The only civilian to fight at Gettysburg, 72-year-old John Burns. The half-stocked sporting gun he used is next to him. Courtesy Library of Congress.

MUZZLE-LOADING SHOTGUNS

If the smoothbore musket was in gradual decline throughout the early eighteenth century, exactly the opposite was true of the second most widely used long gun, the double-barrelled shotgun. While the benefit of the musket was its ability to fire ball or shot, the double-barrelled shotgun, or 'scattergun' as it was widely known, had initially been viewed with disdain for any purpose other than taking game birds. In the latter part of the eighteenth and early nineteenth centuries, most American-made shotguns looked virtually identical to the military muskets of the period, being single-barrelled, fully stocked, and with round or sometimes half-octagonal barrels of anywhere between 44 and 46in in length. Imported double-barrelled English flintlocks were very popular as sporting guns, their shorter barrels, of between 30 and 36in, making them more practical for quick alignment on fast moving birds, and there was little doubt in the minds of the backwoodsmen and settlers that their more convenient size allied to their ability to fire two shots made them invaluable in wooded country.

The ball fired by a 10- or 12-bore shotgun was almost twice as heavy as that fired from a .54-calibre musket, and while it did not have the range of a well-patched musket ball, it was devastating enough close to, particularly if loaded with the 'buck and ball' combination of bullet and shot. By the turn of the century, the double-barrelled shotgun was gaining acceptance as a practical and economical gun and some American gunmakers had acknowledged this by starting to produce shotguns in the European style. The steadily increasing number of pioneers heading West in the 1830s brought with them a demand for more shotguns. They were more practical for those unused to handling a firearm and the poorest of shots could almost guarantee hitting a target at close range. William Hamilton, a plainsman who went West with a party of trappers in 1842, commented that the men used two large shotguns for night guard on their camp as 'they were the most effective weapons at close range, being loaded with a half-ounce ball and five buckshot'. This was proven the following year, when his party was attacked by Indians. The trappers, experienced enough not to waste ammunition:

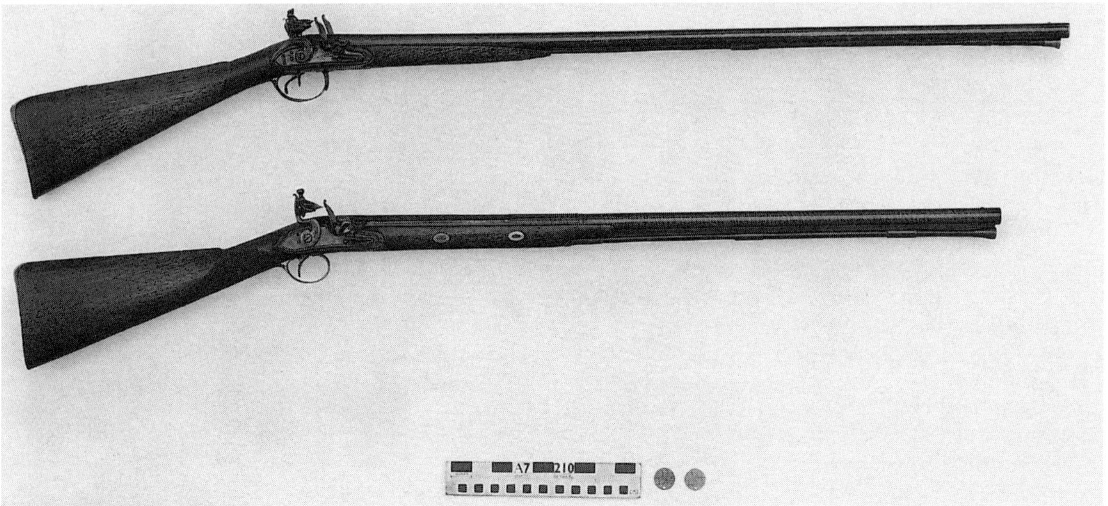

Top: a flintlock double-barrelled shotgun of early American manufacture, circa *1790. Beneath is a single-barrelled smoothbore sporting gun retailed by Meade of St Louis. Private collection.*

> ... held our fire until the [Indians] were within seventy-five yards, and then opened up. Almost every shot counted. Many Indians fell from their horses and ponies fell pinning their riders. Then seven double-barrelled shotguns poured in their fire on the Indians who had halted ... the shots created havoc ... and they fell back, leaving many wounded.[6]

An English adventurer, John Palliser, who spent several years roaming and hunting in the West, wrote a book on his experiences, in which he gave some hard-earned advice for travellers on the subject of firearms, and shotguns in particular.

> The most valuable and indispensable is the plain, smooth-bore double-barrelled gun, about fourteen or twelve to the bore. Let it be made by a first rate maker ... for in a country where there are no gunsmiths to run to ... the breaking of a trigger or the failure of some screw of inferior metal or workmanship may involve the most serious of consequences. For close and dangerous shooting I know nothing equal to the double-barrelled smoothbore gun. You can load it more rapidly and handle it more quickly ... than any other, also ... sufficiently depend on it for accuracy as far as sixty or seventy yards.[7]

The loading procedure for shotguns was no different from that of a smoothbore musket. The powder charge was poured down the barrel, followed by a felt or card wad, then a charge of shot and another wad that were firmly rammed down with the ramrod to ensure the shot and powder were properly seated in the breech. Although many shooters carried their powder and shot separately, it had become increasingly popular to use paper cartridges of a type similar to those used in muskets, where powder, shot and wads were pre-prepared. The loading of shotguns had been improved still further by the invention by Eley Brothers in the late 1820s of a patented wire mesh cartridge – a method of loading that speeded up the process considerably.

Throughout the early 1800s, American gunmakers began to manufacture the shotgun in increasing numbers, and production was boosted by the introduction of the percussion lock that simplified manufacture and made the guns more

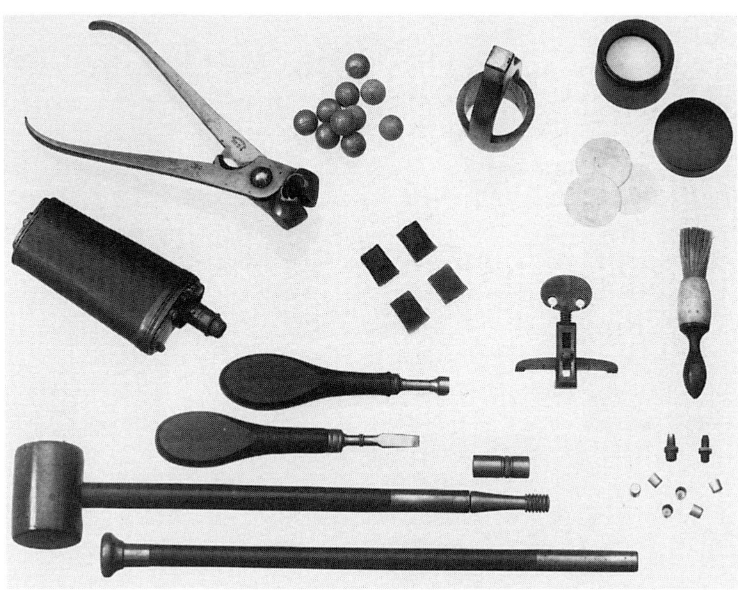

Tools typical of those carried on the Frontier for use with a flintlock or percussion musket. Clockwise: a flask, mould, bullets, punch for making wads, pan brush, spring-clamp, spare nipples and caps, cleaning rod and small mallet, turnscrews and in the centre, spare flints. Courtesy of the Trustees of the Royal Armouries.

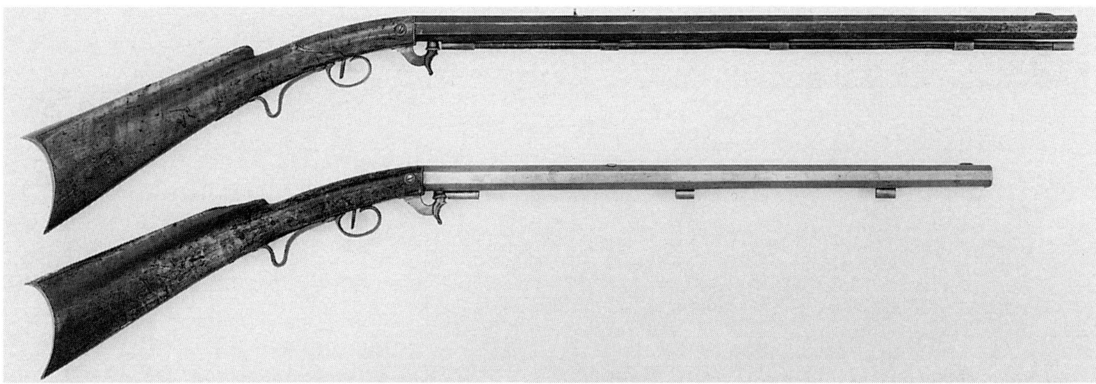

Two underhammer percussion rifles. The upper rifle is a 'buggy' rifle by Nicanor Kendall of Windsor, Vermont, in .42 calibre, the lower is a Smith's Patent in .38 calibre. Courtesy of the Trustees of the Royal Armouries.

affordable. In 1840 a new, average quality imported shotgun would have cost as little as $10–15, a good American gun around $25 or upwards while a best British gun, by a top-quality maker such as Manton, would cost $80 or $90, a very considerable sum in those days. Their usefulness had not escaped the notice of many plainsmen and mountain men, who preferred their versatility and lighter weight. The famous scout and adventurer, Kit Carson, habitually carried a percussion shotgun made by a St Louis gunmaker, Frederick Hellighaus, believing it to be the best weapon for use in wild country. As a Plains rifle often weighed upwards of 15lb (7kg), and a shotgun was around 10lb (4.5kg), the weight saving meant that extra powder, ball or supplies could be carried. Throughout the 1840s, the shotgun started to take on a life of its own, with the old single-barrelled guns steadily being replaced by the double, and the plainsmen who were escorting the burgeoning numbers of settlers along the Santa Fe and Oregon Trails habitually carried them. The demand for these guns and many other types was being met by an expanding number of gunsmiths and retailers who purchased guns in large numbers at bulk prices from America, England, Belgium – in fact anywhere they could be sourced. Retailers such as Meade, Wilmot, Dimick, Albright, Curry and Goodrich all offered double guns to the masses who passed through the staging cities of St Louis or New Orleans on their way west. Such was the popularity of the shotgun that even the august *New York Tribune* noted in 1855 that gentlemen in buggies were 'almost invariably armed with double-barrelled shotguns', and these developed into a form of shotgun or rifle called 'buggy guns'.

If town-dwellers had little real excuse for carrying a shotgun, then the same could not be said of the ranchers and settlers who were gradually inhabiting the Western plains. Indian depredations were increasing, and no family could be assured that the friendly tribes with whom they had traded goods one week, would not be the hostiles who raided them the next. The uncanny ability of Indians to apparently materialize from nowhere kept the settlers on edge – not for nothing were Jim Bridger's words burned into many minds 'Wh'ar ye don't see no Injuns, thet's whar they're thickest'. One pioneer woman recounted how her mother fed a band of wandering plains Indians, while her son sat behind a blanket dividing the room off, with the family's shotgun across his knees.[8] *The San Antonio Herald* reported a rancher by the name of Bowles who beat off an Indian attack by the simple expedient of loading nine revolver balls and thirty buckshot into *each* barrel of his shotgun. He killed two Indians and seriously wounded a third.[9] There is no doubt that the percussion shotgun, in larger

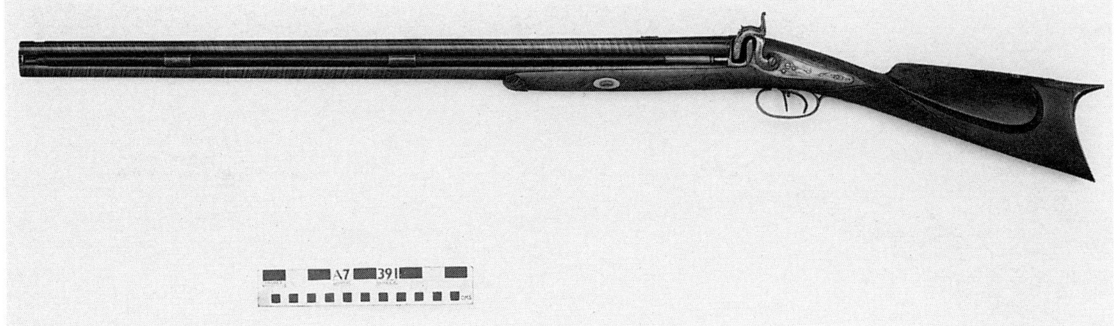

An American manufactured over-under double-barrelled percussion shotgun, maker unknown, circa *1850.*

bores such as 10 or 8, was certainly a formidable weapon for close work. These large guns were fine for delivering substantial charges of shot against birds but suffered from the usual problem of inaccuracy at the sort of ranges that most game in the West needed to be hunted. There was, however, one game animal that these mighty shotguns could be used against with great effect and that was the buffalo. Provided that a hunter had the nerve to gallop close up to the animal, the large lead bullet was deadly, as Francis Parkman recounted: '... we were badly mounted ... but by hard lashing we overtook them and Shaw, running alongside a bull shot into him both balls of his double-barrelled gun.'[10]

By the 1850s an American style of shotgun had become fully developed. This gun was not dissimilar to the English guns – fully stocked usually in walnut, with the barrel retained by metal sliders rather than pins making it quickly detachable, with an under-barrel ramrod. Their distinctive external hammers, with almost vertical thumb pieces, earned them the name 'hammer guns', and it was a term that remained in use for double shotguns right through until the early 1880s, when the first hammerless guns began to appear. An almost infinite number of barrel lengths and bores were offered, from 20in to 38in and from 20 bore to 8 bore. One Henry Boller was cautioned by seasoned travellers before he left St Louis not to bother with his lightweight shotgun but to exchange it for a large bore, heavier gun as:

> ... a heavy double smooth bore [is] a more useful gun than the rifle, adapted to a greater variety of game ... hunters out west prefer a double shotgun that will carry a bullet ... the rifle is only used for long ranges and very accurate shooting.[11]

No one could have predicted the chain of events that would follow the discovery of gold by a prospector named James Marshall in January 1848. The gold he found at a small creek near Sutter's Mill in California was to herald the biggest goldrush ever witnessed. Gold fever swept across the country and men of all ages, professions and temperament were seized with the desire to 'Go West' and make their fortunes. Within a month, San Francisco was reported to be a ghost town with three-quarters of the male population having left to stake claims in the goldfields. Some idea of the scale of immigration can be seen from the fact that 30,000 men had gone to California by the end of 1849; by 1851 another 100,000 had followed and a further 50,000 in 1852. These figures do not include the foreign immigrants – some 50,000 Englishmen and 25,000 Chinese[12] arrived and they all needed clothing, feeding, equipping – and arming. Many, bearing in mind the amount of supplies and equipment they needed to carry, elected to buy pistols, but a goodly number heeded the advice given by seasoned travellers to carry a shotgun.

Sir Richard Burton, an eminent and unconventional Victorian explorer, was as experienced with

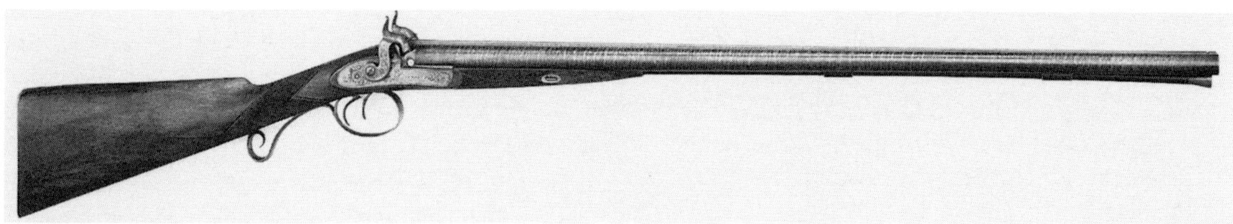

A St Louis-made muzzle-loading double-barrelled shotgun, carried by a pioneer party to Oregon in 1852 and kept by the family ever since. Private collection.

firearms as any man alive, but recalled in his memoirs being taken to one side prior to leaving for a visit to the goldfields, by an old mountain man who warned him to take great care when travelling through Indian territories. He later wrote that he was strongly advised to take a double-barrelled shotgun loaded with buckshot, and he clearly believed the advice to be sound, for he subsequently carried a 26in barrelled double, which he stated 'if Indian fighting was in prospect, the best tool without any exception [is] a ponderous double barrel, 12 to the pound [12 bore] and loaded as fully as it can bear with slugs'.[13]

There was no shortage of retailers to sell the guns to the willing gold-seekers and an understanding of their needs was evidenced by the fact that makers of ammunition, such as Eley, were producing an increasingly large range of projectiles for the shotgun. Not only the famous patented wire cartridges, but also solid slugs were available in ball, conical bullet and even flat-nosed form. As with any endeavour that brought large numbers of humans together, lawlessness and violence broke out. The sprawling mining camps had no official law and disputes were often settled quickly and violently. *The Denver Rocky Mountain News* reported in 1860 that a fight between 'Doc' Stone and Lew Bliss was settled at close range, both men using double-barrelled shotguns loaded with one-ounce balls. Bliss is recorded as having emerged the victor, having presumably shot his opponent Stone dead. There was also a growing breed of criminals politely referred to by the newspapers as 'road agents', or less politely by everyone else as outlaws, who were becoming increasingly prevalent, preying on travellers, prospectors – in fact anyone who may be carrying anything of value. Many were heavily armed, with braces of pistols, but most also elected to carry shotguns, generally with cut-down barrels, not, as is often thought, because of the short range at which they were used, but simply because of practicality. A short-barrelled or 'sawn-off' shotgun was easy to conceal, light to carry and quick to point, the length of the barrel not in fact making very much difference to the spread of shot, that was typically one foot of spread for every inch of barrel length. There was always something deeply menacing about having the twin railway tunnels of a 12 bore pointing at one's chest and it soon became the favourite of many outlaws such as Montana's Henry Plummer and his gang, whom settler Bill Herron bumped into. He noted that their hitched horses had 'their dreaded shotguns on the pommels of their saddles'.[14]

The camps and settlements that had sprung up had, by the early 1850s, begun to form their own 'system' of law and order, comprising vigilante groups, answerable to no-one, who were judge, jury and often executioners. The group that Herron joined, comprising seventeen men in total, were all armed with shotguns and such groups were becoming more common in the wake of the rising tide of lawlessness. US Marshalls were appointed, but they were too few and the area they covered too huge for them to make very much difference. In his story of life on the early Frontier, James Chisholm commented that the level of lawlessness in the city of Cheyenne in the early 1860s had become so bad that:

> … the vigilantes are abroad and there may soon be the necessity of putting the city under martial law. I am roaming with the US Marshall of the territory … and we each have to keep a double barrelled shotgun at the head of our couch ….[15]

Technically, by the 1860s the percussion shotgun had become about as refined as it was possible to be. European manufacturers were working hard to supply the guns needed on the rapidly expanding Frontier, where demand was in danger of outstripping supply. Not only was this demand emanating from the gold territories of the West, but back East increasing numbers of settlers were heading westwards to make their own luck in California or settling on the vast prairies where, it was rumoured, a handful of wheat thrown carelessly on the ground would sprout into a bushel virtually overnight. In actual fact, these pioneers were not necessarily well acquainted with guns and it is a curious anomaly that the use of firearms in early America was nowhere as widespread as history would have us believe. Certainly, from the earliest days of settlement on the James river, it was a requirement that every freeman own a gun to protect himself and his dependants, but recent research is disproving that the mass of early settlers were expert marksmen who carried a gun as a matter of course. Of 1,000 probate records checked between 1765 and 1850, nowhere is a firearm mentioned among the minutiae of household goods listed. In fact only 15 per cent of the wills list a firearm of *any* sort, the research suggesting that less than 10 per cent of the American population owned guns prior to 1850.[16]

For Easterners heading West the obvious choice was either to take the heirloom Revolutionary War musket from its place over the fireplace or to opt more sensibly for a practical shotgun, with the choice from the better supplied and wealthier dealers being enormous. American makers such as Parker, Stevens and Evans, English guns by Manton Purdey, Greener and Mortimer, as well as German, Belgian and French guns all lined the racks of the gunshops and the choice for the prospective buyer was almost overwhelming. A large gun dealer in St Louis could stock up to twenty different makes of shotgun at prices to suit all pockets and tastes, from $15 for a cheap import to $300 or more for a cased English gun. There the percussion muzzle-loading shotgun might well have stagnated had technology not yet again moved ahead in the shape of a simple invention called the pinfire.

BREECH-LOADING SHOTGUNS

For years, gunmakers had looked to breech-loading as a means of speeding up the loading process; indeed, there were breech-loading muskets in the sixteenth century. The problem with the muzzle-loading shotgun was the slowness of reloading. Pouring powder wads and shot down the barrel was difficult enough in ordinary circumstances, but to do so when your life was threatened required very cool thinking and a steady hand. Pre-formed cartridges were one answer, but they still needed ramming down and were easily damaged or deformed. In 1835, a French gunmaker and designer, Casimir Lefaucheux had patented a simple self-contained copper cartridge with an internal primer called a pinfire. He had also patented and manufactured a double-barrelled breechloader, whose barrels unlocked and swung downwards on a pivot, exposing the open breeches. It is a system familiar to almost everyone today, but then it was quite revolutionary. A decade later, another Frenchman, named Houllier, further improved the pinfire cartridge into its perfected form, which was a simple copper cylinder, open at one end and filled with gunpowder and capped by a conical bullet, with a short brass or copper pin protruding at right angles from the base. When struck by the hammer, the pin was pushed down onto an internal percussion cap that exploded, firing the cartridge. By the early 1850s, the pinfire was as refined as it was ever going to be and was increasingly being adopted for sporting guns and pistols and for shotguns in particular. But a new use for the shotgun had appeared in the momentous war years between 1861 and 1865. Apart from a few men who enlisted clutching much loved muzzle-

General Crook in Arizona in the 1880s. He habitually carried a sawn-off double-barrelled shotgun, visible here on his saddle pommel. Arizona Historical Society.

loading shotguns, the use of the shotgun was virtually unknown in warfare. This was to change because of a gradual shift in cavalry tactics away from their traditional use as a battering ram to defeat infantry. In the face of ever-increasing accuracy from rifles, such tactics were proving suicidal, so cavalry was used more and more for reconnaissance, hit-and-run raids behind enemy lines, and skirmishing. Although they were heavily armed, the cavalrymen had little use for weighty infantry muskets, or even sabres. They armed themselves with pistols, sometimes as many as four or more, rifled carbines – or shotguns. The shotgun had a much shorter range than a carbine, perhaps 40yd (35m) as opposed to 300yd (275m), but a cavalry skirmish hardly ever involved the need for comparatively long-range, accurate shooting. Mostly it was hand-to-hand combat, or snap-shooting at fleeing infantry, for which the shotgun was perfect. Many were very short-barrelled, typically 18in, but with buck and ball charges could deliver a devastating short-range blast sufficient to hit several men.

The main problem was that once fired it was well-nigh impossible to reload a shotgun on horseback during combat, so the introduction of the breech-loading system had great advantages and a number of pinfire types saw action, although the majority used were ordinary muzzle-loading hammer-guns. At least one sawn-off double gun was recovered after a skirmish with Confederate troops, the barrel of which was faintly engraved 'Purdey'. After the war, there was renewed interest in breechloaders and some enterprising American gunmakers began to produce their own. The main problem was that the market was saturated with surplus military firearms and there was even a thriving trade in reaming out and shortening the barrels of rifled muskets. The woodwork was cut down and a small German silver bead sight soldered on in place of the standard blade foresight. One of these 'reconstituted' shotguns could be purchased for as little as $4 and they represented excellent value for money. Even the cheapest quality imported Belgian or German guns were double the price, so for huge numbers of rootless veterans, for whom the lure of the golden lands of the West was a powerful incentive, these cheap muzzle-loaders were ideal, and they purchased them by the thousand. In the post-war years, many gunmakers began to look to the new breech-loaders as the way forward and Lefaucheux's idea had been quickly taken up by the English gun trade. Within a few months makers such as Lancaster, Daw, Needham and Westley Richards had all produced lever-latching breech-loaders. Initially, interest in these new guns was lukewarm in the West; after all, the muzzle-loaders had proved their reliability time and again, were simple and tough, and more importantly, didn't require expensive cartridges that could not be easily reloaded.

The Civil War had seen some extraordinary advances in firearms' technology and the commercial sporting gun manufacturers were not slow to recognize these changes. One of the most far-reaching had been the use during the war of the rimfire cartridge, which had a fulminate priming compound in the rim of its copper case. It was reasonably effective for medium-calibre rifles and pistols, but did not lend itself well to being manufactured in large-calibre shotgun sizes – the rims and bases had to be made quite thick to prevent them rupturing on firing, which caused a number of problems with reliable ignition. The invention of the centrefire cartridge was to change firearms' design forever. The earliest cartridges had begun to appear around 1868 and one of the first makers to produce a workable shotgun was Daniel B. Wesson, of later revolver fame, whose fine 12-bore breech-loader was patented in 1867. It used a thumb lever latching mechanism and was built to compete with the best English guns, but it suffered from the same problem as most American made breech-loaders of this period – that is, it was expensive, the price of a basic gun being $250. Both Eli Whitney and Ethan Allen had patented breech-loading pinfire mechanisms about the same time, which were later modified for centrefire cartridges. The Allen used a simple double-width breechblock that was hinged on the left, but it was expensive to make and retailed at over $100. The Allen was only a little cheaper at $70. As a St Louis reporter dryly commented in 1868 on this new breech-loading fad '[the use] of a breech-loading shotgun, which is a curiosity here, and which is valued at $300 awakens general comment …'.[17] Few of these guns stayed in production for any length of time – Wesson ceased production in 1871 and Whitney in 1874.

The war years had certainly given a boost to the British gun trade and many of the leading makers had been working on improving their guns and producing more effective breech-loading mechanisms. In fairly quick succession between 1862 and 1867, Daw, Purdey, Pape, Gibbs and Greener, amongst others, had patented breech-loaders for use with the new centrefire cartridges. Of the early post-war American manufacturers, only Parker Brothers of Meriden, Connecticut were to prove truly successful, producing nearly 240,000 shotguns from their inception up to 1945. Parker's had been a general hardware manufacturer in the early 1830s, producing such vital household items as coffee mills and waffle irons. Always with an eye to the future, Charles Parker had been very quick to adopt mechanical power and had a steam engine for manufacturing in 1844. Like many others, he entered the firearms' business as a result of wartime demands when his company produced some 15,000 contract Springfield muskets, the rights for which he subsequently sold to the Remington Company. After the war, he converted many of these rifles to single-barrelled shotguns. The Parker brothers, Charles and John, appreciated that this new technology had to be made available at an affordable price, so in 1868 they began manufacturing a double-barrelled centrefire gun that was both well designed and constructed. Most importantly, the basic model retailed for $50 and was available in 10,11, or 12 bore and a variety of barrel lengths from 24 to 32in. Special order models with engraving and choice stocks could be had, costing up to $300 – on a par with the best English guns. Parker's soon began to gain a reputation for reliability and value, and sales climbed steadily. These breech-loading guns also had the practical advantage of comparatively cheap ammunition with cases that were capable of being reloaded several times which, as always, was an important consideration in the remoter regions of the West.

The gradual expansion of the Frontier through the 1860s and 1870s did much to increase the demand for shotguns. The stagecoaches that plied the remoter routes between Western towns were a tempting target for outlaws. Many stages carried gold or cash and passengers were frequently accompanied by all their worldly wealth. Englishman Granville Stuart travelled across America in 1866 and made the pertinent comment that 'A party of passengers crowded into a coach have no chance against a few road agents armed with double-barrelled shotguns'.[18] This was a perfectly reasonable observation, and many bandits chose the shotgun out of preference to any other weapon.

One of the West's more colourful characters, Charles Boles, alias Charles E. Bolton, alias 'Black Bart', specialized in stage hold-ups, doing no less than twenty-eight using a sawn-off Loomis-made shotgun and it certainly served its purpose, for not once in that time did he ever actually resort to using it. Many said that he never even loaded it in case someone got hurt, and certainly the 6-year sentence he received when he was caught seems to bear this out, for it was extremely lenient. Bart was only the tip of the iceberg too, for in one month of 1877, Wells Fargo coaches were robbed 200 times and the stage drivers and guards were not slow to copy the road agents. Many of the larger stage companies furnished their men with shotguns. J. Morley who worked as a driver for the Wells Fargo Company in the late 1870s wrote that:

> We stage drivers were furnished with … sawed-off shotguns especially made in the East for the company. The shot-gun barrels were charged with 7½ grams [115 grains] of powder and loaded with 16 buck shot in four layers, with four shot to the layer.

Drivers and guards were always advised to remove the cartridges from their guns whenever they left the stage, to prevent them being used against them by opportunist thieves. It was not only the lawless who found the lure of the shotgun appealing, many lawmen appreciated the value of a sawn-off 12-bore. John H. 'Doc' Holliday habitually carried a Belgian-made double, with barrels cut down to just 12in (30cm), which, as one observer commented, 'made it whip like a rattlesnake' when fired. He carried the gun slung on a long leather strap over his shoulder and was reputedly faster with it than the best gunslingers.

After the famous OK Corral shoot-out in 1881, Wyatt Earp, no mean hand with a revolver, used a double to kill Frank Stilwell. Earp was carrying an issue Wells Fargo shotgun, with cut-down barrels, which he rammed straight into Stilwell's chest. He later described the shooting:

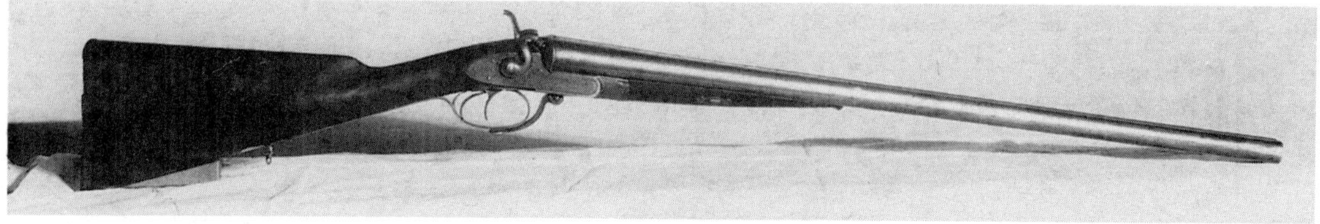

Gunfighter Ben Thompson carried this breech-loading hammer shotgun prior to his death in a shoot-out in 1884. Photo courtesy of Kansas State Historical Society.

> Stilwell caught the barrel of my Wells Fargo gun with both hands … I forced the gun down until the muzzle of the right barrel was just underneath Stilwell's heart … he found his voice. 'Morg' he said and then a second time 'Morg'. I've often wondered what made him say that. I let him have it. The muzzle of one barrel was just underneath the heart. He got the second before he hit the ground.[19]

At point-blank range, there was no question of the outcome of such an encounter.

Even Wild Bill Hickock, increasingly paranoid about the reputation he had acquired in Abilene as a gunfighter, took to carrying a double-barrelled shotgun with him. By the 1870s, many American gunmakers who had previously ignored the shotgun began to have second thoughts, and offered rifle actions converted to shotgun. This was not a new practice, Christian Sharps, Whitney and the Maynard Gun Company had all done it in the years prior to the Civil War, offering optional smoothbore barrels. In fact, the Sharps company had made more than 300 smoothbore breech-loaders from their M1853 rifles, and were to produce more based on the action of the model 1859. The ever-increasing demand in the 1870s had other, more established rifle manufacturers looking towards the new market. The well-respected firm of Remington had not been resting on its laurels either. They had been manufacturing excellent rifles for both military and sporting purposes, and decided to enter the shotgun market, initially by simply replacing the barrels on their Rolling Block rifles with smoothbore ones, in either 16 or 20 bore at a competitive $22. However, in late 1874, they began to produce a double breech-loading shotgun based on a patent taken out by Andrew Whitmore, sensibly calling the gun the Remington-Whitmore. As with many guns of this period, it borrowed heavily from British designs, in this case the long-suffering Purdey double underlug action, a snap-action using a locking latch above the breech that had to be pushed forwards. This system not only brought the hammers to the half-cock position but actuated a sliding underbolt that ejected the cartridges at the same time. It was available in several bore sizes, barrel lengths or even with one rifle and one shotgun barrel. This was not, in fact, an innovation as such guns, called 'drillings', had been very popular in Germany since the early nineteenth century. Indeed many had been imported into the United States where their useful combination proved an excellent practical compromise that many adventurers and hunters took a liking to. Theodore Roosevelt wrote of the drilling that he always carried '… the Winchester rifle, but in riding around near home … it is best to take a little ranch gun, a double barrelled No 16 with a 40-70 rifle underneath the shotgun barrels'.[20]

Remington followed up the success of the Model 1874 with the model 1882 double-barrel hammer gun, which was to remain in production for a comparatively short seven years, with under 8,000 being produced and they rapidly went through a number of no less than four 'new' models, the 1883, 1885, 1887 and 1889, none of which varied very much except in fine details. Remington were not the only manufacturer striving to make inroads into the shotgun market. For many years, Stevens had produced a large range of low priced pistols and small game rifles, but entered the shotgun market about 1872 with a small frame 14-bore gun which was soon joined by 12- and 16-gauge options. Within five years, Stevens had become a major force in the shotgun war with a very modestly priced but well-made breech-loading double gun that used an unusual trigger latch in front of the normal triggers, which allowed the gun to be broken open for loading. It was at $45, within reach of the average person and Stevens were to carve their own important niche in the market.

Meanwhile, the ammunition manufacturers had not been idle since the introduction of Eley's Patent Wire Cartridges. Improvements in the design and manufacture of centrefire cartridges had been going on through the late 1860s. One enterprising maker even produced a shotshell with a clear wad at the case-mouth, so illiterate shotgun owners could see at a glance what type of shot they were using. Suffice to say, that by the early

1870s most of the big ammunition manufacturers such as Eley, Colt, Union Metallic Company and Remington, were making Boxer or Berdan centre-primed cartridges that suited almost every make of gun. Although some continued to sell shotguns that only worked with proprietary cartridges, the gunmaking industry had, by 1880, settled into supplying guns for what had become the standard centrefire cartridge. It was not only the rifle manufacturers who had been eyeing the lucrative shotgun market, for one of the giants of American gunmaking, Colt, had also been looking towards expanding its share of the market. Colt were not, in fact, new to the shotgun business having produced a Paterson framed revolving shotgun early in 1839. It was never a commercial success and they are extremely rare today, but Colt did not entirely drop the idea and made another revolving shotgun in 1855. The trouble with all revolving long arms was their tendency, if loaded without sufficient care, of chain firing the chambers, sending a blast of shot straight into the left hand of the shooter. Wise owners held the guns underneath the cylinder, but it was not a design that readily lent itself to easy handling. In 1878, Colt abandoned the revolving rifle and produced instead a double gun based on the almost inevitable Purdey action, worked by a top lever and underbolt. It was, as could be expected, a very well-finished gun but the reality was that to compete on price with Parker, Stevens *et al.*, Colt had to import Birmingham-manufactured barrels and fit them with their own actions. This enabled them to undercut much of the competition, for their basic price was $50. Not everyone was thrilled with Colt's methods of doing business however, for at least one retailer wrote to Colt complaining that:

> The breech is not heavy enough … and the barrels not sufficiently tapering, the hammers stand up too high … also the price is high in comparison with English makers. The chief objection made by jobbers to American guns is that owing to the plan of lists and discounts, they cannot make a paying profit on them.[21]

Even the Sharps company, by then renowned for their large calibre hunting rifles, were still being tempted by the shotgun market so they took a leaf out of Colt's book, albeit going a step further, by having double shotguns manufactured for them under contract in England by Webley and Sons, the top ribs of which were trademarked 'Old Reliable', the generic term given to all Sharps rifles. Few were actually manufactured, probably less than 200, and Sharps wisely turned back to doing what they did best, manufacturing rifles.

One of the disadvantages of these hammer guns was the vulnerability of the hammers to damage. If dropped or knocked, the cocking piece of a hammer was easily broken off, and once this happened it made pulling the hammer back against a strong spring very difficult indeed. The solution, concealed hammers, had of course been around for many years. At least one British gunmaker, Henry Nock, had produced a hammerless enclosed-lock flintlock sporting gun in 1775 but the idea was not entirely appreciated at the time. Attitudes changed gradually and by the early 1880s there had begun a broadening acceptance of the hammerless shotgun. They had been popular in England and Germany for some years, having several advantages over the old hammer guns. Most obviously, they had self-cocking actions which worked as soon as the breech was closed on the cartridges. It meant that a gun could be carried with the action broken open, but the moment it was closed, it was ready for firing. Short pins, or indicators protruded from the rear of the breech to show that the weapon was cocked and a safety catch was usually fitted to prevent accidental discharge. Secondly, with no hammers to snag, the outline of the gun was smoother and they became easier to handle. Lastly there was no likelihood of shearing off the hammers or their spurs, thus leaving oneself with a gun that was virtually useless.

Colt were one of the first American makers to offer hammerless guns in 1883 but Remington, who had been producing excellent hammer guns, chose to ignore the new trend and continued with their traditional line of guns. They did eventually bow to demand and produced a hammerless gun in the shape of the Model 1894 which was a traditional break-open design available in 10, 12 or 16 bore, with an almost limitless number of grades, barrel lengths, special stocks, steel or Damascus barrels and engraving.

Other makers had also begun to appear, many having little experience in gunmaking and while some were to fall quickly by the wayside, others carved a niche for themselves in the market. There was also emerging a subtle difference between American and British-made guns. Prior to the Civil War, American industry had begun to lead the way in manufacturing technology, and post-war this gap had widened. Although the British and Continental firearms' industries had begun to adopt American manufacturing techniques, particularly for military arms, the traditions of fine hand-built craftsmanship still lingered in England. This produced a widening disparity between the prices of home-made and imported guns. The importers of British shotguns were keen to advertise the quality of their wares, frequently advertising them as 'superior quality', which may have been true in the 1860s but was barely true twenty years later. American makers had sprung up all over the country; Baker, Parker, LeFever, Lovell, Forehand and Wadsworth, American Arms, Ithaca, Harrington and Richards, L.C. Smith, Hopkins and Allen, to name just a few. All were producing well-made competitively priced guns that compared very favourably in quality of manufacture, finish and fit to the British guns. This narrowing quality gap was not lost on the buying public in America who, in the 1880s, were increasingly turning towards home-made shotguns for sporting or defensive use. After the Chicago Exposition of 1893, an engineer who had closely examined both types of gun reported the situation accurately. He stated that the difference between British and American shotguns was so minimal that, aside from the hand fitting of components:

Johnny Baker, trick shot with Buffalo Bill's Wild West show holding a smoothbore Sharps rifle that he used during his displays.

> ... which made British guns so expensive, 'in mechanical terms' ... the American guns are made almost entirely by machinery, which enables them to be sold much cheaper and in much larger quantities. The idea so long prevalent that close-fitting joints can not be made by machinery was demonstrated to be an error by many if not all of the American ... firearms. To show how finely fitted the joints of the working parts were, a pencil mark was made on some of the parts and so close was the fit that a single movement of the barrels completely removed it; this was on a gun taken from regular stock and not one specially prepared for the exhibition.[22]

Clearly, mass-production techniques were eclipsing the time-honoured methods of hand building, and Americans were happy with this. It was at about this time, that American gunmaking began to diverge from the mainstream of what were generally considered to be 'traditional' forms of shotgun, and to produce their own very singular designs, the repeating and pump-action guns. Despite the popularity of the double gun, there had always remained a big demand for the single-barrelled shotgun. Not everybody wanted the weight of a double, and singles, as well as being lighter, were simpler and more importantly, cheaper. Their downside was, of course, the lack of a second shot should the first one miss, and since before the Civil War manufacturers had looked at how to overcome this with some form of magazine or multi-chambered cylinder.

REPEATING SHOTGUNS

One of the few reasonably successful early designs had been the Spencer-Roper that had been patented in 1863. It used a wooden fore-end attached to a

A pair of Wells Fargo company guards, with a brace of double-barrelled shotguns, Model 1894 Winchesters and Colt Single-Action revolvers in their belts. Courtesy Wells Fargo Bank History collection.

sliding rail underneath the barrel, the action of which both loaded and cocked the mechanism, taking cartridges from a tubular magazine underneath the barrel. Once the first cartridge was chambered, squeezing the trigger fired it in the normal manner. Pulling back the sliding fore-end then opened the chamber and ejected the cartridge whilst bringing the sprung shell carrier into line with the chamber. Sliding the action forwards pulled the cartridge off the carrier, into the chamber and, once in its forward position, ensured that the breechblock was locked in place ready for the next shot. While cocking the firing pin was done automatically, the Spencer had the added benefit of a separate 'trigger' that could be used to re-cock the gun should there be a misfire. Although it appeared cumbersome, the motion required to load and fire one of these slide (or 'pump') actions was very fluid and in practice one could be fired almost as fast as the trigger could be pulled. There was, of course, the added benefit of a magazine holding six cartridges. It was to prove an enduring and peculiarly American design that was never quite accepted in Europe. Even in the twenty-first century, a gentleman is not generally accepted on the grouse moors or even at a clay shoot unless he is armed with a double gun. Americans, more generally concerned with practicality than etiquette, took to the new pump-actions like ducks to water and they became immensely popular. Before long, pump-action shotguns were being manufactured by makers such as Stevens, Remington and even Winchester.

Winchester had never really had much of a love for the smoothbore, their reputation having been built on their fine repeating rifles, but they had dabbled in the double-barrelled shotgun market with their Model 1879. This was not quite what it seemed, for they contracted out the manufacture to a number of English gunmakers, including C.G. Bonehill, W.C. Scott & Sons and W. McEntree & Co., all of the guns produced having their top ribs marked 'Winchester Repeating Arms Co'. Partly because of their quality and partly because of Winchester's name, these guns sold very well, some 10,000 being supplied. In 1884, they were discontinued when Winchester, impressed with the success of the new pump-action guns then appearing, looked more closely at the marketplace and decided to introduce their own singular design. This had been brought about by an invention of a lever-action shotgun in 1885 by the brilliant John Browning. Browning had always liked the concept of the pump action and believed it had great possibilities but Winchester, ever mindful of their reputation, were keen to base the gun on their tried and tested lever action. The result was the model 1887, that looked superficially similar to the Winchester rifle, with a tubular under-barrel magazine and combined lever action and trigger-guard, although its action

Wells Fargo Express wagon near Deadwood, South Dakota, around 1890. Two guards carry Winchester M1887 shotguns, the others have double-barrelled shotguns. Library of Congress photograph.

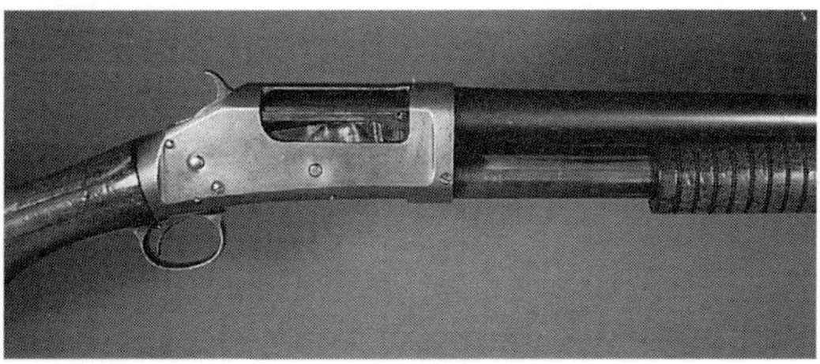

Winchester's popular Model 1897 pump-action shotgun. Courtesy of the Trustees of the Royal Armouries.

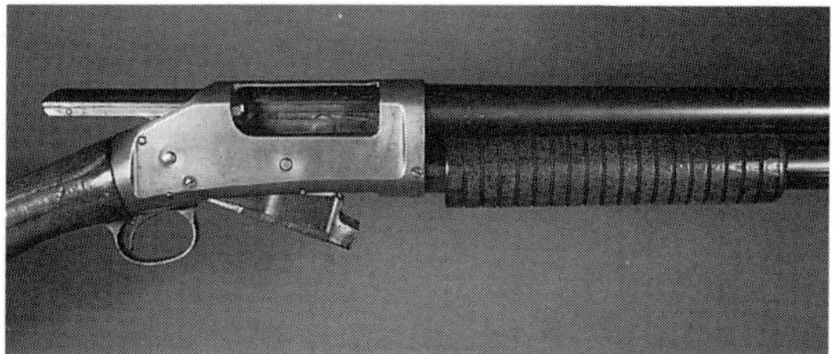

Winchester's Model 1897 with the action open. Courtesy of the Trustees of the Royal Armouries.

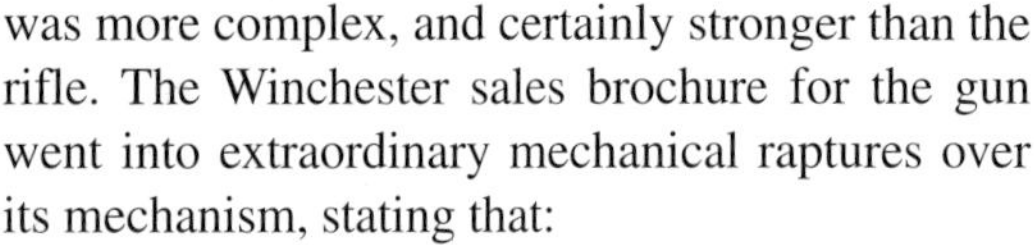

was more complex, and certainly stronger than the rifle. The Winchester sales brochure for the gun went into extraordinary mechanical raptures over its mechanism, stating that:

> The system contains sixteen parts in all ... The breech block and finger lever form one piece and move together in opening and closing. The hammer, placed in the breech block is automatically cocked during the closing motion; but can also be set at cocked or half cock by hand. The trigger and finger lever are so adjusted that the trigger cannot be pulled prematurely, and the gun cannot be discharged until closed. Anyone accustomed to shooting can readily shoot double birds with this gun.[23]

Some thought the new Model 1887 was not as easy to cock and fire as the pump-action, although in tests in New Jersey in early 1887 the Winchester proved marginally faster firing than the Spencer. It retailed in plain form at $30 and soon found many supporters who were familiar with the rifles of Winchester, and who trusted both the name and the engineering behind it. It was available in 10- and 12-bore and had a magazine capacity of five rounds, plus one held in the chamber. A year after it was introduced, John Browning, taking two years' sabbatical to perform as a Mormon missionary, saw a model '87 in a sporting goods store in Georgia. Curious, he and his Mormon companion went in and asked to see the gun. The ease with which he stripped and examined the gun aroused the curiosity of the store's owner, who enquired of his friend how this rather dishevelled Mormon seemed to know so much about a comparatively rare shotgun. 'Ah,' said Browning's friend, '... he ought, he invented it'. The disbelieving shopkeeper can hardly be blamed for promptly removing it from Browning's hands and putting it back in the window. Winchester introduced a new model in 1893, but unusually it proved to have mechanical problems, although this was due in part to stresses caused by the increasingly prevalent use of new smokeless powder cartridges that produced much higher breech pressures than black powder. The new gun was withdrawn from sale and work was begun on what was to become the benchmark for pump-action shotguns, the Model 1897, which was to remain in production until after the Second World War. The action of the '97 was reputed to be unbreakable and it became an immediate success, within a short time being offered in a wide range of options including Brush, Field, Pigeon, Riot, Standard, Trap, Tournament and even Military, with provision for a bayonet. The '97 was to become the mainstay of Winchester's shotgun manufacture, seeing the company through well into the twentieth century and beyond the Frontier era.

Although largely ignored by firearms' historians, who prefer the romance of the rifle and six-gun, the smoothbore, whether a single-shot flintlock or a multi-shot pump-action, played a fundamental part in the history of the West. It put food on countless tables, drove off wild animals, saved families from Indian attack and taught generations of youngsters how to handle and shoot a firearm with confidence and safety. The story of the West could still have been written without the shotgun, but it would have been all the poorer for it.

2 Muzzle-Loading Rifles

It is not possible to write about the development of the American rifle without looking at something of the pre-history of the longarm that was to become the most potent symbol of the American desire for independence. Since the colonists first took up arms against the English King, the rifle has become an icon for all that the United States stood for. It came to represent the fight against tyranny, the struggle for personal and political freedom. Even today in a surprising number of homes across America, an old flintlock or percussion musket hanging on a wall is talked of in terms of being a family heirloom as precious and revered as gold or silver. Regardless of its age, it will nearly always be fondly referred to as 'our revolutionary musket'. So why did the rifle become such an important tool in developing America? The entire purpose of the rifle can be summed up in one word, accuracy. The spiral grooves that were bored through the barrel enabled the soft lead bullet to grip the bore and impart spin on it, giving it a measure of gyroscopic stability. This enabled it not only to travel far more accurately to its target, but it had the added benefit of giving it a greater range than a bullet fired from a smoothbore musket, due to the close fit of the ball in the barrel. This, to a certain extent, overcame that scourge of the smooth-bore muzzle loader, windage.

By far the biggest obstacle in the path of widespread rifle manufacture was the sheer effort and cost of producing one. In an age when all manufacturing was done by hand, cutting the spiral grooves in a barrel was exacting, time-consuming and expensive. Of course, the rifle had come into existence long before the first settlers headed for the New World.

Its antecedents stretched back some two centuries, although no one is sure who invented the rifled barrel. The knowledge that an arrow with angled fletchings spun in flight and was more accurate was well known, so it was really only a matter of time before a gunmaker applied the same principles to a lead ball. By the late sixteenth century, there are many accounts of target matches using wheel lock rifles, whose ignition system relied on a winding mechanism and rotating serrated wheel in much the same manner as a cigarette lighter. They were expensive to make but far more reliable than the burning cord of the matchlock. It is easy to dismiss these early firearms as crude and ineffective, but one wheel lock shooting match in 1547 that was held in Mainz, Germany recorded that a member of the Sharpshooters' Guild, firing freehand, scored nineteen hits out of twenty shots in the bull's-eye at a distance of 200yd (180m). At a time when the average musket was incapable of even firing an aimed shot beyond 100yd (90m), this was impressive indeed.

While there were many benefits to rifling, it did create one added problem in that the more often a rifle was fired, the more black powder residue created fouling in the barrel, as this lodged in the grooves of the rifling. Thus it became harder for the shooter to ram the ball home and cleaning the gun became an urgent necessity. It was a problem that was never entirely solved during the lifespan of the muzzle-loading gun, and only really ceased with the introduction of breech-loading in the mid nineteenth century. To comprehend the ever-increasing demand for rifles, it is important to understand the wind of change that had blown across America following the arrival of the first pilgrims in the early seventeenth century. For decades, Americans had been fascinated by tales of a wondrous western land across the Appalachians. This land was, by all accounts, an earthly paradise, where game without number roamed freely and crops grew almost as fast as they could be planted. These rumours had been given credence by the amazing journey of Lewis and Clark, whose expedition to the Pacific Ocean in 1804–06 had opened a crack in the door that had, until then, been firmly closed to all but the most adventurous or foolhardy. They were quickly followed by Zebulon Pike, who travelled from St Louis to the foothills of the Rockies. The age of Western exploration began in earnest in the first decade of the nineteenth century, and was to continue unabated until the 1880s, by which time there was little left to discover and much of what had been discovered had been destroyed forever. The earliest mountain men, such as the legendary Jedediah Smith, had been trapping in the Rockies since the early 1820s and had no illusions about the weapons or equipment they required.

A contemporary account describes a fully attired mountain man as follows:

> His waist is encircled with a belt of leather, holding encased his butchers knife and pistols, while from his neck is suspended a bullet pouch securely fastened to the belt … and beneath the right arm hangs a powder horn transversely from his shoulder, behind which, upon the strap attached to it, are affixed his bullet mould, ball screw, wiper etc. with a gun-stock made of some hard wood, and a good rifle placed in his hands carrying from thirty five balls to the pound [.50 calibre] the reader will have before him a genuine mountaineer when fully equipped.[1]

Accounts by early trappers and explorers are frustratingly vague when it comes to the guns they carried. The term 'rifle' was often used indiscriminately and was frequently taken from the corrupted and broken English used by French, Russian or German trappers. In fact, the earliest known examples of rifles in America were those carried by the Russians, called *samopals*. These used a simple and early version of the flintlock mechanism known as a 'snaphaunce' and were generally long barrelled, up to 46in, and of relatively small calibre. The length of the barrel meant that they were frequently fired like the matchlock using a simple stick or forked rest to take the weight of the gun and steady the aim, a trick much copied in later years by buffalo hunters. The Spanish brought

A re-creation of the clothing and musket of a late seventeenth-century settler. His long-barrelled matchlock was aimed using the forked rest in the right of the picture. Powder was carried in the wooden bottles slung around his shoulder. Photo courtesy of Geoffrey Mayton.

'miquelet' rifles into the Southwest, but in comparatively small quantities and the French carried long 'fuzees', a corruption of the term 'fusil', at that time a commonly applied word that meant almost any long gun. Certainly the limitations of smoothbore muskets were very apparent to the frontiersmen who required a longarm for their livelihood and most vexing was the lack of accuracy at range. What the colonists needed were rifled longarms that could perform accurately out to 200 or 300yd (185m or 275m), were of effective, but not excessively large calibre, and were light in weight enabling faster target acquisition and less fatigue when being carried. The military pattern muskets were heavy and of course smoothbore, so the first colonists began to adapt the design to suit the specific requirements of the first traders and trappers who began to venture West, early examples looking very similar to the military pattern, although of smaller calibre.

In the middle eighteenth century, a more specific form of rifle began to appear that was to become forever associated with the pioneering spirit of the West. These longarms were variously referred to as Pennsylvania or Kentucky rifles and although broadly similar, different styles of rifle began to emerge from Virginia, Pennsylvania and a large area west of the Appalachians at the same time. These differed in almost every respect from the heavy, inelegant matchlock or flintlock military muskets that were their ancestors. Over a period of time, the two types have become so intertwined that it is now difficult for any but the expert to determine which pattern of rifle is which. Their calibre was reduced from the standard military .78 or .65in to a more compact average of around .40in, although this could vary widely from gunsmith to gunsmith, from as small as .30in up to .60in. Reducing the bore size enabled a number of improvements to be made. The barrel became thinner and lighter, there was less recoil from a reduced powder charge, and this enabled the stock to be slimmed down, saving valuable weight. The barrel was lengthened to aid accuracy, but this did have the unfortunate side effect of making the weapon more awkward to handle in a confined space. Most used maple or American walnut for their stocks, which had a distinctive and graceful curve, down to the buttplate that was noticeably indented to accommodate the shoulder. Almost invariably a patchbox, of the type found on the Jäger rifles was let into the right side of the stock and a curled brass trigger-guard, also a characteristic of the Jäger, was also typical. Some of the earliest examples of these 'long' rifles were made by a Maryland-born gunsmith called Philip Creamer who was, in the first decade of the century, living by the Mississippi River, supplying large trading companies with rifles. Other established Eastern gunsmiths began to take an interest in the demand for the Pennsylvania rifles, and makers such as Frederick Goertz of Philadelphia and Henry Deringer in Pennsylvania started to produce rifles in 1810, that were mostly sold through the Western trading posts.

Demand continued to grow, as a stream of easterners headed west. Lancaster County in Pennsylvania was to become the hub of the gunmaking industry in the first half of the nineteenth century with gunmakers such as Dickert, Gill, Gumpf,

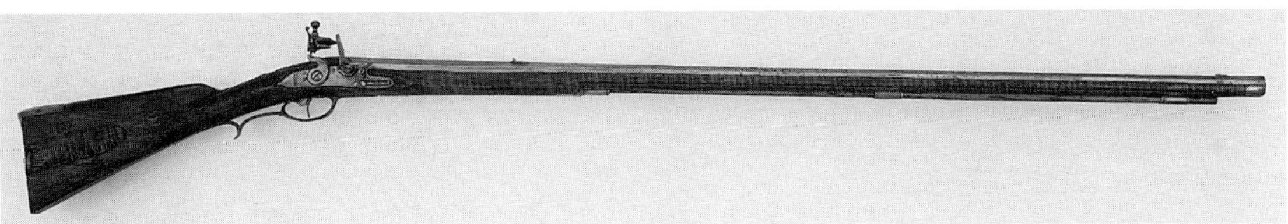

An early .45 calibre Pennsylvania long gun, maker unknown. It dates to about 1760 and is very similar in form to the military musket, lacking the later traditional curved stock. Courtesy of the Trustees of the Royal Armouries.

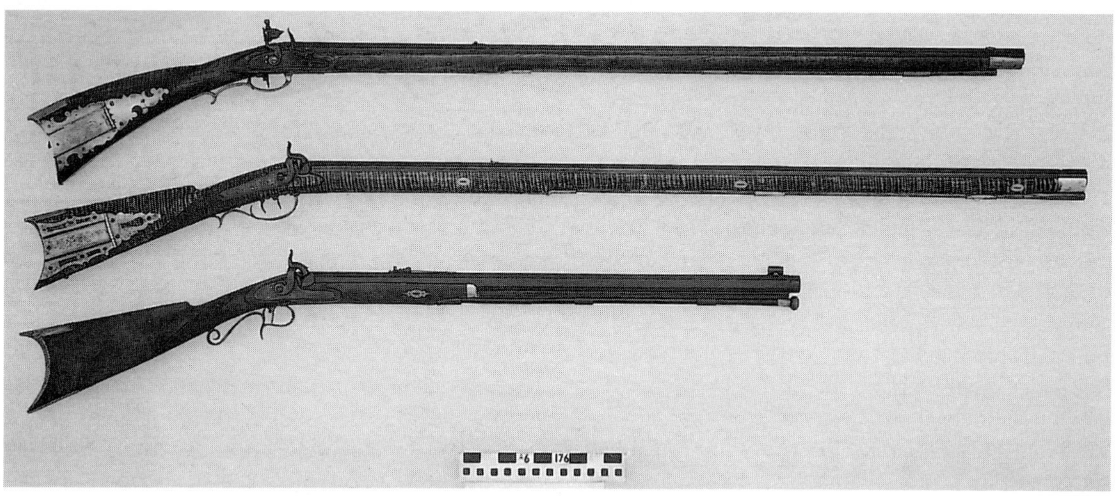

Three American sporting guns. Top: a rifle by Deringer showing the typical curved stock and brass patchbox. This is in .40 calibre. Centre: a fine fully stocked percussion Tennessee rifle with set triggers, in .53 calibre. Bottom: a percussion Hawken in .50 calibre, dating to about 1865. Courtesy of the Trustees of the Royal Armouries.

Brandt and John Henry producing large numbers of fine Pennsylvania rifles. In fact, Henry and Deringer began to dominate the market, trading heavily with the American Fur Company from the late 1820s onwards. To describe a Henry-manufactured rifle of this period is really to describe a typical Kentucky. It was a flintlock often incorporating a roller detent, a simple roller bearing on the frizzen or steel that gave smoother, faster ignition, with a barrel of between 42 to 44in and a calibre of between .49 and .54in. Its stock was maple or possibly black walnut and the brass buttplate was sharply curved for the shoulder. The patchbox and trigger-guard were also brass and the all-up weight of the rifle would be around 10lb (4.5kg). Interestingly, in view of the comments of frontiersmen like Ross, Henry rifles were generally made in a larger calibre than other Kentuckies, more similar to the Tennessee, but there were never any hard and fast rules about the manufacture of these rifles. The Tennessee was a slightly different form of the Kentucky rifle that had appeared around the same time as the Kentucky, but was generally carried by mountain men who came from the hill country of North Carolina, Virginia and Tennessee. Their rifles strongly resembled the Kentucky, but were generally of larger calibre, around .45 or 50in or upwards and of a plainer and heavier construction. The difference between these rifles may appear marginal, but was important as the Tennessee was to eventually evolve into a still more specific type of gun, the Plains rifle.

This gradual change was important, for it heralded the introduction of a new type of rifle that was moving away from the graceful long guns of the turn of the century and which was to hark back to the days of the early German Jäger rifles. A rifle designed for mountain or plains use had begun to evolve from the late 1820s, which reflected the specific needs of the mountain men and plainsmen. These 'mountain' or 'plains' rifles were shorter barrelled – between 36in and 42in, frequently octagonal and of between .48 and .55 calibre, with steel furniture and were being manufactured to order by American gunsmiths, particularly the Henry company in Nazareth, Pennsylvania.

The first mountain men and trappers had flourished in a period of over four decades when there was unparalleled economic expansion and bitter rivalry between the fur trading companies, who had made huge investments in the business, and for whom the rewards were equally huge. Powerful business interests such as the American Fur Company and The Hudson Bay Company were the global traders of their day, and wielded almost limitless power and influence. But from 1830, large numbers of 'free trappers' began working in the mountains, who owed no allegiance to the fur companies, but worked as independents. They were trapping very substantial numbers of animals and undercutting the big companies and this over-exploitation was to have serious repercussions that were exacerbated in the late 1830s by nothing more important than a shift in the public taste for fashion. Beaver fur was becoming too expensive due to over-exploitation, and Eastern fashion dictated that a man wore one of the new silk top hats that were all the rage in Europe. As a result, trade in fur went into a sharp decline, to the extent that in 1840 the last of the famous mountain men rendezvous on the Green River was held. After that, there was precious little living to be had as a mountain trapper and instead the trappers and hunters began to turn their attention towards the apparently limitless Western plains and their buffalo. For this, their light rifles were of no real use, and they needed a more robust and heavier calibre gun.

Although Pennsylvania was the traditional home of the earlier rifles, it was St Louis that was to become the centre for the manufacture of the new rifles. The man who was to play a fundamental part in its development was Jacob Hawken. Jacob had learned his trade working on early rifled muskets that had found their way West, in particular Kentucky, Pennsylvania's and the Model 1803 Harper's Ferry. This military rifled musket had been the choice of Lewis and Clark for their epic journey of exploration and it was unusual in that it broke with many of the traditional designs for military pattern muskets, and its design and construction interested Hawken. With the death of his first partner in 1825, Jacob joined forces with his brother Samuel who had already opened a gunsmiths shop in St Louis in 1815, supplying the demanding Missouri river trade, and between them they repaired dozens of Kentucky rifles and many Model 1803s. Nor were they alone, for a number of makers were then based in St Louis supplying the Western trade – Altinger, Brown, Jackson, Hoffman, LeBeau; indeed, by the early 1840s, there were some eighteen gunsmiths working in the city, all of whom produced good-quality rifles for the Western trade.

One of the problems faced by hunters and trappers was the relative power of these long rifles. In tests carried out in Arizona by *American Rifleman* magazine in the 1950s, it was found that an original rifle loaded with a .45-calibre ball produced an astonishing muzzle velocity of 2,410ft per second (fps). This compares quite well to a twentieth-century bolt-action military rifle such as the Lee-Enfield that propels its .303in streamlined bullet at 2,600fps. Other tests achieved lower but still respectable velocities of around 1,700fps and even at this lower velocity lead balls of .50 calibre fired from test rifles were able to penetrate ¾in of wood at 300yd (275m). Accuracy tests showed that a competent shot, armed with a Kentucky or similar rifle, could achieve on a regular basis, 2 or 3in groups at 100yd (90m) which, in practical terms, meant a near certain body hit at 300yd, which was impressive given the standards of the time. The problem was the speed with which the light round balls lost velocity. A .70-calibre ball weighed around 730 grains, a commercial .54 around 370 grains. Since much shooting was done on dangerous game, such as bear, mountain lion and large animals, such as elk and deer, the problem was simply the lack of penetration of the lighter calibre bullets. There are many references to this; an account by an early settler, Alexander Ross stating that:

> Observing the effect by guns of different calibres, it was found that the rifles of small bore [.40 to .43 calibre] very frequently do not kill although they might hit; while rifles from [.49 to .54 calibre] seldom missed killing on the spot.[2]

The dilemma for the frontiersmen was in finding a happy compromise, for lead is a heavy item to carry, and a smaller calibre meant being able to carry more bullets to the pound. If, however, they were of insufficient weight to kill, then this was negated by the number of potentially wasted shots. Plains' hunters and frontiersmen had lectured long and loud about the shortcomings of these rifles – their inability to take larger game animals, particularly buffalo, how the full length wood stocks warped in wet weather, affecting accuracy, and the problem of their length when on horseback. The brothers Hawken had patiently listened to these comments and quickly realized that combining the better points of the Harper's Ferry with those of the Kentucky would provide the basic blueprint for the type of rifle that was clearly wanted. As a result, they began to manufacture their own flintlock 'plains' or 'mountain' rifles. In their early form, Hawken later recalled that such good reports were made of the quality and accuracy of his rifles that 'every man going west wanted one'. A Hawken cost about $25 in St Louis, the price rising rapidly the further west one went. At least one customer, William Ashley, reputedly turned down $150 for his Hawken rifle while in the Rockies. The early Hawkens were fully stocked and not entirely dissimilar to the Kentucky, with barrels of between 42 and 44in in length, and of average calibre, .35 to .50in. A visitor to the Hawken gunshop in 1825 sold his rifle to buy:

> … a regular mountain rifle. This was of very heavy metal carrying about thirty-two balls to the pound [.53in] stocked to the muzzle and mounted with brass, its only ornament being a buffalo … looking exceedingly ferocious which was not very artistically engraved on the trap of the stock. [3]

This certainly mimics the ancestry of the Kentucky rifles, but post-1830 the Hawken rifle had begun to evolve into a more distinctive type, and became half-stocked, with a heavy round or octagonal barrel of some 38 to 40in and a calibre of .50 to .53in. The wood also changed, from the attractive curly maple to a stronger straight-grained maple or walnut with iron fittings. Gradually the distinctive patchbox was omitted from the stocks of these plains rifles as their owners preferred to carry patches separately, or even use pre-patched bullets; indeed the use in England of lead balls pre-wrapped in greased leather for hunting and target shooting was certainly common by 1800. Most of these rifles were fitted with slow twist rifled barrels. This meant that the machined spirals that comprised the rifling (the 'lands' and 'grooves') had a gentle rate of spiral up the bore, enabling the ball to grip the rifling as it moved along the barrel, rotating at a constant speed so as to leave the muzzle with a consistent rate of spin. Using fast [tighter] rifling meant that, particularly with larger powder charges, the ball could be propelled so fast that it simply failed to grip the rifling at all, resulting in very poor accuracy. Crucially it was also realized that although there was a weight penalty, heavy iron barrels markedly helped to damp out vibration created when the gun fired. This technology still holds true today, for most target rifles have far heavier barrels than their military counterparts. In expert hands a good Hawken was accurate to 300yd or possibly 400yd (275–365m) and the larger calibres were powerful enough to fell any animal likely to be encountered. Many other American makers quickly adopted the Plains rifle style. The cost of a Hawken was at the upper end of the home-manufactured price range, for a good Kentucky or Tennessee rifle would cost between $15 and $25, a large enough sum in the early nineteenth century. Nevertheless, the expensive imported English guns still accounted for about one-quarter of all the rifles sold in the United States at this time. British longarms had always had a reputation, mostly well deserved, for quality and craftsmanship. *The American Shooters Manual* even went so far as to state that 'The English are, without a doubt, the neatest and best gunmakers in the world',[4] and those who could afford them carried rifles by one of the better English makers. Not all English guns were of such high quality or as expensive and many English gunmakers manufactured perfectly good quality rifles for the Indian trade market, also selling them to the domestic market. Indeed, the quality of construction and reasonable price of most English

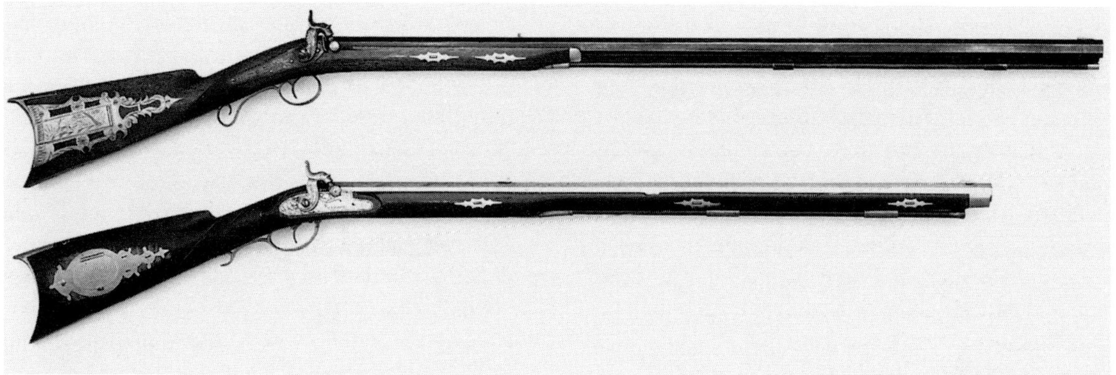

A British-made half-stocked long rifle circa *1850 with brass inlay and octagonal .54-calibre barrel, by Cooper. Beneath is a Hawken-type, maker unknown, with cut-down barrel and fore-end. Photo courtesy Lewis Collection.*

trade guns was good enough to appeal to many trappers and frontiersmen. Ketland, Manton and Tatham plus a dozen others found the trade with the expanding American territories very fruitful, selling their guns at prices comparable to those of Hawken. A typical English rifle differed slightly from its American counterpart, the most striking feature being the typical straight stock and flat butt plate.

The gracefully curved and very distinctive American style never appealed to the English sportsman, and it was this that always made an English gun stand out, although several makers did produce copies of Pennsylvania rifles specifically for the US market. For the most part, there was little difference in barrel length or calibres in the English guns. Barrels were browned, partly to protect the surface from rust and partly to give a better sight of the target. It had long been understood that a polished barrel would reflect light into the shooter's eyes, causing glare in bright sunlight and making target acquisition, with the small blade foresights then fitted, very difficult. Indeed, many shooters took to using lamp black to darken down their foresights. The barrels were normally round but occasionally octagonal and the guns were stocked to the muzzle with brass pipes, trigger-guard and buttplate. While brass was the most common material for fittings, steel had increasingly begun to replace brass from the 1830s. This was mainly due to practicality for, as one experienced observer commented in 1833:

> Rifle barrels should be stained in dark brown. Bright barrels reflect too much light for accurate vision, and are too easily seen ... for the same reason steel mountings are preferable to those of brass or silver.[5]

However good British guns were, it did not stop many English adventurers from acquiring American-made rifles, and Hawkens in particular. Even experienced explorers such as Sir Richard Burton, used to carrying fine English guns on his travels, appreciated the finer points of these plains rifles.

> For the benefit of buffalo and antelope, I had invested $25 at St Louis in a 'shooting iron' of the 'Hawkins' type – that individual now dwells in Denver City. It was a long top-heavy rifle, it weighed twelve pounds and carried the smallest ball – 75 to the pound – a combination highly conducive to good practice.[6]

Burton was unusual in using the smallest calibre rifles he could, firmly believing, with some justification, that accurate shooting was the key to killing anything. Unfortunately, not everyone had the consummate shooting skills he possessed, and most plainsmen, particularly those killing buffalo, felt that the larger calibres gave them an edge when it came to hunting or defending themselves against the Indian attacks that were a constant threat. Not that the frontiersmen were given to wasting bullets, for reloading a rifled musket was a time-consuming business, enabling no more than two aimed shots per minute to be fired. Indians were rightly wary of the accuracy of these rifles and, despite Hollywood's passion for depicting them riding in circles around corralled wagons like a fairground duck-shoot, Indians very seldom made frontal attacks unless they were in overwhelming numbers or believed their opponents to be poorly armed. Because of the danger from the native tribes, trappers invariably travelled together for mutual protection. Two men could alternately load and fire continuously, whereas one would be rushed as soon as he had fired his first shot. Jedediah Smith had graphic experience of this when attacked by a party of Mojaves in 1827. Between them his men had only five guns, and Smith wisely instructed that only three should be fired at any one time, and only then when there was a certain target, two being kept loaded and ready. That they all survived was proof of the wisdom of this strategy.

PERCUSSION RIFLES

By the 1820s, many American gunsmiths had begun to experiment with the new percussion system that had been largely perfected in England in 1807 by a pastor and part-time chemist, Alexander Forsyth, and had been steadily sweeping across Europe. It was to usher in a new era in firearms' technology that was to become the mainstay of firearms' industries around the world for the next forty years. It certainly had its advantages as there were serious drawbacks with the flintlock system. It worked poorly in the wind, which was never in short supply in the West and could actually stop the spark from reaching the primer or was often strong enough to blow the powder from the pan. Rain was a problem too, the powder in the pan becoming easily saturated and the moisture sometimes affecting the main charge as well. Carrying a loaded flintlock in poor weather meant that the likelihood of a misfire was high, flints had to be in good order to spark properly and needed regularly replacing and the frizzen would quickly rust in the wet, presenting a poor striking surface for the flint. This was certainly not what a hunter wanted when faced with 1,000lb of angry bear or a hostile native. The idea of using a fulminate compound to create primary ignition had been around for many years, descriptions of its properties going back to the mid seventeenth century. A number of inventors had lost vital body parts, or even their lives through experimenting with this very volatile chemical. In 1805, Forsyth came up with the simple idea of using a measured amount of fulminate to deliver an ignition flame down a hollow tube. Within two decades, a copper percussion cap containing a tiny charge of fulminate was in general use by sportsmen in Europe and America. The main advantage of this form of ignition was that for the first time, a musket could be carried loaded, and ready for immediate use in any weather. Once the cap was fitted over the nipple, the barrel was effectively sealed, and the gun could be fired by simply pulling the hammer from half-cock to full cock, and squeezing the trigger. American gunsmiths adopted the system with enthusiasm; although flintlocks continued to be used until the cartridge era of the 1870s. The percussion rifle was to become the mainstay of the hunter, traveller and frontiersman.

However, the introduction of the percussion ignition system was not wholeheartedly welcomed in America, for new inventions were often regarded with suspicion and not everyone embraced the new technology. The Indians much preferred the practicality of the flintlock despite its shortcomings and so did the majority of the pioneers heading west. One wagon train leader, John Bidwell, took several parties of emigrants across the plains in the early 1840s and his comments regarding flint and percussion locks are worth repeating.

> My gun was an old flintlock, but a good one. Old hunters told me to have nothing to do with cap [percussion] locks, that they were unreliable, and if I got my caps or percussion wet I could not shoot, while if I lost my flint I could pick up another.[7]

One of the main complaints about early percussion rifles was simply the problem of running out of caps when supplies could be weeks away, and the other was the efficiency of the caps themselves. Early caps were made in a number of forms, the most common resembling a tiny ribbed copper bucket. They were fiddly to handle, particularly with cold or wet hands, and their reliability could be questionable as the science of lacquering their insides to protect from damp was still somewhat hit or miss. A typical example was the experience of a hunter by the name of Sibley who was faced with a grizzly bear at point-blank range. He raised his new percussion rifle and pulled the trigger.

> Snap, snap, snap was all I could get … which no persuasion could induce to go off and O! that I should live to record the fact, the bear got away … Now my opinion is, that any man … who will not use a percussion, when he can procure one in lieu of a flint lock should be … furnished with a straight jacket at the public expense.[8]

By the mid-1830s, the percussion mechanism was making strong inroads into the firearms' market, and it was to lead to the development of the final Hawken rifle that was to characterize this type of plains rifle for evermore. Of course, most gunsmiths became very adept at converting the old flintlocks to percussion. This conversion was done by the simple expedient of boring a hole on the right side of the breech and threading a simple drum on to it. This drum had a nipple screwed into it and the flintlock cock was replaced by a hammer. The end result, if not pretty, was a perfectly functional percussion rifle. Many frontier guns received an extended lease of life through this conversion, as shown by the comments of a Santa Fe-based Indian trader:

> Many years before, a trapper … had taken it on a trapping expedition in the Blackfoot country. The Indians killed him and took his gun. Years later Messrs Bent, St Vrain and Company sent an expedition to that nation on a trapping and trading trip, and traded for the old rifle … At the fort it was restocked [full length] and altered from flint-lock to percussion, and kept at the fort for a target rifle for some years. In 1846 I had it newly grooved [rerifled], half stocked, and a new lock and breech pin, and have carried it in all my travels. In 1849 a man from Boonville, Missouri … came into the store when I was cleaning it up and said 'My father made that gun. There are his initials, it must be very old, for he has been dead many years.' This is the history of my old and trusty friend … Old Blackfoot, the name it was known by at the fort and which I have always retained.[9]

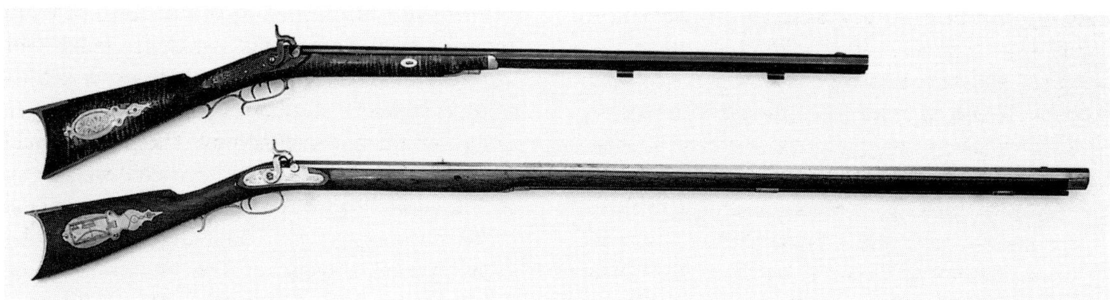

A half-stocked percussion conversion of a Hawken rifle, in .54 calibre, and a fully stocked Hawken plains rifle in .50 calibre by Golcher. Courtesy of the Trustees of the Royal Armouries.

Jim Bridger's Hawken plains rifle, circa *1850. Octagonal .54-calibre barrel with iron fittings and a lock by Gibbon. Photo courtesy Montana Historical Society.*

The basic Hawken rifle changed very little from the late 1830s to the early 1860s, retaining its maple stock, iron mounts and octagonal barrel that was usually around 36in long and of .53 calibre. Double-set triggers were invariably fitted, although not everyone appreciated them. At least one hunter, surprised by a bear, tried in vain to fire his Hawken by repeatedly pulling the wrong trigger. But Hawken's were by no means the sole suppliers of plains and mountain rifles. If demand in the West for the Pennsylvania and Kentucky had waned, the New England gun trade had not diminished in stature, and continued to produce a wide range of sporting percussion guns, even to the extent of supplying rifled barrels under contract to the Hawken brothers. In the East, Kentucky rifles were still being manufactured and Kentucky-made Plains rifles by makers such as Dickson began appearing west of the Missouri in the late 1830s. One of the most prolific of the Kentucky makers was Horace Dimick, who had left his home state and opened a shop in St Louis. These rifles were very close to Hawken's in appearance but he also manufactured very good-quality target rifles, sometimes using barrels supplied by other makers. That well-established firm in Pennsylvania, James Henry, also produced some very high-quality rifles, but also supplied many hundreds to the trade on contract, many of which were then sold under the name of the retailer. Large numbers of these guns found their way to Texas, then in a state of almost constant armed insurgence. Other gunmakers had moved West and established themselves in Oregon and California, and post-gold rush they found their services in heavy demand. On the goldfields, the 'forty-niners', short of everything, could and would pay large sums for the most basic of goods, and there are many instances of firearms being sold for four or five times their true value. One poker game ended with one miner owing another $80,000, for which he offered all his worldly goods, including his wife and Hawken rifle in payment. A commentator who clearly held a very practical outlook on frontier life, pointed out that while he could easily get another wife, where on earth could he buy another Hawken?

One of the more prolific manufacturers was Henry Leman of Lancaster, Pennsylvania. He had long been producing moderately priced guns for the frontier trade, and had begun to establish strong trading links with dealers in St Louis, and his fully stocked, simple percussion rifles were to see use throughout the West. The New York and New England gun trade were also busy in the fruitful years of expansion during the 1850s, and many Easterners headed west with guns by Hart, Tomes, Gillespie and a dozen others, mostly following the Kentucky pattern of medium-calibre rifles. As ever, the British gun trade continued to supply fine percussion rifles to those who could afford them although not everybody was able to acquire one in the manner that Granville Stuart did in 1858, swapping his Kentucky for a Westley Richards owned by a travelling companion named Jacobs. The 24in barrelled rifle fired a .65 calibre one 1oz (28g) ball, but weighed only 8lb (3.5kg). He commented:

> I tried the rifle and found it a fine shooter when enough powder was used and found that Jacobs used only half enough because he feared the recoil, which was tremendous, for it would turn me half-around to the right every time I fired it. We were ... in no danger of starving after I traded for that mighty tiger rifle. [10]

Perhaps fortunately, such punishing rifles were rare on the frontier, but the British could no longer consider themselves the masters of their art, for several American gunmakers had been looking very hard at manufacturing techniques and in particular experimenting with new methods of assembly. One such was Edwin Wesson, whose brother Daniel went on to form the famous Smith and Wesson company. Edwin had been manufacturing rifles of very high quality since the early 1830s and had been particularly interested in the accuracy produced by using different forms of rifling, experimenting with a new type of rifling, 'gain twist'. This used a slow rate of twist at the breech but it became progressively faster as it neared the muzzle, imparting a faster rate of spin and giving the bullet greater stability and accuracy. The levels of accuracy attainable were fast becoming a subject of great interest to a very specific group of shooters.

PERCUSSION TARGET RIFLES

It was not only the hardy trappers and plainsmen who used the rifle, for there had been a long tradition in the United States of target shooting, a tradition that stretched back to the days of the earliest settlers. There are many accounts of target shooting using flintlock smoothbores and rifles, although it should be said that it was not always the gun that was to blame for poor performance. In Pennsylvania, after a public shooting competition by the local militia, in which not one soldier managed to hit the target, the newspaper expressed some surprise, as it dryly pointed out that 'The size of the target ... was precisely the size and shape of a barn door.' The development of good rifled barrels allied to the introduction of percussion ignition gave considerable impetus to target shooting, and it became a popular sport across the country, where any form of sporting pastime was a welcome relief from the harsh life. Prowess in shooting had long been a fundamental part of the upbringing of many young men, especially in rural areas where the ability to hit a running squirrel or a deer made the difference between food on the table and being hungry. Turkey shoots, where the target was quite literally the head of a live turkey, had been popular since the mid eighteenth century, but the growing interest in firearms for recreational purposes had spread West with the Eastern emigrants. Gradually a new form of rifle began to appear in the 1830s – the bull-barrelled target rifle. These guns were primarily made for extreme accuracy in target shooting, and manufacturers such as Wesson, Marshall Tidd of New York, and Alvan Clark in Massachusetts had begun producing a very distinctive form of percussion rifle.

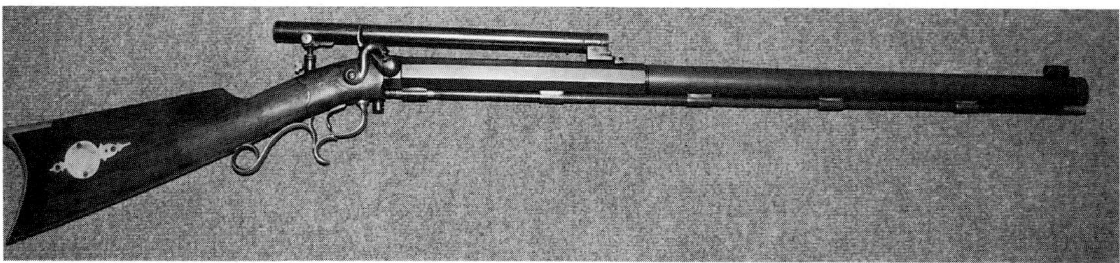

A fine .45-calibre target rifle made by Marshall Tidd of Woburn, Massachusetts with Wesson-made bull-barrel, made about 1850. The maker of the optical sight is unknown. Photo courtesy of Roy Jinks.

Typically they had extremely heavy octagonal barrels, which alone could weigh 15lb (6.8kg), heavily scrolled trigger-guards and lock mechanisms with a very short, smooth hammer drop. The complete rifles could weigh 25lb (11kg), and were not designed for shooting from a standing position. Despite their size, they fired relatively small calibre bullets, typically .36 to .45 inch. Neither were these projectiles the traditional spherical type but conical, or 'picket' bullets that, it had long been understood, were far more accurate than spherical bullets. No matter how carefully a spherical bullet is cast, it will never be uniformly dense and will always have a weight bias at some point on its circumference, that will inevitably lead to imbalance in flight, affecting its stability and ultimately, its accuracy. Conical bullets not only had a greater surface area for gripping the rifling, but rotated around their own axis, giving enhanced stability and better accuracy. This enabled faster twist rifling to be used to its full effect. There was a problem however, for the conical bullets were harder to load than ball. The ever-present problem of windage had to be avoided at all costs, so a patch was used but the flat base of the bullet made loading with a patch nearly impossible. As it engaged the rifling at the muzzle, the patch would inevitably tear and the faster the twist, the more likely this was to occur. If the patch were made thicker, it simply became too difficult to ram the bullet home without deforming it. The most obvious solution, flaring the barrel at the muzzle does not work for, as many rifle and musket owners discovered, any irregularity on the internal portion of the bore at the muzzle led to very erratic accuracy.

A simple answer to this was found by that master of the percussion sporting rifle, Alvan Clark, who arguably did more for the science of accurate shooting than any individual before him. He patented a tapered brass false muzzle in 1840. In his 'Essay' he explained:

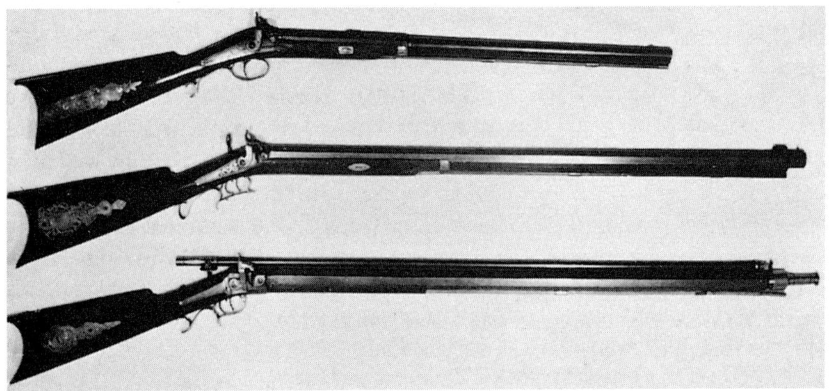

Three Edwin Wesson rifles 1839–49. Top, a short sporting rifle, while below are two heavy-barrelled target rifles, the lower having an early optical sight and false muzzle. Photo courtesy of Roy Jinks.

(Below) Whitworth rifle, with the long-range target rearsight fitted. Courtesy of the Trustees of the Royal Armouries.

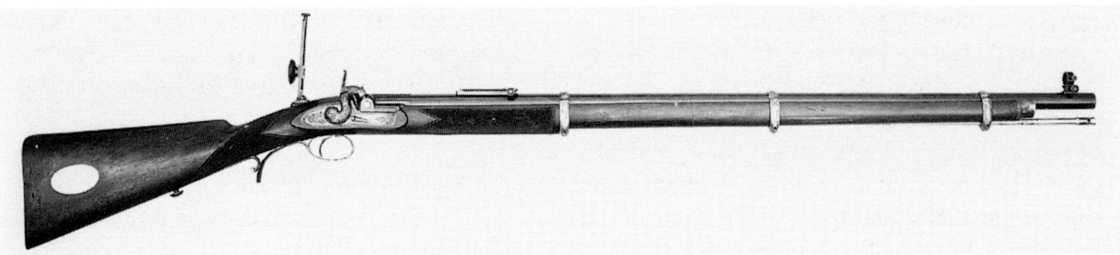

> I have always found it impossible to load sufficiently snug to prevent all windage, without either disfiguring the lead or cutting the patch, or both, unless it is done by enlarging the muzzle. To secure the patch from injury, and to facilitate loading as tight as can be wished … I have fixed upon the detachable loading muzzle. In using the gun, the operations of wiping and loading are performed through it, in which case it shields from wear that part of the gun [the muzzle] which must give direction to the ball. Passing through this tapering muzzle, the patch and lead are compressed to fit, and fill the rifling, and get a more fair and uniform bearing than can be obtained in the usual form of loading. After loading the muzzle is removed and in discharging, a very uniform delivery is effected.[11]

In conjunction with the false muzzle, Clark also used a bullet starter, a short length of brass the same calibre as the bullet, with a concave end into which the nose of the bullet rested as it was rammed into the bore. This ensured it was inserted parallel which was crucial to obtain the accuracy that was required, and these two simple inventions were to become standard accessories for any shooter looking for serious performance. Interestingly, Clark was probably the first gunmaker to understand and develop what was, a century later, to become known as the 'squeeze-bore' principle. He found, through experimentation, that by fractionally reducing the diameter of the bore towards the muzzle he obtained increased velocity and better accuracy. Certainly, his rifles were proof positive of his ability as a gunmaker, one test at 200yd placed twenty .40-calibre bullets in a 3 × 5in bull. Many of these target rifles were to find their way across the continent, and although their weight was a drawback, hunters and frontiersmen found that their accuracy and tough barrels outweighed that penalty. There was, however, a problem with these single-shot muzzle-loaders that was not to be solved until the production of the first repeating arms in the 1860s, and that was the difficulty of making a quick second shot. In the 1850s and after, these rifles were able to challenge the supremacy of the traditional English-made Enfield and Whitworth target rifles and they won a considerable following on the target ranges of America.

DOUBLE RIFLES

One drawback of the single-barrel rifle was the time taken to reload, and it was readily appreciated that in many circumstances two barrels were more useful than one, but the problem of building accurate double-barrelled rifles was much greater. In the past, there had been a number of attempts at manufacturing multiple-barrelled or single-barrelled, multi-shot rifles, usually using superimposed loads, the majority of which either discharged their charges simultaneously regardless of whether or not they were designed to, or simply did not fire at all. Besides, multi-barrelled guns were always heavy and cumbersome and reloading was a time-consuming chore. Double rifles were a good compromise, *if* the gunsmith was skilled enough to build one properly. For the gun to be any practical use, the barrels had to be perfectly harmonized, which in the days of hand manufacture required a skill of almost supernatural level. If they were not harmonized, the first shot may well hit the target, but the second could cross over or run wide. Neither did the double rifle have the range or accuracy of a single rifle. John Palliser, an English adventurer and hunter with considerable shooting experience, maintained that:

> … experience has indeed satisfied me that for a very long shot, you can never count upon the same precision with a double as with a single barrel … would not expect too much from it, or reckon that its accuracy of execution beyond one hundred and fifty yards is equal to that of a good single-barrelled rifle.[12]

This was not usually due to lack of ability on the part of the gunsmiths but was brought about by the conflicting stresses that existed in a double rifle. On firing the first barrel even-expansion of the steel was made impossible because it was firmly soldered to another barrel. This was a perennial problem for the gunmaker who had to compensate by using his skill, experience and a certain amount of trial and error. If this were not complicated enough, he also had to allow for differences in the type and thickness of the steel used in the barrels and also variations of calibre, for most doubles were of reasonably large calibre, of between .450in and .577in. Many rifles produced in the 1870s were chambered for the new, powerful Express cartridges, which only exacerbated the problem. Nevertheless, when properly built, a double rifle was an excellent gun. In his interesting contemporary book on American rifles of the period, A.C. Gould put the problem into a nutshell.

> There are but few gunmakers who can successfully accomplish it, and the cost is excessive … the makers of double rifles … are obliged to use the greatest care in putting the barrels together … in order to regulate the arm so as to have both the barrels shoot on the same line of elevation, as well as to keep the shots from crossing or shooting out. I have no doubt that no double rifle can have anything like the accuracy of a single shot and believe [they] do not possess accuracy enough for hunting certain game found in America.[13]

As a result of the labour-intensive production, double rifles of the type made by Alexander Henry, Rigby or Gibbs were indeed expensive, costing $300 or more if cased with all accessories, a veritable fortune in contemporary terms. Despite their rarity some did find their way into the West, brought over by European adventurers and hunters and there are a surprising number of accounts of doubles being carried and used. Francis Parkman in his engaging book on early life on the Oregon Trail, refers several times to English sportsmen and their double rifles:

> English sportsmen were well equipped for the journey … besides ammunition enough for a regiment … they had also … English double-barrelled rifles of sixteen to the pound [.66 inch] slung on their saddle dragoon fashion.[14]

It was not only the British who manufactured double rifles though, for a few American gunmakers had been making them since colonial days, and it is worth remembering that in 1777 the British General Simon Frazier had been killed by a bullet from a double rifle fired by Timothy Murphy. Boyer and Schuler in Pennsylvania made doubles and a number of Kentucky-based makers also produced variations on a theme, with the two barrels mounted side by side on the stock, but not joined together, thus obviating the need for very time-consuming harmonizing. Another variant was an old idea, long used on European flintlocks, of having an over-under barrel arrangement. This was in many ways an ideal compromise, for on firing the top barrel, a latch mechanism was released that simply allowed the second barrel to be rotated into the upper position. Regardless of whether it was a flintlock or percussion mechanism, the second barrel could be left primed or capped, and was instantly ready to fire. More importantly, it was easier for the gunmaker to harmonize the barrels, and the famous trapper and mountain man Jim Bridger was known to have carried a swivel percussion double rifle.

Unlike the double-barrelled shotgun, the advent of breech-loading was not to give the double percussion rifle the same lease of life and it was a technology that was to virtually kill off the double rifle in the United States. At best, these guns had been a compromise between the need for firepower and the practical realities of weight and cost, but the near simultaneous combined introductions of breech-loading and centrefire ammunition gave the impetus for an entirely new range of sporting longarms. These rifles were to be almost wholly identified with the opening, and ultimately the end, of the Frontier, and they were the breech-loading single-shot rifle.

3 Breech-Loading Single-Shot Rifles

Seldom is a technical innovation truly original. More often it is merely an old idea that over a period of time has been re-examined and improved upon in the light of newly available knowledge. It will surely come as no surprise to readers to know that working breech-loading guns were known to have existed in the fourteenth century, and there are records of 'guns with pots' (a removable, reloadable chamber) in the inventory of Edward III. These were most likely light hand-cannon rather than true handguns, but some 139 breech-loading rifles using an iron cartridge were held in the private collection of King Henry VIII in the sixteenth century. But why was there such interest in developing a reliable breech-loading system? There were several very good reasons, some technical and some simply to do with the properties of the gunpowder used in all firearms until the late nineteenth century. It is a substance that today would probably be near the bottom of a list of chemicals chosen as a good propellant for firearms. One of its many less endearing traits is the fouling it leaves behind in a barrel after firing which forced gunmakers to cast bullets undersized to permit easy reloading, thus causing windage with all of its associated problems. This was compounded by the increasing use of the rifle, whose grooved barrel accumulated fouling more readily and made loading physically even more difficult. Certainly the last thing any gunmaker wanted was to produce a rifle that had to shoot undersized bullets that failed to grip the rifling. There were other drawbacks with muzzle-loading, not the least of which was speed of loading. With the best will in the world, the fastest that a smoothbore musket can be loaded and fired is four shots a minute, and that was for military volley fire that required no marksmanship other than pointing the muzzle in the general direction of the enemy. Experienced shots such as trappers would hold lead bullets in their mouths and could exhibit considerable skill at rapid shooting.

> Captain Scott proposed to me we should take an old ... yager [Jäger] he had, and determine which could load and fire three shots in the shortest time. Captain Scott then took the rifle uncharged, with the powder flask at hand and the balls and patches in his mouth and he made three shots 'offhand' in one minute and twenty seconds. We ... found the three balls in one mass, all having passed through the same aperture of the [playing] card.[1]

Impressive though this was, such skill was exceptional, and under stress most men spent anxious seconds, that seemed like a lifetime, fumbling with flask, ball and ramrod. While it is quite feasible to lie down to reload a musket, it is a clumsy procedure and markedly slows down the reloading time. In practice, most men who reloaded a musket had to do so standing up in full view of their enemy, and to all intents they were helpless until they had managed to reload. The traditional method of carrying powder was in a flask of horn, although as the nineteenth century progressed, copper gradually took over. The copper flasks could deliver a measured charge, but the process of patching and ramming still had to be completed, and in the event of a misfire, removing the ball was a very time-consuming task, during which it effectively rendered the musket useless. Clearly it made perfect sense to be able to load a longarm from the breech, as this would solve all of these problems at a stroke and breech-loading produced its own secondary benefits. The bullet could be made a perfect fit for the bore, ensuring accuracy and much reduced fouling, as the tight fitting bullet effectively scraped the bore clean of the accumulated debris left behind by the previous shot. Speed of loading was vastly improved by the use of a combustible paper cartridge, of the type issued for use in military muskets. It was inserted into the chamber, the end torn to expose the powder ready for ignition by flint or percussion cap and any misfire was easily and quickly remedied. To give some idea of the capabilities of a breech-loading rifle, it is worth quoting a short extract of the demonstration performed by Captain Patrick Ferguson, with his breech-loading flintlock rifle in 1776. In front of an astonished Board of Ordnance:

> First he fired … at a target 200 yards distant, at the rate of four shots a minute. Secondly he fired six shots in one minute. Thirdly he fired four times per minute advancing at the same time at four miles in the hour. Fourthly he poured a bottle of water into the pan and barrel of the piece when loaded so as to wet every grain of the powder and in less than half a minute fired with her as well as ever, without extracting the ball.[2]

Nor was Ferguson alone in appreciating the benefits of breech-loading, even if the Board didn't share his enthusiasm. Commercial English gunmakers such as Durs Egg and Henry Nock also made breech-loading sporting guns, although their cost made them available only to a wealthy few. In America, a mechanical genius called John Hancock Hall had begun to look in detail at methods of breech-loading. In 1811, he took out a patent with William Thornton, a Washington architect, on a single-shot breech-loading rifle with a novel breechblock mechanism that could be removed in its entirety from the rifle. Produced initially as a commercial firearm, many found their way west via Texas, where it found greater fame as a military weapon in the Mexican wars. There could be little doubt that the breech-loading mechanism was an improvement at almost every level in terms of a firearm's performance, as was pointed out in a traveller's handbook produced in 1859 called *The Prairie Traveller*. The author, Randolph Marcy, makes a pertinent comment on the new breech-loading rifles then appearing:

> My own experience has forced me to the conclusion that the breech-loading arm possesses greater advantages over the muzzle-loading, for the reason that it can be charged and fired with much greater rapidity … and I cannot resist the force of my conviction that if I were alone upon the prairies, and expected an attack from a body of Indians, I am not acquainted with any arm I would as soon have in my hands as this.

By the early 1850s, percussion breech-loaders were beginning to herald a new era of firearm development although there were relatively few commercial single-shot rifles available before the Civil War. The Hall, originally manufactured as a flintlock, was converted to percussion in some numbers, but of the manufacturers who began producing percussion breech-loaders in the first half of the nineteenth century, the most prominent was undoubtedly Christian Sharps.

He had formed the Sharps Rifle Manufacturing Company in late 1851, but had been producing breech-loading percussion rifles since 1849 that used a unique rotating capping wheel and a vertically falling breechblock worked by an under-lever. It was a simple design – the massive block, when locked into position was incredibly strong and would enable the rifle to digest any cartridge that the rifle could be chambered for, and these early rifles were easily identified by their distinctive slanted breech. They were also capable of rapid fire of around ten times a minute, although Sharps himself could demonstrate one at eighteen rounds per minute. It quickly generated considerable interest from both the military and civilian markets, and its use by Kansas abolitionists in 1855 resulted in the famous quote by Henry Ward Beecher that:

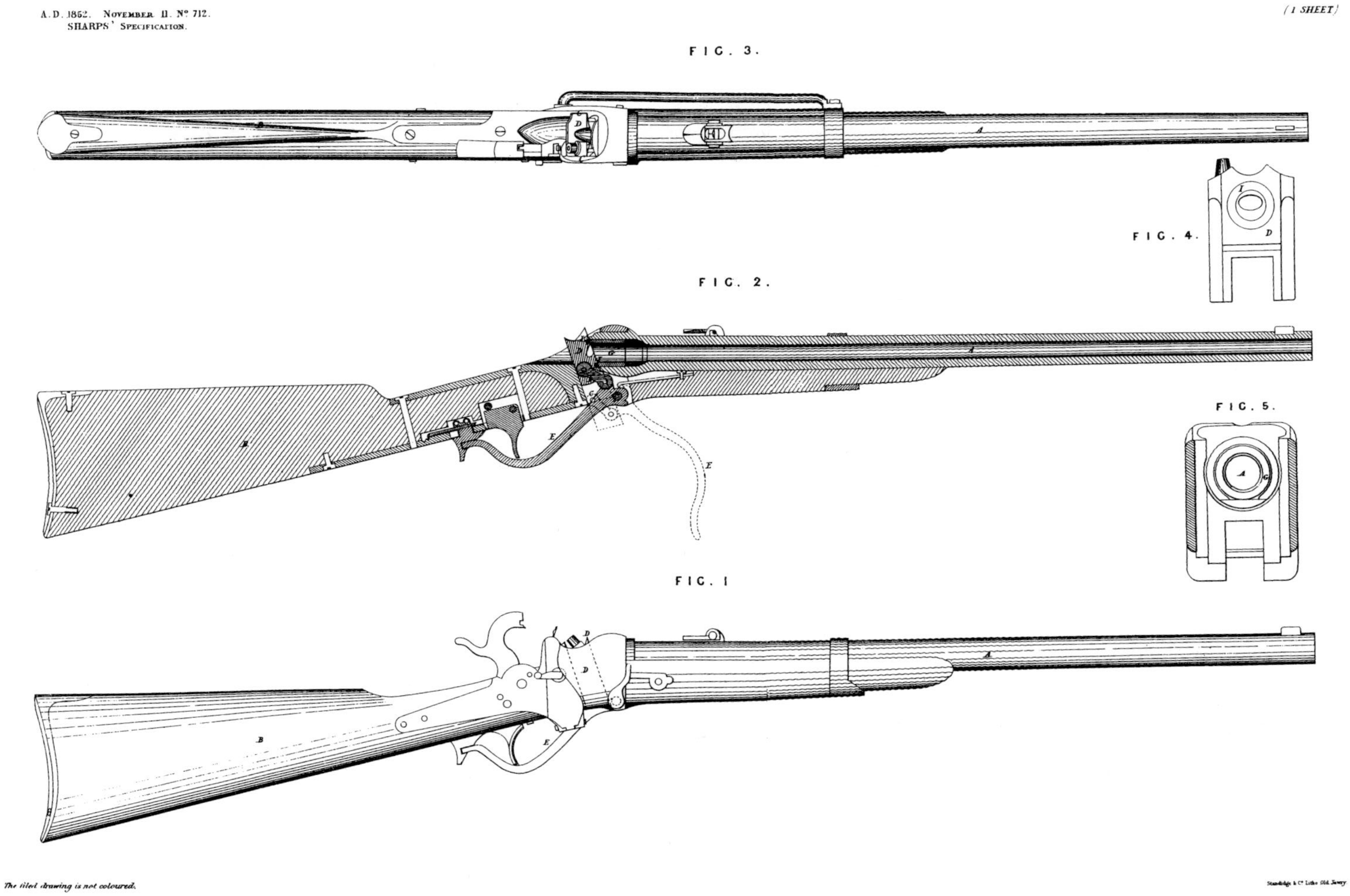

A. D. 1852. November 11. N° 712.
SHARPS' Specification.

(1 SHEET)

FIG. 3.

FIG. 4.

FIG. 2.

FIG. 5.

FIG. 1

The filed drawing is not coloured.

Standidge & C° Litho Old Jewry

Christian Sharps' original patent for his breech-loading rifle. Dated 1852.

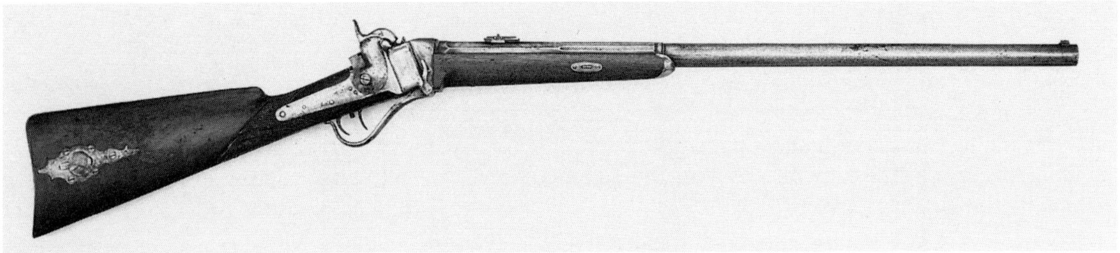

A factory special-order percussion, Sharps 'slant breech' sporting rifle with brass patchbox, silver fore-end cap and half-octagonal barrel. Photo courtesy of Lewis collection.

> You might just as well read the Bible ... to buffaloes as to those fellows who follow [abolitionism] but they have a supreme respect for the logic that is embodied in Sharp's rifles.[3]

This resulted in the Sharps being nicknamed 'Beecher's Bible' for many years thereafter. Sharps quickly introduced improved models in 1852 and 1853. These early rifles used an improved Maynard patented disc primer system, not unlike the caps used in modern toy pistols, although the caps themselves proved unreliable. In five years, the factory made over 13,000 longarms, some 25 per cent of these being pure sporting rifles that found a loyal following among the frontiersmen, hunters, adventurers and settlers heading west. Their combustible linen cartridges were easy to use and the range of the long-barrelled rifles was astonishing. Frederick Olmstead compared the Sharps favourably to the old Kentucky rifles, stating that it was capable of sending its bullet '... through a four inch white fencepost, and to constantly striking a piece of water a mile and a quarter distant with the ordinary purchased cartridge.'[4]

CARTRIDGE RIFLES

One major advantage of these capping breech-loaders was their ability to be muzzle-loaded like an ordinary musket should the breech seize due to fouling or the supply of pre-prepared cartridges run out. They did suffer from an inherent defect, which was obturation, the loss of propellant gas from the slight gap between the mating faces of the chamber and breech. Although not dangerous, it allowed powder fouling to accumulate, and could seize the block in place unless regularly cleaned. In practical terms during the short span of about a decade before the Civil War, breech-loaders actually made rather slow inroads into the Frontier. Most men preferred to retain their faithful muzzle-loaders and one observer noted that of all the weapons carried by emigrants across Kansas in 1859, the vast majority had muskets and shotguns, with virtually no breech-loaders or repeating rifles of any sort in evidence. There was still one major obstacle to perfecting the breech-loading system, and this was the development of an efficient self-contained metallic cartridge. Despite the many and varied attempts by a host of inventors such as Pauly, Benet, Martin, Tibbals, Prince, Pottet and many others to develop an efficient centrefire cartridge, one of the biggest problems was not the ability to ignite a charge in a tube (which is effectively all a cartridge is), but to make the tube light, strong and above all, cheap.

Two systems appeared in quick succession, the first true metallic cartridge was to be the rimfire, the other, the Boxer or Berdan primed centrefire. There is not space to give a full history of the development of these cartridges; suffice to say that a functioning form of the rimfire appeared in 1858, being sold for use in the popular .22-calibre pistols and produced by Horace Smith and Daniel Wesson. It consisted of a simple rimmed copper case filled with a charge of black powder and with a fulminate priming compound packed into the rim. There were some inherent problems with the rimfire cartridges though, for they could not be reloaded, clearly not a practical proposition in the wilderness. Secondly, by virtue of its design the copper of the rimfire case had to be thin enough to be crushed by the hammer, thus igniting the primer. This meant that the copper case always had an inherent weakness, for putting a large powder charge and thickening the case would prevent it igniting, but using thin copper would cause the case to rupture on firing, jamming it in the breech. This effectively limited the power of a rimfire cartridge, which was not a problem when it was used in carbines or pistols for close-range work, but it did prove a serious drawback in situations where distance and power were required. The rimfire immediately attracted the attention of rifle-makers who appreciated the advantages of the new self-contained cartridge, and they began to develop mechanisms to handle it. Probably the most successful were Christopher Spencer and Benjamin Tyler Henry who both produced repeating breech-loaders. The outbreak of the Civil War saw a proliferation of single-shot breech-loading rifles being manufactured and used in quantities that a few years before would have been unimaginable. Before long, a truly bewildering number of makes appeared, some of which will be looked at in more detail in the chapter on military longarms.

Meanwhile, in the late 1860s, the centrefire cartridge had almost simultaneously been perfected on two continents, by two colonels. One was an American, Hiram Berdan, and the other British, Edward Boxer. The technology of brass metallurgy being in its infancy, the Berdan was manufactured as a copper case while Boxer used rolled brass foil, with a separate riveted iron base. Each had a small priming cap inserted into the base. Initially both cases proved structurally weak and prone to deformation or rupturing and it was not until around 1870 that the technology was at last available to manufacture solid drawn brass cases. This was of considerable importance for the use of cartridge firearms on the Frontier, as a cartridge case that was too fragile to be reloaded was of no practical use. Hunters and travellers were limited in the amount of ammunition they could carry, for a large number of filled cartridges were heavy and bulky, and they needed to carry powder, spare caps and bullets with them to reload their fired cases. Postwar, demand for muzzle-loaders dwindled rapidly, not helped by the availability of plentiful and very cheap surplus guns. In 1866, the arsenal at Denver was advertising 'Army carbines at prices between $1 and $4.60.' There were tens of thousands of these surplus military arms postwar to be disposed of, and tens of thousands of disenchanted ex-soldiers who were anxious to buy them as they looked for a better life 'out West'.

As with the Gold Rush of 1849, the discovery of huge silver deposits at Comstock in Nevada in 1859 attracted huge numbers of men and women, hardly surprising when you realize that even in the early 1870s these mines were producing $35 million of bullion per year. The vast prairies that separated East and West America were destined to be rapidly diminished once President Lincoln had agreed to the building of the railroad from the Missouri River to the Pacific Coast in 1861. By 1872, 61,000 miles (98,150km) of track had been laid and this railroad was to change the face of the West forever.

The availability of cheap guns was of particular interest to the streams of settlers on the wagon trails from the East. Firearms were not a prime consideration for many of them and the cheaper a gun the better. The surplus single-shot rifles available to them worked on a variety of breech mechanisms. The .52-calibre Starr was a lever action, with a falling block, as was the Sharps. The Maynard had a hinged barrel that tipped down in the manner of a shotgun, whereas the Sharps and Hankins used a sliding barrel and had the distinction on some models of having the naked barrel covered in leather to prevent burning the left hand when firing. The Burnside had a lever action that unlatched a pivoting breech and the Joslyn a simple hinged block. Some, like the Warner, were not quite as user-friendly, having a breechblock arrangement that when unlocked had to be swung upwards and to the side, giving access to a manually operated extractor mechanism. Some of these models had never

E. MAYNARD.

Breech-Loading Fire-Arm.

No 26.364. Patented Dec. 6. 1859

Witnesses.

Inventor:

(*Left*) *The 1859 patent for Maynard's breech-loading carbine.*

(*Right*) *A typical advert for general hardware goods and firearms, from Spies of New York,* circa *1853.*

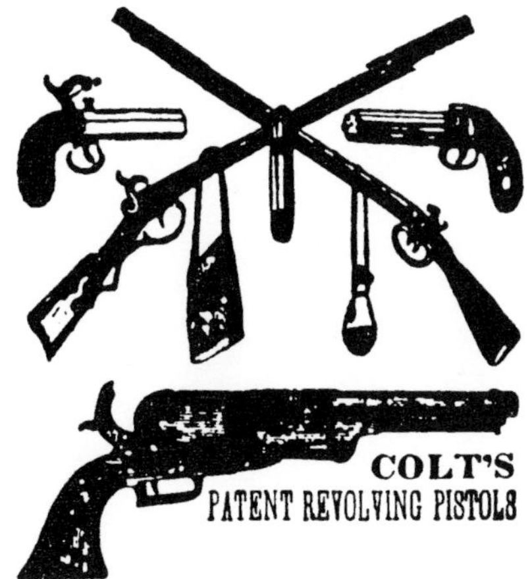

A. W. SPIES & CO.,

IMPORTERS OF

GUNS, PISTOLS, RIFLES,

GUN MATERIALS,

FOR MANUFACTURING

GUNS, GUNSMITHS' TOOLS, POWDER FLASKS,

Belt Pouches, Sporting Implements,

And every article needful for Sportsmen.

RODGERS' MOSTENHOLMS,

AND OTHER

FINE CUTLERY.

GENERAL HARDWARE.

91 MAIDEN-LANE, New-York.

SHIP'S ARMS, CUTLASSES, BOARDING PIKES, &c.

been issued to the army before hostilities ceased in 1865. There were even some precursors of the new age of firearms, such as the Palmer, a little known carbine that used a bolt action with interrupted threads that locked the breech, but had an external hammer for its .56-calibre rimfire cartridge. The great majority of these guns were carbines, manufactured for the cavalry service and their cartridges were generally low-powered, with a charge of between 45 to 55 grains of powder. Compared with the standard 80 grains of a rifle, this gave only an effective range of perhaps 300yd (275m) in skilled hands. But they were plentiful and cheap; there were some 25,000 .50-calibre Smith carbines alone sold off after the war and many of the guns were brand new, either through being stored and never issued or simply having been end-of-contract guns produced too late for the hostilities. Many of these guns were to be swiftly advertised for sale to the public. In 1866 some thirty-five brand new, unissued Starr carbines were advertised in the *Montana Post* along with 3,000 rounds of ammunition, and the *Galveston News* of 1867 carried a similar advert for 'Sharps, Maynard, Ballard, and Henry's rifle … Ball's Patented Repeater, Palmer's single breech-loading carbines'.

This did not put off potential civilian buyers, who found their light weight and short barrels extremely convenient for carrying across the saddle horn, or for tucking out of sight next to the seat on a wagon. The single shot breech-loader had many inherent advantages over most of the other systems that had begun appearing in the mid 1860s. Repeating rifles could certainly fire more shots more quickly, moreover, the simplicity and strength of the breech mechanisms of the later rifles meant that they could accommodate any of the most powerful black powder ammunition then available. There were many small manufacturers of sporting guns vying for trade in the immediate postwar years, such as Ballard, Lee, Peabody, Phoenix, Remington, Stevens, Sharps, Springfield and Wesson. All produced good rifles that found a ready commercial market. One of the most significant of these guns to emerge, although few today have heard of it, was the Ballard rifle.

It was designed as a military rimfire in .44 and .56 calibres but was quickly adapted to take commercial ammunition, so that by 1865 it was available in .32, .38 and .46 calibres. In view of the problems associated with the rimfire, of greater importance to the frontiersmen and hunters was the Ballard's mechanical action.

The design of its sliding breech meant that a cartridge could be pushed into even the most fouled of breeches, whilst still being easy to extract on unlocking, as the block slid downward and backwards, giving very positive extraction. In addition, it also had a separate chamber insert that meant, if required, it could be loaded and fired using loose powder and ball while still utilizing its breech mechanism. By 1866, the Ballard was available in a number of centrefire calibres, including the substantial new .50-70 centrefire, and its ability to be loaded with loose powder and ball made it particularly appealing to frontiersmen. It became a very popular rifle on the plains, but by the early 1870s it was under stiff competition from Springfield, Remington and Sharps. In 1873, Brown Manufacturing, the makers of the Ballard, had gone out of business, but the Ballard was too popular and its manufacture was taken over by a gunmaker called John Marlin. Marlin had been playing with lever-action rifles and adapted the Ballard to include a self-ejecting mechanism. Ever enterprising, he also fitted the rifle with a reversible firing pin,

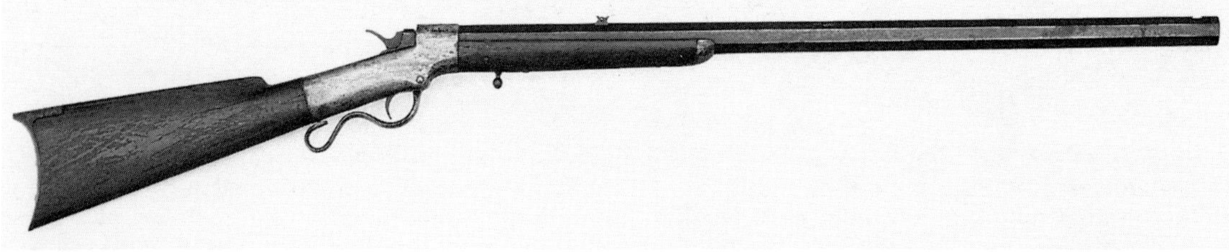

A Ballard breech-loading sporting rifle with heavy octagonal barrel, chambered for the .45-70 cartridge. This model had a firing pin that could be reversed to use centrefire or rimfire ammunition. Photo courtesy of B. Lees.

enabling centrefire or rimfire cartridges of the same calibre to be used.

The Ballard was chambered for a very wide number of cartridges, from .38-50 through to government .45-70 and eventually .45-100. All Ballard's were available in a variety of barrel lengths and finishes, priced from $22 for a small-calibre gallery gun up to $70 for a full sporting rifle with target sights and special stock, about two-thirds of the price of comparable repeating lever actions. John Marlin was well aware of the demand for rifles in the West, and he advertised heavily in the Western press, often stating that the rifle was 'specially adapted to far west trade'. The Ballard continued to sell well but Marlin was eventually producing his own repeating lever action and the single-shot Ballard was eventually destined to slip quietly into obscurity.

BUFFALO RIFLES

From the 1860s, steadily increasing streams of men and women were pushing back the Frontier, and buffalo hunters such as William Cody had begun to obtain contracts to supply meat to the newly established forts and shanty-towns that were springing up. While the commercial requirement for furs had dwindled, the demand for buffalo hides had begun to increase dramatically. America had for thousands of years been the home of the bison, erroneously but universally called 'buffalo' by early explorers who mistook it for a breed similar to the African buffalo. Exactly how many existed pre-Civil War is not known, but reasonable estimates are in the region of 40–50 million. They lived in two vast herds, one in parts of Texas, Kansas, Nebraska, Southern Wyoming and Oklahoma and the other in Montana, Northern Wyoming, the Dakotas and up to and across the Canadian border. Aside from being the traditional food source of the Indians, who as a nomadic people relied for their entire way of life on the animals, buffalo proved to be, quite literally, easy meat for the hunters and travellers who began to swarm across the postwar plains. As a result, demand grew steadily for rifles capable of felling a buffalo from at least 200 or 300yd (180 or 275m), far enough away for the report of the shot not to cause a stampede. For the most part, the rifles being used by the hunters were of large calibre, with a powerful charge – 60 grains and upwards, for despite their poor senses, buffalo were very tough animals to kill, requiring an exactly placed shot to the heart. In 1834, a naturalist called Townsend, having been told that a buffalo's skull was impervious to a bullet, fired a .62 Hawken rifle at close range into a buffalo's forehead, without apparently doing any more than mildly irritating it. When it was finally killed, the ball was found flattened against the otherwise unharmed skull. Buffalo even provided entertainment for travellers, who would ride the trains and shoot at the passing animals in the manner of a live fairground attraction. Not that it was difficult to miss. One herd in 1867 was so huge that it stopped a train quite literally in its tracks, taking three hours for the animals to pass by. Even in Europe, the demand for their hides was increasing for it was supple, thick and immensely durable, so much so that the British War Department took out contracts with American suppliers to supply hides to manufacture leather for the army.

It is estimated that from 1865, over the fifteen years that the buffalo were hunted, some 12,000 full-time 'runners' (the name by which professional hunters were known) worked the plains. They learned quickly that only a rifle of large calibre was capable of killing quickly and cleanly – a wasted shot was wasted money and when a skinned hide fetched only $2, and a cartridge was 20 cents, margins were slim. Equipping himself for hunting was not cheap for a runner, for a rifle cost between $100 and $300, normally being purchased in a wooden travelling box complete with every accessory needed to keep the hunter functioning in the remote plains, all of which had to be carried across hundreds of miles of rough country. One hunter in 1882 calculated exactly what was required to put together a hunting outfit, and it makes interesting reading.

> We required … two wagons, two four-horse teams, two saddle horses, two wall tents, one cook-stove with pipe, one .40-90 Sharps rifle, one .45-70 Sharps rifle, 50 pounds of gunpowder, 550 pounds of lead, 4,500 primers, 600 brass shells, 4 sheets patch paper. The entire cost of the outfit was $1,400.[5]

The runners used a very broad spectrum of weapons ranging from fine English rifles to surplus US Army weapons, but three types proved to be the primary choice for buffalo killing, Springfield, Remington and Sharps. The Springfield rifled musket had been in service with the army since before the war, but in 1865 some were converted to breech-loading by means of a simple hinged breechblock, that unlatched and flipped upwards. These 'Allin' conversions proved effective and durable and these 'Trapdoor' Springfields became a common sight in the hands of civilians on the frontier – more so than the government liked, for many soldiers deserted taking their Springfields with them, trading them at the first opportunity for rifles that were less conspicuous. Initially chambered for a .58-calibre rimfire, then the .50-70 cartridge, they were subsequently produced to chamber the Government .45-70 ammunition. One of the earliest hunters, William 'Buffalo Bill' Cody used a .50-calibre Springfield rifle, nicknamed 'Lucretia Borgia', with which he shot an incredible ninety-six buffalo in one day to win a bet. His technique

J. H. BARLOW'S PATENT IDEAL RE-LOADING IMPLEMENTS.

FOR LOADING CARTRIDGES COLT'S ARMS.

N. B.—When ordering tools be sure and specify not only the Calibre, but the name of the arm as well, as there are various cartridges of same Calibre, all being very different and a tool correct for one is of no use for any of the others.

REGULAR LIST.

Price, $2.25.

No. 1 is a light tool, designed especially for loading the smaller pistol cartridges, and is capable of performing all the operations required in reloading.

ADAPTED FOR
.32 short .32 long
.38 short .32 long, outside lubrication.

Price, No. 4, $2.50.
Price, No. 6, $3.00.

This is a very popular tool, no extra pieces to get lost or carry, and performs all the operations required. It moulds the bullet a trifle above the standard size, which after they are lubricated can be forced through the sizing die which packs the grease firmly in the grooves, removes the surplus, and makes the bullet perfectly round and of the correct diameter.

ADAPTED FOR
.32 Colt's L. M. R., .38 Colt's L. M. R., .44 Colt's L. M. R.,
.41 Colt's D. A. and .45 Colt's Army Revolvers.

Price $2.00 for Rifles;
$2.50 for Shot Guns.

Price, $1.10.

Price, $0.50 each.

Bullet Moulds with Wooden Handles.

All regular sizes, . .	$1.10.	Moulds for Round Bullets,	$1.50.
Express Mould, . . .	2.00.	Moulds for New .38 and .41 Colt's Long, . . .	2.00

SPECIAL LIST.

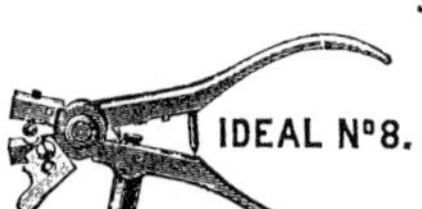

No. 8 is made especially for the new .38 long Colt's and .41 long Colt's, INSIDE LUBRICATION. We also make it for the cartridges, .450 and .455 BRITISH, AS APPLIED TO H. M. WAR DEPARTMENT. Adapted to the New Service Webley, Mark I. Revolvers, Colt's, Smith & Wesson and other Double Action Pistols and for Target Pistols. The Shells as made by Messrs. Eley Bros., of London, or The Union Metallic Cartridge Co., of Bridgeport, Conn., U. S. A., may be used. We find the shells made by the U. M. C. Co. to be better for reloading purposes and we recommend them. This tool will not reload the OLD OUTSIDE LUBRICATED .38 long or .41 long Colt.

.38 Long Colt's Inside Lubrication, $3.00 | .41 Long Colt's Inside Lubrication, $3.00
450 "British" as supplied to H. M. War Dept., $3.00
455 " " " " 3.00

Price of separate moulds for any of these bullets (Hollow base), $2.00.

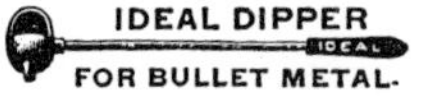

Dipper, Pot, and Cover.
Just what you need.

They are indispensable in casting bullets. No spilling of metal. Good full bullets guaranteed when they are used according to instructions.

Melting Pot. Cut ⅓ size.

Special Cover for holding Melting Pot. Will fit any stove.

HOW TO USE THIS DIPPER.

Dip full from MELTING POT, do not pour, but connect mould with nozzle, turn DIPPER with mould connected to a vertical position, and the weight of metal in Dipper above mould, will secure a good, full, smooth bullet.

Price, $0.50 each.

A popular selection of cartridge reloading tools.

was unusual even by Western standards and required strong nerves, excellent horsemanship and a steady aim. Mounting his horse, Brigham, without saddle or reins, he would head straight into the herd where he would pull the blind bridle from Brigham's head.

> The moment the bridle was off he started at the top of his speed … and in a few jumps brought me in alongside the first buffalo. Raising old 'Lucretia Borgia' to my shoulder I fired, and killed the animal at the first shot. My horse then carried me alongside the next one, not ten feet away, and I dropped him at the next fire. As soon as one buffalo would fall, Brigham would take me so close to the next that I could almost touch it with my gun. In this manner I killed the eleven buffalos with twelve shots.[6]

Some idea of the level of slaughter can be judged by the fact that by his own calculations, Cody alone shot 4,280 buffalo in eighteen months. Many hundreds of the early rimfire Springfields were sold off as surplus after the war and there even existed an army directive giving permission for Fort Commanders 'at exposed frontier settlements, in case of emergency [to] direct the sale of arms and ammunition to the settlers for their protection'.[7]

The Trapdoor was particularly practical as a plains rifle, for parts were readily available from any Army post, they were simple and relatively cheap, around $15 for a surplus rimfire model, and the introduction of reloadable centrefire brass cases in the early 1870s made them still more attractive, as converting the rifle to centrefire was a straightforward procedure for any gunsmith. Not that the Springfield was without its faults, suffering from ejection problems and an unpleasant habit of springing its breech open at inopportune moments. The Trapdoor was available as a special order gun, known generally as the 'Officer's Rifle', that boasted a detachable pistol-grip and tang sight. General George Custer was particularly fond of his customized .50-70-calibre M1866 Trapdoor which had been modified by reducing the length of the fore-end, fitting double set-triggers and a scrolled trigger guard.

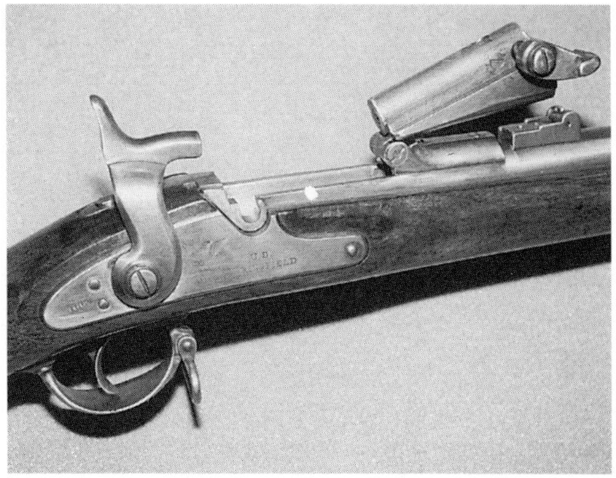

The open breech of a 'Trapdoor' Springfield. Photo courtesy of Jim Lewis.

The factory also produced other special order rifles, built along the lines of the best quality sporting rifles, and they were greatly prized. Some gunmakers offered them with other refinements, such as very heavy octagonal target barrels. In the late 1870s a Springfield with heavy barrel, special sights, set triggers and chequered sporting stock was retailing at a competitive $25. They were particularly attractive to English sportsmen who went to hunt buffalo and other game. One such was James Mortimer-Murphy, who was hunting in the Far West in the 1870s, and who commented on his Springfield:

> The most effective weapon that I have ever used was a fifty calibre Springfield rifle, which was resighted so that its point-blank range was one hundred and fifty yards. This was almost as accurate at three hundred yards as it was at half that distance and I have killed a wolf with it at nearly four hundred yards.[8]

Along with the Trapdoor, the demand for plains rifles was to produce another important type, the Remington Rolling Block.

Although largely unknown now, in fact the Rolling Block was a far greater commercial

The Remington Rolling Block action, with breech open, showing the firing pin. Courtesy of the Trustees of the Royal Armouries.

success than any other contemporary rifle because of its subsequent great popularity abroad as both a military and target rifle. Introduced in 1865, the Remington used a split-breech system which had a pivoted breechblock that unlocked and dropped backwards and downwards, exposing the chamber for loading. When the cartridge was loaded and the block was pushed back, it was locked in place by an 'L'-shaped hammer. It was very simple, very quick to operate and immensely strong, being able to handle any size cartridge then in existence, although it was initially designed for the weak .56-50 Spencer rimfire and the .46 Long rimfire also chambered by the Ballard. The Rolling Block rifle was often advertised as 'The best rifle in the world' or 'the preferred arms for hunting on the plains', a claim doubtless disputed by more than a few owners, who found it could be troublesome, particularly when the breech was fouled and its manual extraction system proved inadequate. The Remington was produced for the usual range of early rimfire calibres, that is, .32, .38, .44 and .46 and the later centrefires, but demand for heavier cartridges prompted Remington to market a conversion rifle in about 1868, using the Springfield barrel and stock, with rolling-block breech. Many of the heavy framed 'Sporting Rifle No.1s' were purchased by Army Officers and its simplicity and strength very quickly came to the notice of the buffalo hunters on the plains. Depending on its barrel weight and calibre, a rolling block for buffalo killing might weigh up to 15lb (6.8kg) and cost $50, but there was no question about the accuracy of such rifles. One owner was recorded as achieving a ten-shot group of under 1in at 50yd, which, although a short range for a rifle, gives some indication of its potential at 300 or 400 yards and why they became so popular with the runners. Acknowledging the popularity of the design, Remington produced a heavy-barrelled 'Buffalo' model in 1874, chambered for the 'Big Fifty' .50-70 cartridge, that sold at an affordable $30. Of the three most frequently encountered rifles on the plains, it is the Sharps that has gone down in history as 'The Buffalo Rifle'.

The military use of the Sharps will be looked at later, but its popularity for buffalo hunting really began with the adoption of the centrefire cartridge in the New Model 1866, although these were made in fairly small numbers. Earlier converted Government Sharps percussion rifles were far more

'Buffalo' cartridges: .40-70, .45-90, .44-100, .50-90, .44-90, .50-110. Photo courtesy of B. Lees.

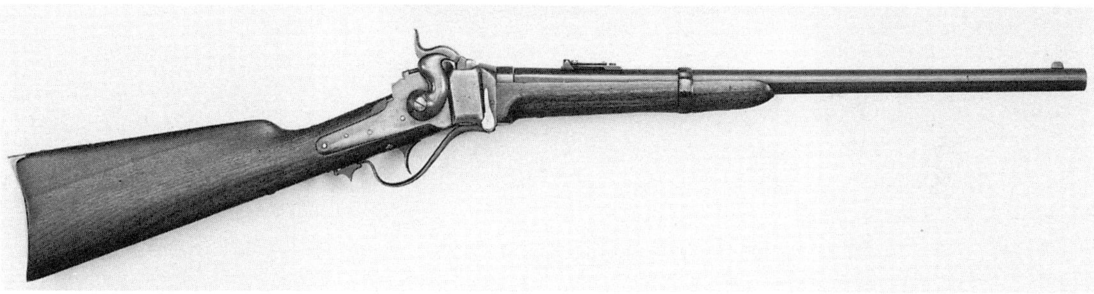

(Below) A Sharps New Model 1863, converted to chamber the .50-70 centrefire cartridge. These rifles saw much service in the Indian Wars. Courtesy of the Trustees of the Royal Armouries.

common, and much cheaper. Altered to take the short .50-70 cartridge, the rifles had 30in barrels, the carbines 24in and demand for them was soon outstripping supply. In 1869, Sharps began to make a half-stocked hunting rifle, following it up with another rifle in 1871 that unaccountably became better known as the Model 1874. As with most other makes, the Sharps was available with a bewildering variety of options, the most popular being the octagonal heavy barrel, set triggers and 'globe and peep' target sights. Where Sharps differed from other makers was his belief that the standard range of calibres offered for sporting rifles was inadequate, and the Sharps company were to produce a greater number of calibres than any other manufacturer. Sharps rifles could, in fact, be purchased chambered for a bewildering number of calibres, .44 Berdan, .40-70, .44-77, .45-70, .45-120, .50-90 and .50-110.

In addition, Sharps also recognized the problem inherent in attempting to shoot very large calibres over long distances. The recoil of repeatedly firing a full charge in a large calibre, such as .58, would make shooting untenable for anything but a short period of time. It was certainly impractical for buffalo killing, where hundreds could be shot in a day.

As a result the majority of these Sharps' cartridges were of the bottlenecked type that enabled a large powder charge to be loaded into a comparatively compact case, achieving higher velocities. At the same time the calibres used could be smaller and the bullets lighter, a vital factor considering the weight

The end of an era. Buffalo skulls in Michigan waiting to go to the Carbon Works. Photo courtesy of Detroit Public Library.

of lead that needed to be carried by the hunters for reloading. Here, too, Sharps' had more flexibility with regards to loading than other makers, for they offered not only a very wide range of calibres but also bullet weights. A standard 430 grain bullet could be replaced by a 230 grain providing greater space in the case for powder, and resulting in still higher velocities. As an example, the standard .45-90-370 (.45-calibre, 90 grain, 370 grain bullet) was able to reach 1,500fps, but use of a lighter 340 grain bullet and greater charge meant that it could reach an impressive 1,830fps, a more than adequate velocity for buffalo. The majority of runners actually reckoned on 1,300–1,500fps as being the minimum for their needs using a .45-calibre bullet. New Sharps rifles were in great demand but were expensive, particularly if they were factory specials, and some were lucky enough to obtain their Sharps second-hand as James Cook, hunting buffalo in Texas, recorded:

> I was fortunate enough to buy … a Sharp's 44 calibre rifle, reloading outfit, belt and 150 shells. The man had used the gun only a short time and seventy-five of the shells had never even been loaded. I got the gun and his entire interest in the buffalo range for thirty six dollars.[9]

Frank Meyer wrote that he bought his first Sharps second-hand for considerably more – $125 – from a Colonel Irving Dodge. It was in .40-90 calibre, had a 32in barrel, fine walnut stock and weighed 12lb (5.4kg) and he considered the price to be a very fair one.

Because of the weight of such rifles, hunters adopted the use of a barrel rest, an old idea dating back to the heavy military muskets of the seventeenth century. This consisted of a pair of sticks lashed together near the top to provide an 'X' support, although some preferred to use a single 'Y'-shaped stick. Another reason for raising the rifles from the ground was to reduce the reverberation of the report. Fired from ground level a black powder rifle has a distinctive 'boom'; raised up off the ground this becomes a less obtrusive 'bang', much less liable to spook the herd into a panic stampede, a happening dreaded by hunters because of the effort and time lost in repacking their wagons and having to track the herd and set up camp again.

Careful shooting would drop animals in their tracks, causing others to mill about in confusion. In this manner, Mayer reported seeing 200 buffalo killed by one rifle firing 200 shots at ranges from 200 to 600yd (180 to 550m). It was not only buffalo that fell to these rifles, for along with the inexorable Western expansion came increasing conflict with the native tribes. Indeed a brush with a war party of Commanche and Cheyenne warriors in 1874 enabled a Sharps rifle to take and hold the distance record for a one-shot hit from a single-shot rifle. A party of twenty-eight buffalo hunters working in the Texas panhandle had set up camp at a small huddle of buildings called Adobe Walls. They were soon spotted by a large Indian war party, but had beaten them back with their accurate rifle fire. There followed an impasse in which the hunters began to run low on water and food, but it was broken by Billy Dixon using a .50-90 Sharps. Reckoned to be the best shot, he took steady aim and fired at a mounted Indian, knocking him out of the saddle at a range later reputed to be 1,538yd (1,406m). This has been disputed, but even allowing for a reasonable margin of error in calculating the distance it was by any standards an extraordinary shot.

While we may regard such shooting as mere luck, it is worth pointing out that 1,000yd (915m) target shooting was quite commonplace throughout the 1870s and beyond, and many, with a little luck, could have duplicated Dixon's shot. Given still wind conditions, experienced target shooters, such as Irishman James Wilson could, and did achieve 55 out of a possible 60 bulls at that range. Target shooting had long been a popular sport in the East, and many who had journeyed West had taken their love of target shooting with them. The introduction of reliable centrefire ammunition in the early 1870s gave the target shooter a completely fresh perspective on long-range shooting.

By the late 1860s, the pre-war percussion bull-barrelled rifles, based on the heavy German 'schutzen' target rifles of the eighteenth century, were giving way to a new breed of sporting target rifle. There was fierce competition among target shooters, and British, Irish, Scots and European teams would travel to competitions at the world-renowned Wimbledon ranges in England, where American riflemen had proved on many occasions that they were a match for anyone. The manufacture of these new rifles owed nothing to the demands of buffalo hunters or frontiersmen but to

Buffalo skinners. A Sharps carbine is resting eloquently against the carcass. Photo courtesy Western History Collection, University of Oklahoma Library.

the opening in 1873 of a 1,000yd target range on Long Island in New York State, called the Creedmoor range. It became the Mecca for long-range shooters, and within a year it had hosted an international meeting with shooters attending from all over America, as well as Europe. American shooters demanded the most competitive rifles, and both Remington and Sharps looked closely at how their respective rifles could be improved. In 1873, both companies produced 'Creedmoor' models, chambered for the .44-90 cartridge, that were available as special order rifles. Remington offered a model with gain twist rifling, special 'globe and peep' sights and pistol-grip stock that retailed at $100. Sharps offered a Long-Range target rifle, with similar refinements, and began producing a 'Creedmoor' within a couple of years. With a heavy 32in target barrel, special stock and sights it could cost $120. Before very long, most other single-shot manufacturers were also offering 'Creedmoor' versions. Springfield also produced an interesting range of target rifles, sold as the Springfield Long-Range Rifle, and some idea of their exclusivity can be gained from the fact that the factory only produced 176 rifles in three years. Maynard, Ballard, Peabody, Whitney and Wesson all produced variations on a theme and many found their way West. Occasional buffalo hunter and frontiersman Jack Bean used a .45-120 Sharps Creedmoor to shoot an Indian at a range later estimated to have been in excess of 1,400yd (1,280m). Although never common on the frontier, the ownership of any Creedmoor conferred upon the owner a faint sense of superiority and these rifles were to set new standards for accurate shooting.

Ammunition was also a vitally important part of any shooter's equipment, and most chose to load their own. Empty unprimed cartridges could be purchased from between $22–$35 per thousand, depending on size. There were a large number of cartridge manufacturers, the biggest being Union Metallic Cartridges (UMC), United States Cartridge Co (USC Co), Remington and Co, Sharps and Winchester, all of whom produced their own brands. Target shooters and runners alike were adept at casting their own bullets and reloading their empty cases, and most had their own loads that suited their rifles, the ranges they liked to shoot at, and the bullet weights they preferred. Overloading a case was pointless, for it simply wasted powder and made the recoil uncomfortable, but underloading could result in poor performance, or worse, if the shooter was hunting buffalo. Being anywhere near a wounded and enraged buffalo wasn't a wise move. Neophyte buffalo hunters had a great deal to learn about buffalo, who were neither as stupid or passive as they were reputed to be. Many hunters died on the horns of a wounded animal, and while escaping from a stampeding herd on horseback was just about possible, a hunter caught on foot stood no chance. Being caught by a stampede resulted in 'not enough of a man left 'ter bury' as one hunter dryly commented, so most hunters planned their shooting carefully and tried to take as few risks as possible.

One of the great problems faced by all hunters and target shooters was in actually locating their targets at extreme ranges, and this was compounded on the plains, where lack of cover and vast distances often made closing with a quarry almost impossible. American gunsmiths had an early tradition of fitting optical sights to their sporting rifles, and telescopic sights had been fitted to target rifles as early as the 1840s. Alvan Clark of Boston and Morgan James in New York provided some of the best sights, although their low magnification (typically 3×) and extremely narrow field of view would now be considered basic in the extreme. In 1865 one veteran trapper and hunter recounted that he crossed the Rockies carrying:

> … a Sharps rifle, .52 calibre linen cartridge, government caps. The rifle was fitted with a Malcolm telescopic sight. The rifle itself as well as the telescope was something of a novelty in that region in those days and much was the discussion on the merits and demerits of the telescope sight. Within a year from the time I joined the band every one of that little company of hunters and trappers procured, and had fitted, the best Malcolm telescopic sights.[10]

Germany had long had a tradition of producing good optical sights, and Frank Mayer purchased a Vollmer sight of rare 20× power, which he had fitted to his buffalo rifle, and with which he reckoned to have no difficulty killing at 600yd (550m). Many bull-barrelled target rifles also had optical sights fitted. Although never designed for hunting, with the use of a rest they proved to be excellent rifles, although their smaller calibres required accurate placing of the bullet. Much has been written about the Sharps, and along with the Colt revolver and Winchester, one could be forgiven for thinking that no other rifles made their way west of the Missouri. As has been shown, this is far from the truth, for in the boom years after the Civil War there were more single-shot rifles developed than at any other time. Some, such as the Howard, were to have fairly brief lives, for despite the ingenuity of its design it was in production for little more than six years, from 1865 to 1871.

Even the larger manufacturers were not always successful; in the late 1870s, the Sharps Company had begun to develop a new rifle, using the design talents of a German engineer who was to achieve greater fame with semi-automatic pistols. His name was Hugo Borchardt and his design was for a falling block action with internal hammer that automatically cocked the mechanism as the block was closed. Its odd looks and lack of external hammer did not appeal to the Westerners, which was a pity, for the Sharps Borchardt was way ahead of its time. More popular was the Peabody, a rifle that deserved far greater commercial success than it ever actually received. It was patented in 1862 by Henry Peabody and was not dissimilar to the Springfield, except that its breech was hinged at the rear rather than the front as on the Springfield. The block was stronger than the Springfield as well as being less prone to jamming the cartridges in the chamber after firing. The sporting model was initially chambered for a .50-calibre rimfire cartridge with a 50 grain charge, which made it somewhat underpowered, but by the late 1870s it was being offered in .45-70 Government and .50-70 sporting at $42. It simply didn't catch on in its home country although it was to prove very popular in Europe, being adopted as both a military and sporting rifle. A rifle that achieved far more in sales terms was the Maynard, originally adopted as a cavalry rifle during the Civil War and, at the end of the conflict, the Massachusetts-based Maynard Arms Company swiftly turned to the burgeoning sporting rifle market. Maynard produced the Model 1873, a break-open centrefire sporting gun chambered for all of the popular sporting calibres, up to and including the 'Big Fifties'. Available with round or octagonal barrels in a variety of lengths, they had the added advantage of a quick-change barrel, so that a shotgun barrel of 20- or 28-bore could be substituted. They were mechanically

John P. Lower of Denver, Colorado in front of the target he has just shot using the Sharps Borchardt Model 1878 rifle that he is holding. Courtesy Denver Public Library, Western History Dept.

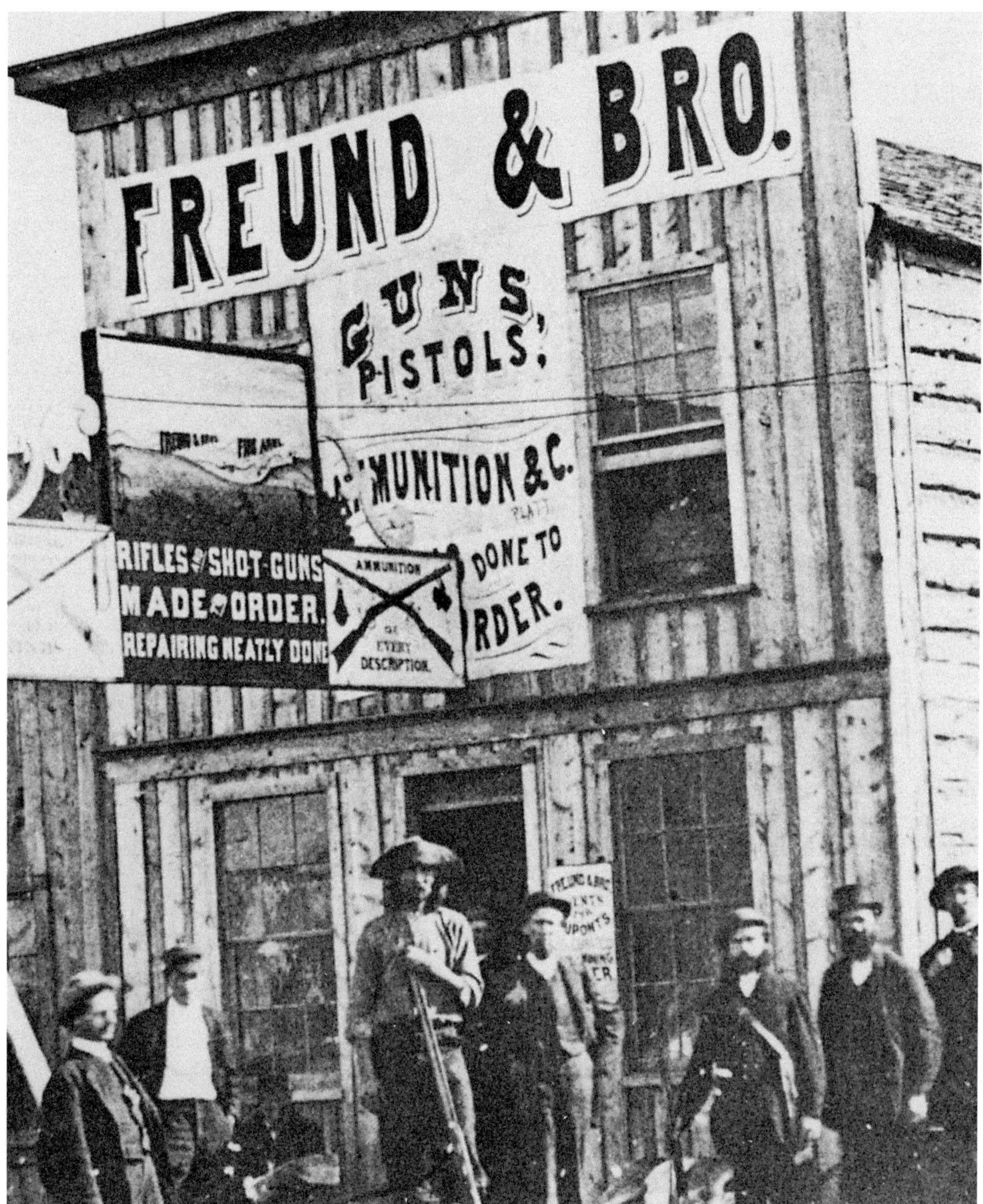

Freund and Bro., one of the Frontier's premier gunmakers in Laramie, Wyoming around 1870. Courtesy of Wyoming Historical Society.

simple and cheap, the basic .35-calibre rifle being a little over $20 and a .50-calibre example, fully stocked with a heavy barrel, could cost $70. Partly because of its robust construction, and its attractive price, Maynard's became common Frontier rifles, although their popularity was hampered by the unusual thick-rimmed cartridge they used. The problem that was to eventually render them obsolete was their inability to handle the new smokeless powder that had been developed in the 1880s. This led to the company's demise and the name was taken over by the Stevens company in 1890.

Other makes that gained some popularity were the Whitney, which appeared late in 1872 and closely resembled the Remington. The New System Whitney was really a blatant copy of the Remington, but with a simplified action and much improved extractor mechanism. There was also a derivative designed by Whitney's son which closely resembled the earlier Warner rifle and was named the Whitney Phoenix. It had a side-hinged breech that opened to the right, which made it perfect for left-handed shooters, but was less than practical for right-handers, and though it had a mechanical extractor the design suffered extraction problems. It was also very prone to locking its breechblock once fired, which probably explained its brief nine-year production life. The Stevens company, better known as makers of shotguns, also entered the sporting rifle market, with a typically simple break-open design. Even Winchester, never known for their desire to be lured away from their profitable repeating-rifle manufacture, produced a falling block rifle, the Model 1885, that became known as the High Wall (small calibre) or Low Wall (large-calibre) Winchesters. They were well designed, naturally, by the brilliant John Browning, and achieved considerable success, with some 140,000 being produced. By the end of the 1880s, a new breed of repeating rifles were supplanting the old single-shots as the most popular rifles in the West. Americans were showing a tendency to demand speed and firepower over accuracy, and the buffalo were becoming scarcer, although big herds still lived in the northern territories and runners were still prepared to hunt them as long as a profit could be made although this was becoming increasingly difficult. For them the single-shot rifles were still the only guns to use.

However well it had stood up to the rigours of frontier life, by the late 1870s the Sharps was becoming old technology and the company had turned to manufacturing other patterns of rifle, such as bolt-actions, in an attempt to stay afloat. However, they were swimming against the rising tide of technology and were forced to close in 1881. With them went an era the like of which would never be seen again, but happily the Sharps rifle was not destined to die. A Cheyenne gunsmith by the name of Frank Freund had long admired the Sharps and had made custom rifles based on their design but using his own mechanical improvement since the late 1870s. When the company went into receivership, Freund began to build his own modified Sharps, which he retailed as 'The Wyoming Saddle Gun'. These were lighter, smaller rifles commonly chambered for the popular .40-90 cartridge and they were beautifully finished with oiled walnut stocks, set triggers and special sight, although they retailed at a staggering $200 each.

Another latecomer to the single-shot marketplace was the Remington-Hepburn that had been patented as early as 1879. Its falling-block action was of the type very commonly found on English sporting rifles, operated by a lever on the right side of the receiver, and it also used a rebounding hammer. It was available in barrel lengths between 26–30in and had as standard a chequered pistol grip, short fore-end and was chambered for several black powder cartridges. Unusually for rifles of this period, it adapted quite well to the use, in the 1880s, of smokeless powder, and it stayed in production until 1907, possibly the last of the true single-shot rifles to see out the old century. A few other makes continued to be offered, such as the simple break-open Stevens and the Wesson, but their days were numbered. While the single-shot rifle undoubtedly served the hunters well, the American fascination with mechanization was to produce a type of rifle that was never really adopted on a grand scale anywhere else, the repeating rifle.

4 Repeating Rifles

The quest for rapid fire has existed since the first simple tubes were filled with powder in medieval times. Removable breeches and superimposed loads worked after a fashion, but even the adoption of breech-loading did not immediately solve the problem of how a longarm could be reliably made to fire more than one shot, without being too cumbersome to carry, or disintegrating at an inopportune moment. It is unlikely that the inventor of the first revolving firearms will ever be identified; certainly there was a Swedish design of revolving musket that was already considered to be old at the start of the nineteenth century. Flintlocks could be, and were, made with revolving cylinders, but the problem of priming each chamber remained and ingenious solutions were applied to the problem. The pan cover could be manufactured so as to be tight fitting enough not to allow the priming charge to escape when it was inverted, but the slightest knock would cause the cover to open, rendering the gun useless. In addition there was a problem common to all revolving cylinder firearms and that was the escape of burning gas from the gap between the cylinder face and breech. Although rarely life-threatening, in a rifle held close to the face it was unnerving to say the least, and could provoke flinching in the most experienced of shooters. More serious was the tendency of the chambers to chain-ignite caused by the flash of discharge in one cylinder igniting all of the others. On a longarm whose barrel was supported by the left hand just forward of the cylinder, a multiple discharge could, quite literally, be disarming. Some early models employed a camming action to force the cylinder forward onto the rear of the breech to form a gas seal, with some success, but though it was a rare occurrence the possibilities did limit the popularity of revolving rifles. Several reasonably workable designs had been produced in England in the eighteenth century, one of the earliest being a 'single-barrelled and poli-chambered gun' patented by an Islington amateur engineer called James Thomson. However, arguably, the best was an American design patented by Captain Artemus Wheeler, of Concord, Massachusetts who produced a seven-shot hand-rotated longarm in mid-1818.

The idea was taken up by Elisha Collier, a Boston engineer who improved the mechanism using a spiral spring to align each chamber with the bore. Collier patented the design in England, where the guns were made until 1824, mostly for supply to India. In reality though, flintlock ignition systems were always going to prove troublesome for multi-shot guns, but things were to change in the 1830s at a stroke with the introduction of percussion ignition. The simple percussion cap solved the problem of igniting the main powder charge because a tight fitting cap would remain in place on the nipple even when the chamber was inverted. Although Sam Colt is generally credited with producing the first percussion revolving rifles, there were actually several earlier makes of quite efficient repeating rifles available in America through the 1830–50 period. Probably the most widely distributed was a revolving rifle produced by William Billinghurst in the late 1830s that was something of a cross between a Kentucky rifle and the Collier revolving gun. A few years later, in 1837 a New Yorker,

An example of the revolving rifle patented in 1818 by Captain Artemus Wheeler of Massachusetts and subsequently made in England by Elisha Collier, also a native of Massachusetts. Courtesy of the Trustees of the Royal Armouries.

(Below) Porter's Patent turret rifle. US Patent No. 8210 of 1851. Courtesy of the Trustees of the Royal Armouries.

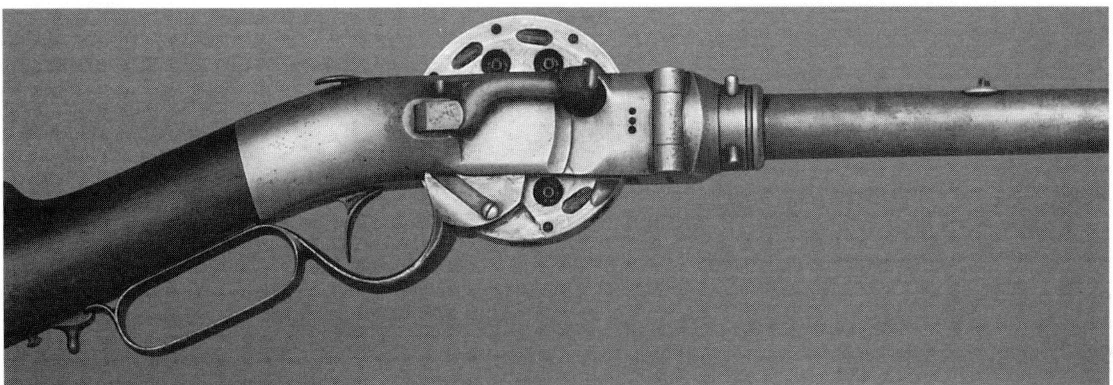

John Cochran, was to patent another multi-shot rifle, although this was of a much different construction from the revolving guns. It was a turret gun, using a thick disc-shaped cylinder that lay flat on the receiver and rotated clockwise. It was a design also retailed in England by Wilkinson and Son, with some success. The nine-shot underhammer that Cochran called the 'monitor' was available in several calibres, .36, 38, .40 or .44, and was advertised by several gun dealers in St Louis. It was not cheap at $35 but found favour with a number of adventurers and frontiersmen who took an immediate liking to its firepower, although this could lead to some confusion. Josiah Gregg, travelling with a wagon train, decided to hunt some buffalo with his Cochran in 1840. Having fired several shots in quick succession, he was surprised by the sound of hoofbeats.

> ... a party of our own men came galloping up from the wagons considerably alarmed. They had heard the six shots and, not recollecting my repeating rifle, supposed I had been attacked by Indians.[1]

Another turret rifle, this time employing a cylinder on its side with each chamber rotating vertically, was produced by Patrick Porter, a gunmaker from Memphis who patented his gun in 1851.

They were actually quite sophisticated, using a tape primer mechanism on the locks; a self-cocking action was available in .36 or .50 calibres, in eight- or nine- shot variants. Ironically, Porter was tragically killed by one of his rifles chain-firing as he was demonstrating it to Samuel Colt, and less than 450 were ever produced. Other multi-shot repeaters were produced by Rufus Nichols and Edward Childs in 1838. They had mechanically rotating cylinders as well as optional barrel lengths, five, seven or nine-shot cylinders and a fine quality wood stock and in many ways was a superior gun to the Colts that were to later dominate the revolving rifle market. Nor was a rotating cylinder the only means of obtaining repeating fire. Harmonica guns also appeared, so named because of their sliding chamber that resembled the musical instrument. Inserted in a slot behind the breech, the chamber was released by a catch and manually pushed along as each chamber was fired. These were a far more practical proposition, and at least two American makers produced reasonably workable examples, a gunsmith called Kendall making, in 1838, what was termed a 'slide repeating rifle' with a five-chambered magazine. Unsurprisingly, the best design was produced by John Browning.

Browning's inventive genius was never still and he had seen examples of the Kendall, which he believed could be improved on, so in 1841 he had manufactured his own solid-framed underhammer slide gun. This had the added benefit of a magazine that could be specified to hold between five and twenty-five charges and, in addition, an extra magazine was supplied with each gun. This gave an owner the potential of up to fifty shots without reloading and Browning slide guns sold steadily albeit in relatively small numbers.

Interesting as these early repeaters were, they all suffered from some inherent defect – whether of weight, mechanical complexity, or reliability. Sold in far greater numbers were percussion revolving rifles that gained much greater popularity. The mention of revolvers of any sort immediately conjures up the name of Colt, but there were several successful revolving rifles produced before his entry into the firearms' industry by the likes of Billingshurst and North-Savage. The Billingshurst design used a smoothbore barrel that also doubled as the axis-pin for the cylinder and it was eventually to evolve into a pistol that became far more famous than the rifle, the Le Mat revolver. Like many successful inventors, Colt's genius was partly in gathering together all of the best functional parts of existing repeaters, and then adding a few innovations of his own. The story of the development of the revolver rightly belongs to the chapter on pistols, but the development of the repeating rifle is in itself an interesting and comparatively little known story.

Colt's revolving rifle was first produced in 1836, and was known as the Colt-Paterson. It had a ring-cocking lever mounted just forward of the trigger-guard and was, eventually, to incorporate a hinged loading-lever, mounted alongside the barrel. In a time where losing a ramrod effectively meant that a muzzle-loader was rendered useless, this was an important and practical consideration. Although the rifle was a single-action, it incorporated a pawl that mechanically revolved the cylinder each time the action was cocked. Although adequate for civilian use, the early revolving rifles required very careful loading to prevent chain fire, and proved too fragile for the military. They were also very costly, at $150 each, which effectively priced them out of all but the most wealthy pockets, and the company soon foundered. A new Colt company was reborn in 1849, and Colt wisely employed a brilliant engineer called Elisha Root, who produced a side-hammer revolving rifle in 1855 that proved more rugged than the Paterson. Root had even designed a bush that fitted into the frame which could be forced against the cylinder, thus minimizing the risk of multiple side-hammer discharge. The Colt side-hammers were as good as a revolving rifle could be, which in all honesty was not brilliant. As one wary user commented of the Colt, 'It was a gun built exactly on the principle of a Colt's revolver. The trouble with it was that one never new just how many shots might go off at once.'[2]

However, according to Colt's own advertising, the Model 1855 six-shot rifles were probably the best guns ever sold to the public. In fact, if one were to believe their advertising, the public were fortunate simply to be able to purchase such a rifle. Colt assured his customers that his guns did not:

> endanger their eyesight or brain [reference to the poor gas sealing at the breech]. They do not stick

fast refusing to either open or shut without the aid of an axe when heated … they leave no burning paper in the barrel after a discharge, to blow the next cartridge into your face as do the guns which open from behind … [an unsubtle swipe at the increasing popularity of breech-loaders, which Colt did not make] They are always worth what they cost – in the Far West much more, almost a legal tender![3]

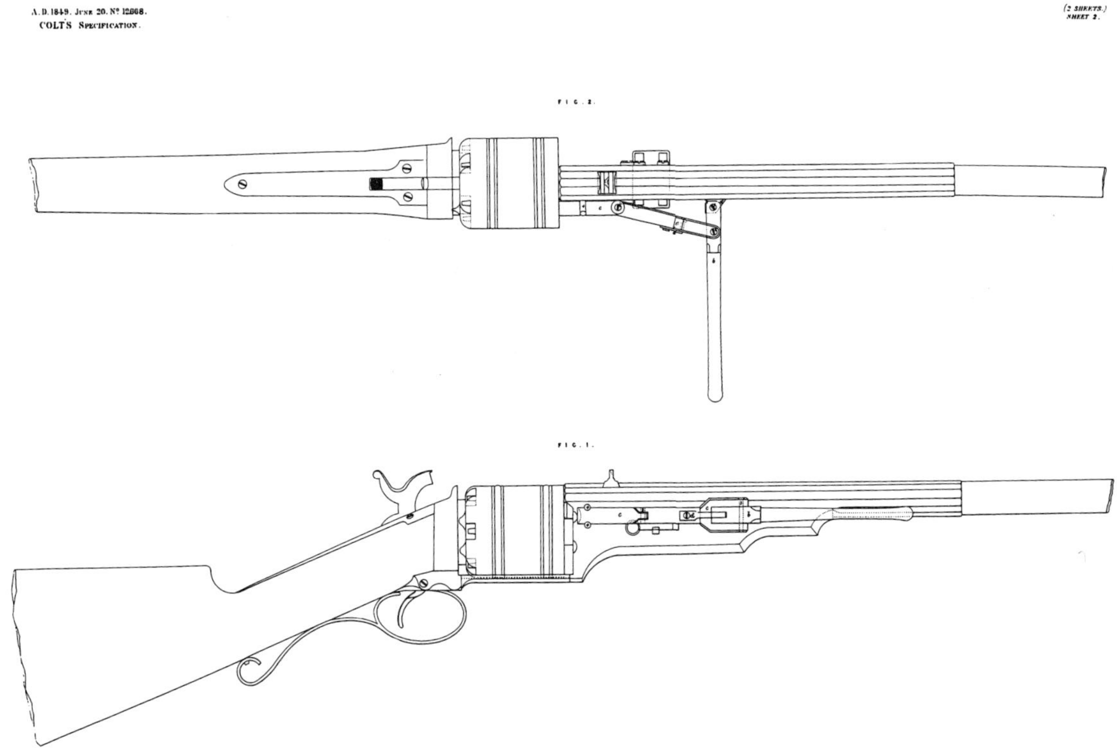

A.D. 1849. June 20. No 12668.
COLT'S SPECIFICATION.

(2 SHEETS.)
SHEET 2.

FIG. 2.

FIG. 1.

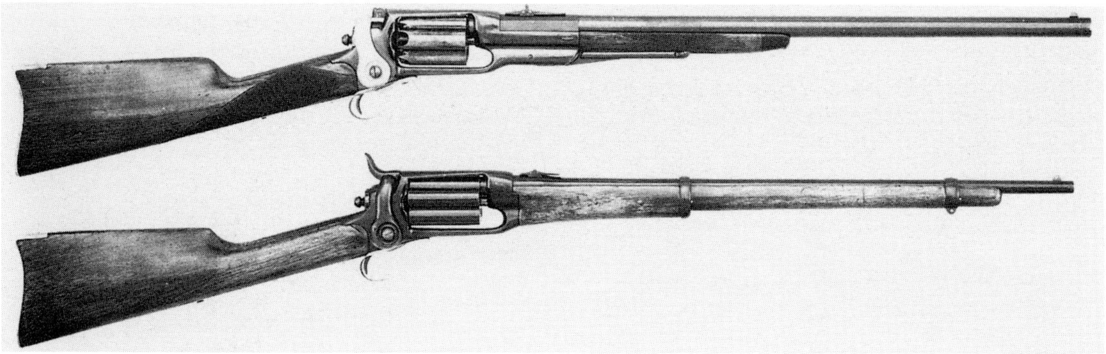

(Top) Colt's revolving rifle patent of 1849.
(Above) Top photo: a Colt revolving .60 shotgun and below, a fully stocked Colt sporting rifle in .44 calibre. Courtesy of the Trustees of the Royal Armouries.

The last point was actually true, as demand in the West was outstripping supply, and a good gun could be traded for almost anything, usually for many times its actual worth. But as with so many innovations, it was only a matter of time until something better came along.

There were several repeating rifles manufactured of rather less efficient design, that surprisingly made it to the production stage. Two models were produced by Orvil Robinson of Plattsburg, New York. The first was a repeater that used a tube magazine and a longitudinally sliding breechblock similar to that of the Henry rifle. However, it relied on the shooter pulling hard on two wings that protruded from the rear of the bolt to unlock it, which was both an awkward and slow procedure. His second rifle used a locking breech that had a toggle bar opened by a lever on the right side of the receiver. It had loading gates on either side of the breech, useful presumably if two people wanted to load simultaneously, and few were made, but Winchester, always protective of its image as *the* premier manufacturer of repeating rifles, very sensibly purchased the rights to Robinson's guns.

Another unusual but more effective design was produced by Warren Evans who patented a lever-action rifle in late 1871, that he made at his factory in Maine. Its basic mechanism was not dissimilar to that of the Spencer, but it used a curious fluted magazine based on the Archimedean screw principle. The magazine had four fluted tubes that held an extraordinary total of thirty-four .44in cartridges. Each time the lever was lowered, the magazine turned one quarter of a turn, feeding a cartridge into the magazine by means of a screw thread machined into the inside wall of the magazine. It was complicated, and the mechanism was prone to locking up solid if it became dry or ingested dirt or sand, all of which were fairly fundamental elements on the plains. Despite at least two dealers in the West offering it for sale, the company went bust in 1880 and examples are rare today.

There were also a number of very well-designed repeating rifles developed during and after the war, but two magazine rifles stand out as having historical significance way beyond the many that were to proliferate in the West in the years immediately post-Civil War. These were the Spencer and the Henry. While this chapter is in no way meant to be an exhaustive history of both makes, their importance certainly warrants a close look at their development and use.

The Spencer was an important design that was to usher in the modern era of repeating firearms. Christopher Milner Spencer was a talented engineer who, for many years, had been playing with the concept of magazine-loaded weapons. In March 1860, he patented a perfected design of a repeating magazine rifle, the first of which was made under contract by a company named Cheney Brothers. Amazingly, in view of the complex mechanism, the first Spencer's worked well from the start, proving the basic soundness of his design. They were lever-action seven-shot repeaters chambering a copper-cased .56-calibre rimfire cartridge that was loaded into a tube magazine through a hole in the buttplate. It was a clever, though not totally original solution to the problem of where to put the magazine and did sometimes prove a weak point, as

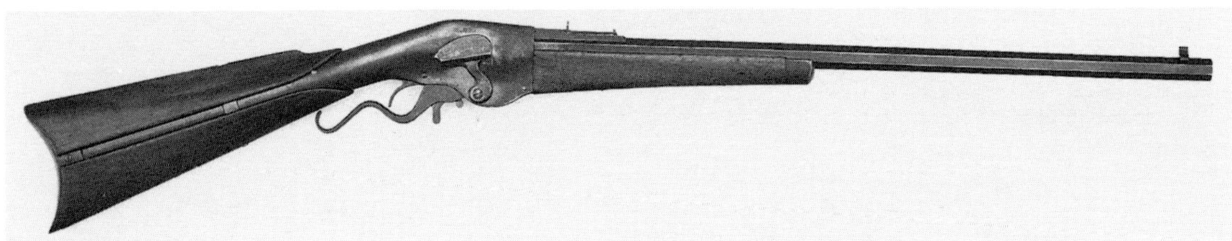

The complex Evans lever-action repeating rifle of 1872. Courtesy of the Trustees of the Royal Armouries.

the tubes could come loose, as William Breakenridge found to his chagrin in Colorado in 1867.

> Suddenly a band of six Indians ran through the edge of town … the men all ran out and one of them took my Springfield...I was forced to get another. It was a Spencer carbine which loaded in the stock … I fired at one Indian … I felt sure that I had hit him and tried to throw another shell into the gun, when I found that the spring that held the cartridges in the breech had come out and all the shells had fallen out of the gun.[4]

Despite this unfortunate tendency, the mechanism of the Spencer proved to be tough and mechanically trouble-free. Unlocking and lowering the lever allowed the rear portion of the block to drop, exposing the chamber. As the lever was closed, the magazine spring pushed the cartridge forwards and the top of the breechblock caught it, pushing it into the chamber. Raising the lever then firmly locked the breech. The hammer had to be manually cocked for each shot, but the Spencer could be fired at a rate of one shot every two seconds. After 1864, the rifles were equipped with a cut-off device invented by Edward Stabler, that isolated the magazine and allowed cartridges to be fed manually into the chamber. The 350 grain bullet and 45 grain charge of the Spencer gave it a maximum effective range of about 400yd (365m), although it lost velocity very quickly at that distance. The Spencer had proven itself in

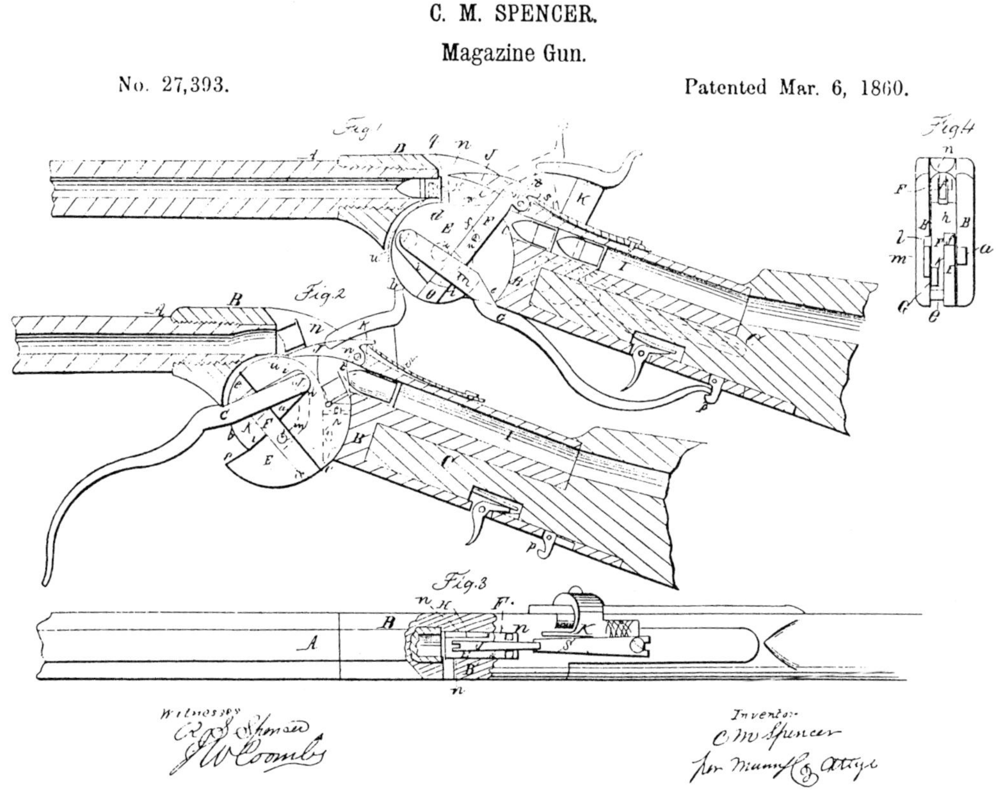

C. M. SPENCER.

Magazine Gun.

No. 27,393. Patented Mar. 6, 1860.

Christopher Spencer's original 1860 patent.

(Top) A commercial variant of the Spencer rifle, half-stocked and with a long-range sight visible just behind the hammer. This example was used for buffalo hunting post-Civil War. Photo courtesy of Jim Lewis.
(Above) A Spencer infantry rifle.

battle and more importantly, carbines and rifles were cheap and in plentiful supply, as some 106,000 had been manufactured during the war. A carbine could be had for as little as $10 and a rifle $12, with cartridges about $2.50 per hundred. The original .56-56 calibre cartridge was powerful enough for use against buffalo but from 1866, .56-52 and .56-50 cartridges became available with 45 grain charges and 400 or 350 grain bullets, which made up in hitting power what they lacked in range.

They proved to be more than adequate cartridges for the early buffalo hunters who were beginning to work the vast herds on the Great Plains. The Spencer bullet was dubbed 'the humdinger' because its low velocity meant that it could be heard humming as it passed by. More important was the repeating firepower of the guns, which was a godsend against the frequent Indian attacks as one traveller on the Missouri in 1866 recounted. Having met a party of woodcutters, Andrew Simmons and his Spencer-armed party noted that:

> … these men were armed with Hawkins rifles … greatly inferior to the breech-loading cartridge guns then in use. We warned them of their danger but with energy and enterprise they possessed also the courage and recklessness of all pioneers. They said they were ready to take chances. Poor fellows! The chances were too strong for them … for afterwards a party of Sioux Indians came upon them … and every one of them massacred.[5]

The mechanism of the Spencer was also used as the basis for modified hunting rifles fitted with improved heavy Hawken barrels by a number of Western gunsmiths, but the major drawback to development of the Spencer was the design of the mechanism, which could only feed a short cartridge. Any attempt to use a longer case would mean a reduction in magazine capacity and require a total redesign of the action. Some Spencer's were converted in the 1870s to take the short .50-70in centrefire cartridge also used in the Sharps carbine, but it was only marginally more powerful than the original .56 cartridge and gave little performance improvement. Although the Spencer company was to continue with other models, the rimfire Model 1865 was eventually to be overtaken by other magazine rifles, one of the most prominent being its arch-rival, the Henry. James Cook, who spent a lifetime working the frontier, summed up the feeling of many regarding the old Spencer:

> One day a Mexican rode into camp with an almost new Henry rifle on his saddle. He wanted to buy some cartridges for it. We had no Henry rifle shells but did have some Spencer ammunition and I succeeded in trading him for his Henry, my Spencer carbine … this rifle proved a most accurate shooting piece, and I had the satisfaction of knowing that nobody … had a better shooting iron than I.[6]

The Henry rifle had a complex beginning, starting life as a design produced in 1849 by an inventor and engineer from New York named Walter Hunt. He had earlier produced a primitive self-contained cartridge called the 'Volitional Ball' or 'rocket ball', which was a simple hollow conical bullet much like a Minié, with a powder charge in its base, sealed by a cork disc, in the centre of which was a priming cap. When struck by a firing pin, the bullet fired and in practice it worked quite well, although the 'cartridge' was somewhat underpowered. It actually owed much to an earlier type, the Flobert, which had proved popular in Europe. The experimental 'Volitional' rifle that Hunt produced had a tube magazine under the barrel and a self-contained firing pin that was released by a spring. He soon sold the rights to a gunmaker called Lewis Jennings, who had himself earlier produced a ring-trigger magazine rifle with pill percussion lock, although it was not a commercial success. Horace Smith, of later Smith and Wesson fame, had taken over the Jennings patent in 1854 and he and Wesson took out a joint patent on a lever-action repeating pistol partly using the Hunt/Jennings system. Crucially for the future of the lever action, the senior machinist at a large firearms' manufacturer named Robbins and Lawrence was one Benjamin Tyler Henry, who had, during his employment with Robbins, been quietly assisting Smith and Wesson with their underlever design.

What they finally produced was a mechanism using a longitudinally sliding breechblock that was locked by an underlever toggle link. It also incorporated a tube magazine mounted underneath the barrel. The carrier for raising the cartridge from magazine to breech slid vertically upwards. Working the toggle dropped the carrier, where a cartridge was pushed rearwards from the magazine onto it. Closing the ring lever raised the carrier and the breech ran forwards, pushing the cartridge into the chamber, and locking behind it, in a similar manner to the shell-loading mechanism of a big naval gun. It was a very clever design, fast and quite smooth to operate. If there was a major obstacle to the design achieving any credibility in the West, where shooting distances could be very great indeed, it was that its bullet produced a slothful velocity of under 500 fps that gave it a short range and miserable stopping power. Smith and Wesson soon realized that the design of the Volcanic was not well suited to a handgun and they abandoned it, being far more concerned with pursuing better pistol designs. In 1854, they sold the rights to the Volcanic Arms company, based in Norwich, Connecticut in which one Oliver Winchester was a major stockholder. Volcanic produced a range of pistols and carbines in varying barrel lengths and calibres of .30 or .36in. They all used the same ring-operated, rising-block mechanism and were chambered for the underpowered Volcanic self-contained bullet. The guns themselves were actually very well made and were capable of good accuracy, albeit at limited ranges. One newspaper report commented on an exhibition of the new repeating guns that they '… seem to be the very perfection of firearms'. Some 3,200 Volcanics were manufactured in a variation of types; pistols, rifles and carbines, but the company never achieved the sales that they needed and, following the death of the Company President, went into receivership in 1857.

This allowed Oliver Winchester to take over the now ailing business, restructuring it and renaming it the New Haven Arms Company, although for a while the guns continued to be marked 'Volcanic'.

No. 30,446. B. T. HENRY. Patented Oct. 16, 1860.

Magazine Fire Arm.

B.T. Henry's patent of 1860 for his lever-action repeating rifle.

Although Winchester had made his money from shirt manufacture he had long been interested in firearms. Crucially, he also employed inventor and engineer Benjamin Tyler Henry as Superintendent of the new company. Henry had filed a patent in 1860 for an improved lever-action rifle that used a new .44-calibre rimfire cartridge and Winchester provided the financial backing for the manufacture of the new Henry rifle that appeared in mid-1862. The performance of the rifle was remarkable for its day. In tests it fired 187 shots in three minutes and thirty-six seconds, and fired offhand it could place all of its bullets in an 18in (46cm) bull at over 100yd (92m). This was a result of both the mechanics of the rifle and its cartridge, for unlike the Spencer, the rifle did not require the hammer to be manually cocked each time. The new rimfire with its charge of 25 grains of powder and 216 grain bullet, gave the rifle a far greater range and much improved stopping power over the old Volcanic. The design was by no means perfect though, for the loading required the front of the magazine under the muzzle to be unlatched and a thumbpiece to be pushed forwards to allow the magazine spring to be compressed to accommodate the ammunition. The slot that this catch ran in allowed water and dirt in. In fact, the swivelling end cap of the magazine was awkward to use and loading itself was not an easy operation. But such minor details were easy to overlook in the face of the performance of the Henry, particularly in the face of the unmatched firepower of the new rifle. By 1862, a number of St Louis dealers were selling it, and for many professional hunters and trail guides it became the pre-eminent arm, despite its fairly hefty $42 price tag. One comment extracted from a letter to the company has more of a ring of truth to it, stating that:

> The recent experience of my men on their journey through Sonora and Arizona armed with these weapons … in the Indian country, so great is the dependence placed upon them that none … care to go on escort duty unless there is one or more of these powerful and accurate weapons in the party.[7]

The Henry's effectiveness at moderate ranges was reinforced in a manner far more eloquent than any advertising testimonials when, in August 1867, a large group of warriors under Chief Red Cloud attacked a wood-cutting party of twenty soldiers and six civilians, at least three of whom had Henrys. One participant, D.A. Colvin was a cool and careful shot, and his actions were later described by another survivor, Finn Burnett, in what was to become known as The Hayfield Fight.

> He was armed with a sixteen shot repeating rifle and he had a thousand rounds of ammunition. He was a dead shot, and if he missed an Indian in that fight, none of us ever knew it. He fired about three hundred shots … and as he did most of his shooting at distances from twenty to seventy five yards, it was almost impossible for him to miss. He was shooting steadily from nine-thirty in the morning to until five o-clock in the afternoon, and the ground … was literally covered with empty shells from his rifle.[8]

The Indians, used to the slow rate of fire of single-shot rifles, were taken aback by the level of fire directed at them, although they continued to press home their attacks. The number killed is disputed but believed to have been around seventy dead and double that number wounded. In 1865, Winchester had employed a new Superintendent of Works, Nelson King, who soon modified the loading mechanism by replacing the magazine with a hollow tube and inserting a loading gate on the right-hand side of the rifle's receiver where it was protected by the strong metal of the frame. This enabled the cartridges to be slipped in nose first, with the rifle held in almost any position. In December of 1866, Oliver Winchester changed the name of the firm to the Winchester Repeating Arms Company and a Western legend was about to be born.

The new Winchester, introduced in early 1867 with its side loading gate, distinctive brass receiver and 18-shot magazine, quickly became known as the 'Yellow Boy', although its true designation was the Model 1866. Aware of criticisms made

SIXTY SHOTS PER MINUTE

HENRY'S PATENT

REPEATING

RIFLE

The Most Effective Weapon in the World.

This Rifle can be discharged 16 times without loading or taking down from the shoulder, or even loosing aim. It is also slung in such a manner, that either on horse or on foot, it can be **Instantly Used**, without taking the strap from the shoulder.

For a House or Sporting Arm, it has no Equal;

IT IS ALWAYS LOADED AND ALWAYS READY.

The size now made is 44-100 inch bore, 24 inch barrel, and carries a conical ball 32 to the pound. The penetration at 100 yards is 8 inches, at 400 yards 5 inches; and it carries with force sufficient to kill at 1,000 yards.

A resolute man, armed with one of these Rifles, particularly if on horseback, CANNOT BE CAPTURED.

"We particularly commend it for ARMY USES, as the most effective arm for picket and vidette duty, and to all our citizens in secluded places, as a protection against guerilla attacks and robberies. A man armed with one of these Rifles, can load and discharge one shot every second, so that he is equal to a company every minute, a regiment every ten minutes, a brigade every half hour, and a division every hour."—*Louisville Journal.*

Address **JNO. W. BROWN,**
Gen'l Ag't., Columbus, Ohio,
At Rail Road Building, near the Depot.

R. NEVINS' Steam Printing Establishment, No.'s 36, 38 and 40 North High Street, Columbus, Ohio.

An 1861 advertisement for the Henry rifle.

over the weight and length of the Henry a carbine version was also made, which held fourteen cartridges. Winchester's promotional literature went to great lengths to extol the virtues of the new gun, stating with some truth that:

> … the gun is made stronger yet light, the magazine is closed and strongly protected; it is more simple in operation, requiring few motions in the one case and fewer pieces in the other. Not only can this gun be fired thirty times in a minute continuously as a repeater, but it can be used as a single loader without any attachment to be changed for the purpose, retaining the magazine full of cartridges … when the whole fifteen cartridges can be fired in fifteen seconds – an effectiveness far beyond that of any other arm.[9]

On the Frontier, the Winchester was beginning to draw an appreciative following and not just from the settlers and adventurers. At least one Indian, having been killed by Finn Burnett who was accompanying a wagon train, was found to be carrying a brand new Winchester, at a time when they were still a rarity in the West. How he acquired it was a complete mystery. Winchester were keen to improve sales, and exploration parties that set out to travel the Colorado river in 1869 and 1871 were almost exclusively equipped with them, which proved useful publicity, but there were still some shortcomings with the rifle. The '66 had some inherent design weaknesses, which were the main reasons for its failure to gain military acceptance in the stringent trials to which it was subjected in early 1872. The mechanism was very susceptible to dirt entering the open top of the breech and jamming the carrier block, so a sliding dust cover was fitted to the top of the receiver to counter the problem. The brass body of the gun, while undoubtedly handsome, was soft, prone to damage and wore quickly, so was replaced with a steel receiver. In addition the toggle-link action was modified to include a separate firing pin, activated by a spring, that alleviated one of the most dangerous eccentricities of the Yellow Boy – accidental misfiring. The resulting rifle was called the Model 1873, and was destined to become a Western icon.

Although the new Winchester was a great improvement mechanically over the Henry, it still relied on the structurally weak and puny rimfire cartridge, which possessed only moderately useful killing power and less than spectacular accuracy at any distance. The answer lay in the adoption of the new centrefire cartridges, that had been in existence since around 1870. Inexplicably, Winchester did not chamber the Model 1866 for them, waiting until the Model 1873 was in production, then offering it in .32-30, .38-40 and .44-40 calibres. Contrary to what many believe, this use of the .44-40 cartridge was not because of its compatibility with similarly chambered Colt

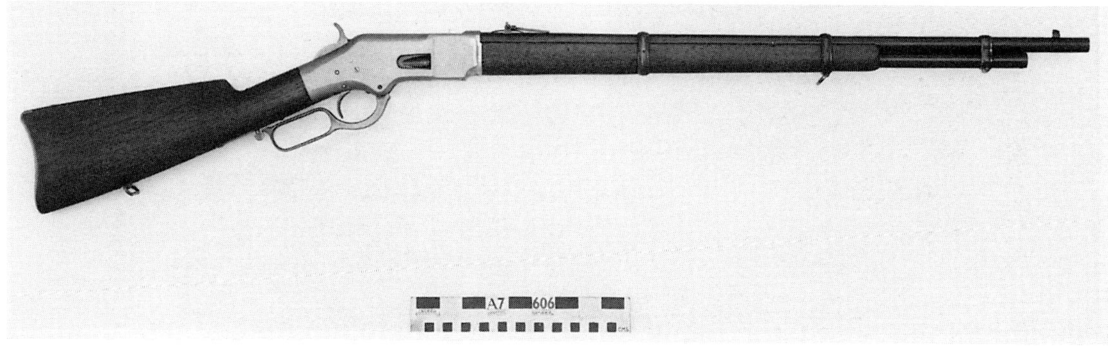

Winchester Model 1866 rifle in .44 calibre. Courtesy of the Trustees of the Royal Armouries.

N. KING.

MAGAZINE FIREARM.

No. 55,012. Patented May 22, 1866.

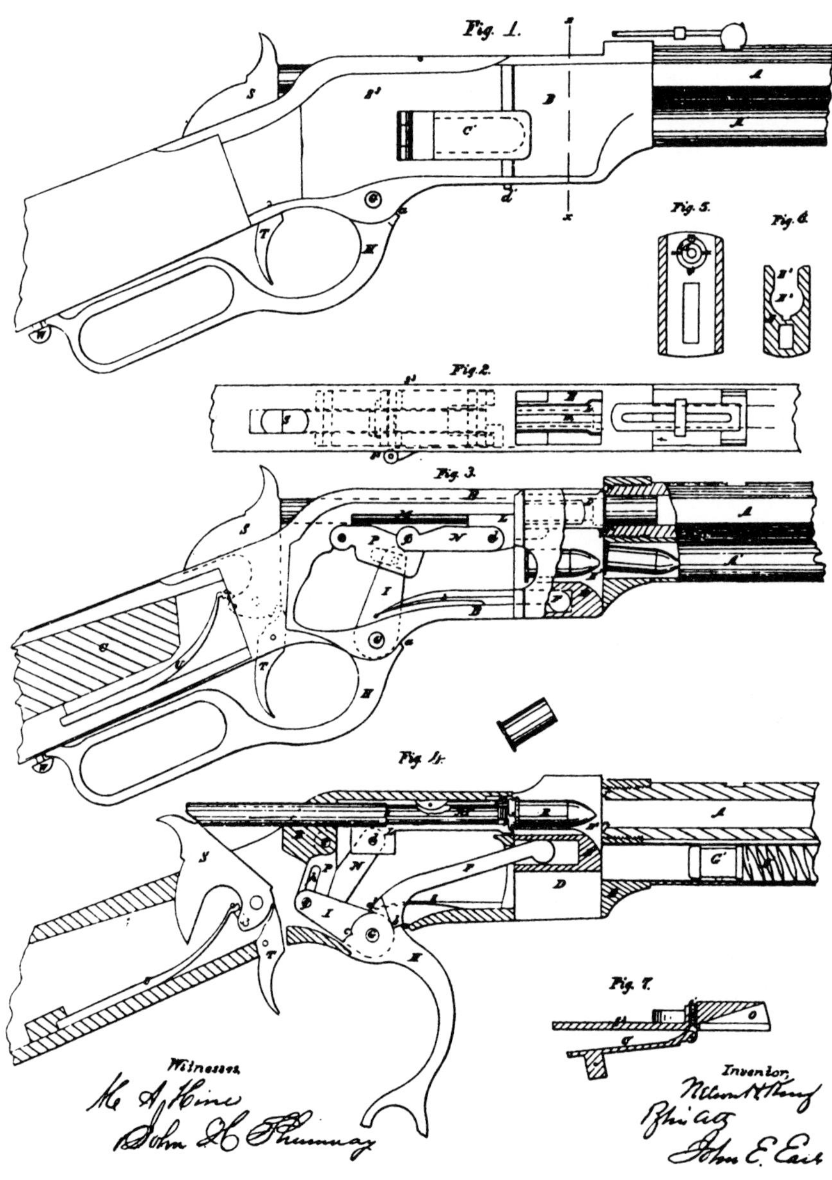

King's patent for the Winchester rifle.

revolvers, for the .44-40 Colt Frontier Six Shooter was not produced until 1878. The .44-40 was a good enough pistol cartridge but a peculiar choice for a rifle, being only a little more powerful than the old rimfire. At 300yd (275m) it was losing power so quickly that trajectory drop was over 12ft (3.7m). Nevertheless, the Model 1873 was produced in a wide variety of barrel lengths, magazine capacities and finishes and despite the limitations imposed by the cartridges it proved hugely popular in the West.

It began to appear in gunshops in St Louis in early 1874, and was soon available in Texas and on the West Coast. It retailed for $50, or $40 for the carbine, and became the chosen weapon of lawmen, Texas Rangers, cowboys and bandits. The Winchester was also used by a number of Western celebrities, including Buffalo Bill, who had forsaken his old Springfield in favour of a Model 1873. With perhaps a more than clear understanding of the benefits of self-publicity, he wrote to Winchester in 1874, extolling the virtues of the rifle.

> I have been using and have thoroughly tested your latest and improved rifle. Allow me to say that I have tried and used nearly every kind of gun made in the United States, and for general hunting or Indian fighting I pronounce your improved Winchester the best. When in the Black Hills this last summer ... Mr Bear made for me ... that bear was not thirty feet from me when he charged but before he could reach me I had eleven bullets in him, which was a little more lead than he could comfortably digest. Believe me that you have made the most complete rifle now made.[10]

That the 1873 was popular is proved by the sales figures. It was in production for forty-six years and in excess of 720,000 rifles were sold. While it was true that nothing could compete with the short-range rapid-fire of the Winchester, the lever-actions in turn couldn't compete in performance with the very powerful, long-range single-shot rifles such as Sharps and Remington, and the company wisely refrained from attempting comparisons. Nevertheless, the factory was keen to introduce a rifle that would

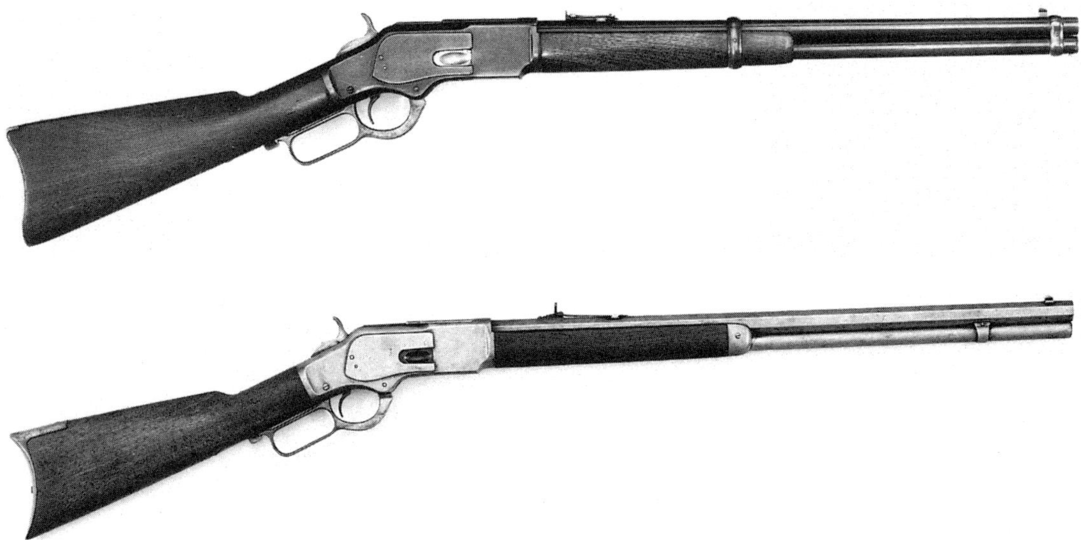

(Top) Winchester Model 1873 saddle-ring carbine. Courtesy of the Trustees of the Royal Armouries.
(Above) Winchester Model 1873, in .45-90 calibre with heavy octagonal barrel. Courtesy of the Trustees of the Royal Armouries.

chamber a more powerful cartridge. The problem was simply mechanical, for the breech-locking system was not strong, and while Winchester would like to have chambered his rifle for the issue Government .45-70 cartridge, it was too long and too powerful and would have meant completely redesigning the action of the '73. The answer was to produce a new model, the Model 1876 that had a longer and heavier receiver and was initially chambered to fire a bottlenecked .47-75 cartridge. Before long, a potent .50-95 was added to the list, and this proved to be about as powerful as the mechanism could handle.

Other models were to follow, and the most significant in Western terms was undoubtedly the Model 1886. This gun was probably single-handedly responsible for the demise of the traditional single-shot rifles such as Sharps and Ballard, which had played such a large part up until then in shaping Western history, and commercially it was an almost overnight success. The '86 was developed by John Browning who had a seemingly impossible brief to design a magazine rifle that would take the most powerful of cartridges, without being too long, too heavy or too complicated. Few engineers could actually have achieved this, but Browning came up with a mechanism that used a longitudinally sliding breech and bolt onto which the loading lever was directly pivoted. (Earlier lever actions had mainly used the receiver to mount the pivot.) He did away with the toggle link and used two vertically sliding locking bolts that worked on either side of the bolt. This met all of Winchester's design parameters as well as giving the '86 a far smoother operating action and a stronger breech than was ever likely to be needed. For the first time a lever action had been produced that could take the most potent cartridge known, and deliver it with speed and accuracy. The new rifle was offered for sale in a range of large calibres, .38-56, .40-65, .45-70, .45-90, and also for the .50-110 Express. This very potent round, introduced in 1899, was a new concept in high-performance black powder ammunition, and it combined a comparatively light bullet allied to a very large charge. This gave an extremely flat trajectory out to about 300yd (275m), and made long range shooting to 800 or 900yd (730m or 825m) perfectly feasible. The new rifle came with a 26in round barrel and magazine capacity of eight or nine, depending on calibre. For big game in both the United States and Africa, the Winchester was equalled only by some of the bigger double rifles and it was capable of felling grizzly bear, moose, rhino and even elephant. It was offered for sale at a basic $45 and within a short time had become one of Winchester's most successful rifles. One problem with the 1886 was the cost of manufacture, which made the gun comparatively expensive, so Winchester simplified the design and reintroduced it as the Model 1892.

The only serious competitors Winchester had at this time were Marlin and Savage. In 1893 Marlin had brought out a fine hammerless lever-action repeater that matched the Winchester in terms of reliability and performance. The rivalry between the two companies was intense, so Winchester countered with their Model 1894. It was not much different to look at from previous Winchesters, but it had been designed with a nickel steel barrel and very heavy vertically sliding breechblock that was mortised into the receiver. This gave it the sort of strength required to handle chamber pressures generated by the new smokeless powders, which were on average 30 per cent higher than black powder and in the region of 40,000psi. The advantages were enormous, for relatively small-calibre bullets could be used that reached velocities well in excess of 2,000fps, unattainable by black powder cartridges. Older guns simply could not handle the new ammunition and Winchester stole a march upon most of their rivals with the Model 1894. It was so successful that it is still in widespread use today. One problem with the new longer cartridges was the use of tube magazines, so in 1895, a Winchester with box magazine was produced and this enabled cartridges such as .30-40 Krag to be used, the .30-30 of the original '94 being deemed only a mid-range cartridge.

If Spencer and Winchester had been the first to start the trend towards repeating firearms, they were by no means the only successful players in the field. The Colt company had watched the

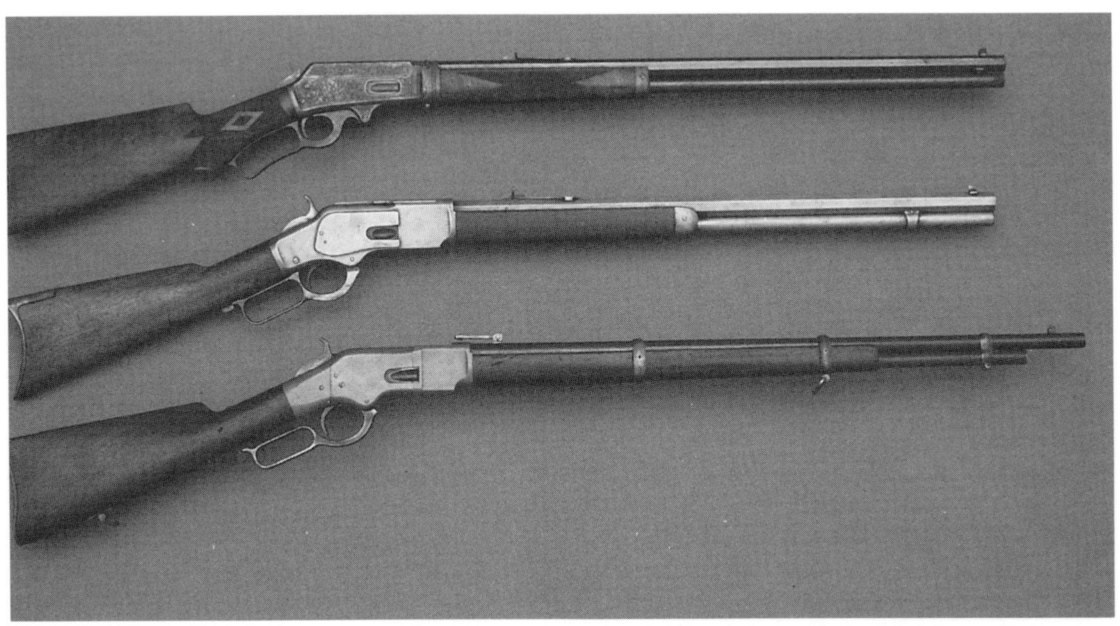

(Above) Top: a Marlin Deluxe Model 1893 Safety, in rare .25-36 calibre. Below are a model 1873 Winchester in .44-40 calibre and an 1866 also in .44-40. Courtesy of the Trustees of the Royal Armouries.

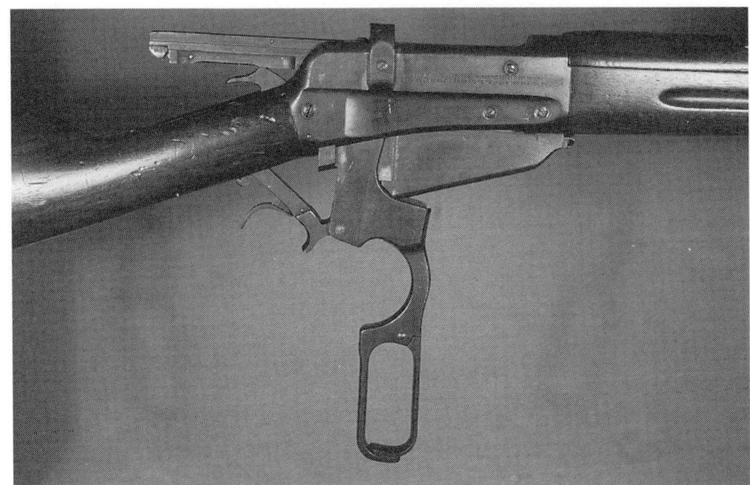

(Right) The open action of Winchester's Model 1895 rifle. Courtesy of the Trustees of the Royal Armouries.

success of the Winchester, in particular the Model 1873, with envious eyes, and decided to enter into direct competition with Winchester, so in 1883 they brought out a lever-action rifle that was strikingly similar to the Winchester design.

The Colt-Burgess was designed by Andrew Burgess but had a far simpler mechanism that used a breech-lever extension combined with a longitudinally sliding breech-block. When the breech was locked, the pressure generated by the exploding cartridge was taken by the breech-lever pivot pin, a far better method than the fundamentally weak Winchester. As a result, the Colt was able to chamber the popular .45-70 Government cartridge, with a tubular magazine that could hold between eight to ten rounds, and a varying choice of barrel lengths and weight as well as set triggers, engraving, special target sights and even lightweight versions. It was offered for sale at a basic $24 for a carbine and $27 for a rifle, and long barrels were charged at $1 per inch extra. It was to prove a considerable commercial success, much to the annoyance of Winchester. In fact, so ruffled were they that Winchester, who had previously purchased some of Burgess's very promising revolver designs, made it clear that they would start manufacturing pistols in direct competition to Colt's popular single action. This threat was backed up by the fact that Winchester also held the rights to an improved Burgess rifle, and were quite prepared to put it into production. A 'gentleman's agreement' was therefore reached between the two arms' giants, that Colt would cease making rifles and Winchester would not manufacture pistols. Some 6,400 Colt-Burgess rifles had been made in a comparatively short period of a year and it is interesting to speculate what sales would have eventually been if production had continued. Despite their 'agreement', Colt did in fact return to rifle manufacture, but not in direct competition with Winchester, for instead of lever-actions they looked at a different end of the repeating rifle market.

There was considerable demand for light-weight guns that were strong enough to use for self-defence in Indian Territory, could down small game, yet were light and simple. Pump- or slide-action shotguns had been around for some time, and Colt applied the principle to a new range of repeating rifles that they introduced in 1883.

Patented by William Elliot, these guns were called the 'Lightning Magazine Rifle', but were

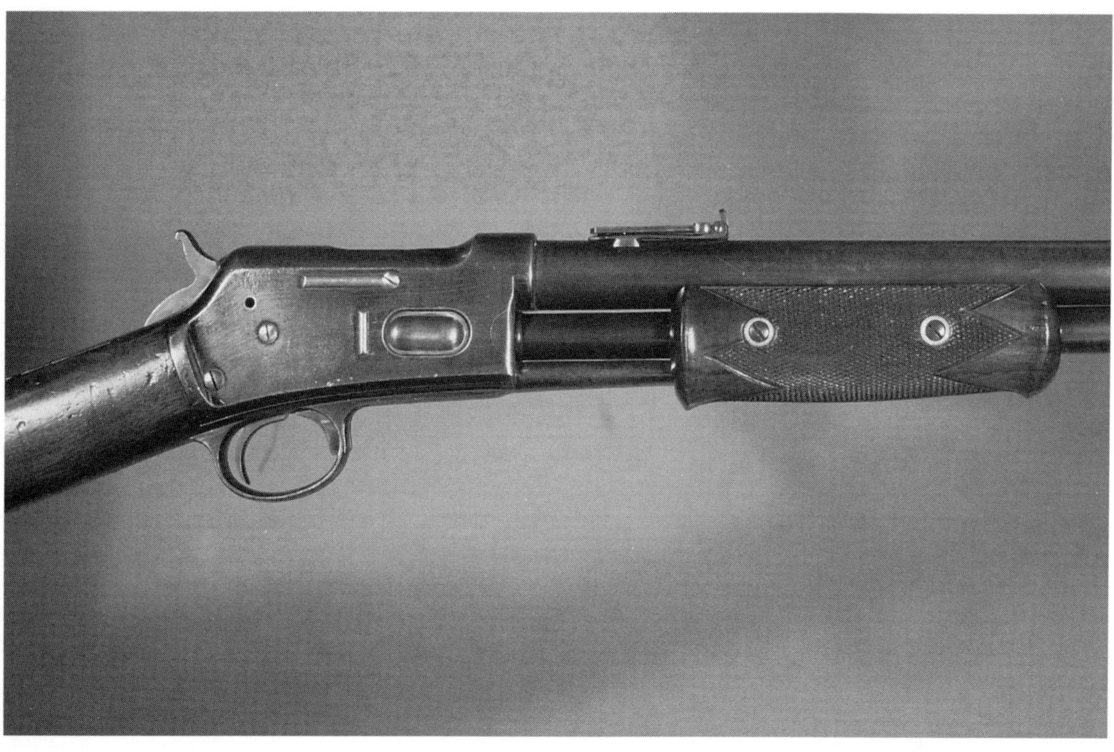

A Colt Lighting pump-action rifle in .38 calibre. Courtesy of the Trustees of the Royal Armouries.

universally known as the Lightning. The sliding fore-end was almost a direct copy of that used on the Spencer shotgun, but the action comprised a longitudinally sliding breechblock worked by the fore-end, under which was a pivoted locking block. This had the benefit of enabling the shooter to keep the trigger pulled, and firing the rifle by racking back the fore-end as fast as possible, giving an astonishing rate of fire of around two shots per second. It was a reasonably simple and strong mechanism, capable of handling most medium calibres. Early production models suffered from ejection problems but this was soon resolved and the rifle became very popular. Initially it was introduced in .32-30, .38 and .40-40, the tube magazine holding fifteen cartridges in the rifle and twelve in the carbine. Lightnings became popular rifles for trick shooting and were used by George Sickles, Johnny Baker and Annie Oakley amongst others. In the more demanding country out west, the light weight of the gun – it weighed 8lb (3.6kg) loaded – made it useful for carrying on a saddle or wagon, and Colt capitalized on this by producing a 'Baby' carbine weighing only 6lb (2.7kg).

Inevitably demand grew for a wider range of calibres and in 1888 Colt produced a larger version, the Express Rifle. This heavy-framed gun was a ten-shot repeater and weighed about 10lb (4.5kg), although a carbine version was also available at 2lb lighter. It was available in a wide range of calibres, mostly .40, .45 and .50 and was the final incarnation of the Lightning. Some 6,500 were sold in total. At the same time, a little .22 version was produced and more of these were probably sold than any other small-calibre rimfire firearm. For generations of youngsters it was the gun with which they learned to shoot tin cans, squirrels or impress their girls at fairgrounds. The Lightning was eventually discontinued in 1900, after nearly 90,000 had been manufactured.

Although Andrew Burgess's name is now virtually unknown, his contribution to repeating firearms' design was immensely important and many guns carried in the West owed their existence to his mechanical genius. He believed in the basic engineering principle of 'keep it simple' and he had a particular love of lever actions. His design of action for lever rifles had not been used exclusively by Colt; some years earlier in 1876, when working in New York, he had produced a lever rifle chambered for the .45-70 government round, which he subsequently displayed at the Centennial Exposition. It was subsequently manufactured under contract by Eli Whitney and sold as the Whitney Long Range Repeating Rifle, a claim that, at the time, Winchester couldn't match. Another version of the Whitney, chambered for the smaller .30-40 and .44-40 cartridges, had an improvement to the carrier mechanism designed by Samuel Kennedy so the receiver was stamped with his name and patent. As a result most of the Whitney-Kennedy rifles became erroneously known as Kennedy's, which must have been less than amusing to Eli Whitney and Andrew Burgess. However, Burgess's design abilities did not end there.

In 1880, John Marlin, who had been manufacturing the popular single-shot Ballard rifles, expressed an interest in entering the repeating rifle trade. As Burgess still had two patents in force that could provide a basis for a design, he set to and produced what was to become the Model 1881 Marlin. Burgess's design used an extension of the cocking lever that projected vertically up into the rear of the breech. With the lever closed, the longitudinally sliding breechblock was pushed forwards against the breech face and the extension, which pivoted on a strong pin, effectively locking the mechanism. It was immensely strong and could chamber nearly all of the large cartridges then in production. The Marlin gained some fame, or notoriety depending on one's point of view, from the fact that it was used in considerable numbers by the runners who wiped out the last buffalo herd in the Northern Territories between 1880 and 1885.

The heavy-barrelled Marlin in .45 calibre had both the power and range, allied to its repeating-fire ability, that few other rifles could match except possibly some of the new Winchesters chambered for the larger cartridges. But Burgess's simpler and

A chuck wagon, probably in New Mexico in the 1890s. The rifle is a Whitney Kennedy, the pistols are probably Colt Single-Actions. Courtesy the Museum of New Mexico.

stronger design won the Marlin a great many admirers and in the late 1880s, capitalizing on its success, Marlin produced a new range of rifles designed by Lewis Hepburn of Remington-Hepburn fame that, like the Lightning, were designed specifically for smaller calibres. This rifle actually owed more to Winchester in terms of design and several models followed, the 1889 arguably being the most popular due to its use of a solid receiver with an ejection port on the right. This improved the resistance of the mechanism to the ingress of dirt and, more importantly, enabled an optical sight to be mounted on top of the rifle, which could not be done with Winchesters. One drawback was that most of these Marlins were chambered for the medium-calibre cartridges, that were simply not powerful enough to be good all-rounders. As a result, in 1893, Hepburn produced a modified 1889 that was mechanically simpler and had an action that had been lengthened to accept the longer more powerful cartridges that were then available and it proved highly popular. In 1896, Marlin also made a hammerless lever action that could chamber the new smokeless cartridges, and this proved to be a big rival to the all-conquering Winchesters.

Although they never entered into the production of repeating rifles, Smith and Wesson were keen to have a place in the market so they compromised and their entry came in the unusual form of a revolving rifle, the New Model No 3 Carbine, introduced in the early 1880s. This was effectively a long-barrelled revolver supplied with a detachable shoulder stock in an option of 16, 18 or 20in lengths. It was a very nicely made gun but the

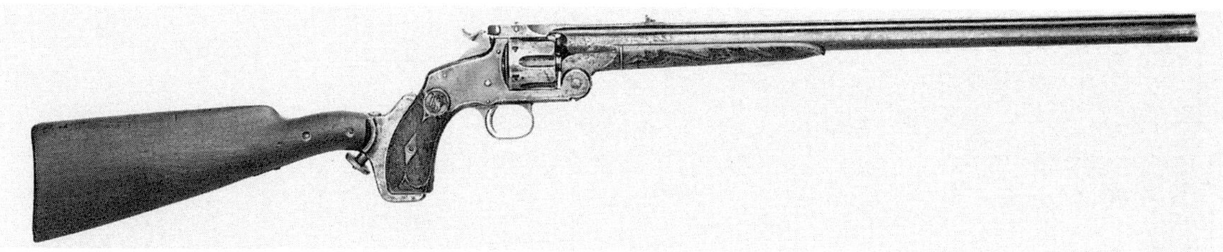

A rare Smith and Wesson revolving rifle, of which only 977 were made. Courtesy of the Trustees of the Royal Armouries.

problem with it was the weedy .320-calibre cartridge it was chambered for, which made it a somewhat underpowered rifle, and only 1,000 or so were sold.

A more conventional repeating arm that appeared in the early 1880s was the Bullard (not to be confused with the existing Ballard) lever action. It was worked by compound levers and a rack-and-pinion assembly that was both complicated and comparatively expensive, retailing at $35 for the basic model. However, James Bullard's design was smooth operating in the extreme and had the added strength, when closed, of being solidly locked by what was in effect a rolling block action, making it the strongest of any lever action, and capable of digesting even the gargantuan .50-115 cartridge. One Bullard enthusiast was Theodore Roosevelt who owned and regularly used one chambered for this cartridge. Despite the competition, the grip that Winchester had on the lever-action rifle market was vice-like, and they sold more rifles than all of the other makes combined.

BOLT-ACTION RIFLES

By the early 1800s, a new form of rifle was appearing that would eventually take over as the predominant longarm of the West and this was the bolt-action rifle. Bolt actions had been in production in Europe since the late 1860s, and both France and the German states had engaged in warfare on a grand scale using them during the Franco-Prussian war of 1870. These needlefire guns were heavy, rather cumbersome, large-calibre rifles that relied on a primitive combustible, centrefire black powder cartridge. However, the actual bolt-action mechanism was simple and fairly efficient, relying on a rotating bolt that was unlocked by means of a protruding lug on the right-hand side. The breech-locking lugs were an integral part of the bolt itself; when the bolt handle was pushed downwards the lugs locked in to the receiver and ensured that the bolt-face was solidly locked into the breech. It gave the new rifles tremendous strength and providentially enabled them to handle the new generation of

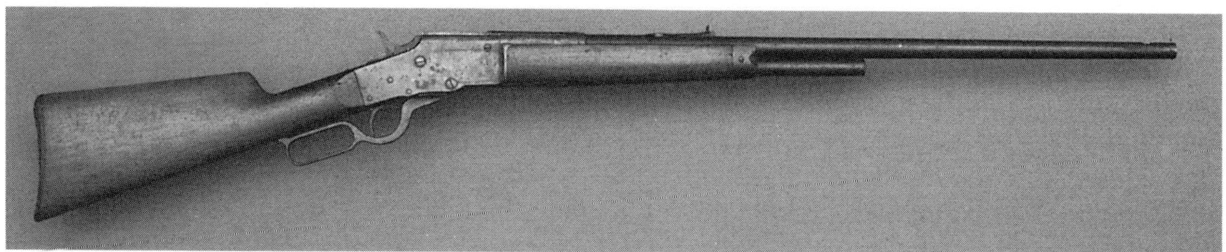

A Model 1886 Bullard chambered for the .32 Special cartridge with its tubular magazine visible beneath the barrel. Unlike the Winchester, it does not have the distinctive loading gate on the side of the receiver. Courtesy of the Trustees of the Royal Armouries.

The Hotchkiss .45-70 infantry rifle. Courtesy of the Trustees of the Royal Armouries.

smokeless powder cartridges that were, in the late nineteenth century, becoming the standard ammunition for virtually all firearms. Initially there was little interest in the new rifles. Most sportsmen and adventurers were conservatives at heart and were happy enough to rely on the technology they knew – lever actions and large-bore single-shot rifles.

As early as 1876, a turning-bolt rifle had been designed by a naturalized Frenchman, Benjamin Hotchkiss, who presented his rifle to the world at the Centennial Exhibition in Philadelphia in 1876. It was an interesting concept, owing a little to the past by utilizing a five-shot tube magazine very similar in design to that of the Spencer, but having a bolt action with a sprung floorplate underneath. When the bolt was pulled back a single cartridge was pushed upward, and the action of pushing the bolt home chambered the round. It is a familiar mechanism to most shooters today, but met with considerable reserve at the time. It was briefly tested by the army, who could see its potential but put their reservations into plain language:

> The manufacturer's experience with this gun proves that difficulties are ever to be met and overcome in perfecting a new invention ... the principle of the Hotchkiss is a good one, but there seems to be a prejudice existing ... against the bolt system and its awkward handle that time and custom may overcome.[11]

Undaunted by early problems, Hotchkiss produced a first model in 1879, chambered for the .45 government cartridge, then an improved second model in 1880. This rifle did away with the tube-type magazine and was loaded by pushing the cartridges directly into the magazine from the opened breech. Its performance was good, a skilled shot being able to fire five aimed shots in around ten seconds. It was certainly efficient enough to interest the Winchester Company, who promptly purchased the manufacturing rights. The final configuration of the Hotchkiss, the Model 1883, was made available as a pure sporting rifle, with round or heavy octagonal barrel and pistol grip. It had a six-shot magazine and a cut-off to enable the chamber to be loaded with single rounds without using the magazine and it was, in form and function, a very modern rifle, retailing at a moderate $25. One drawback was that it was only ever chambered for the Government cartridge that, although powerful enough for most game in the west, was not top of every Westerner's list. Its accuracy was as good as many contemporary rifles and better than some. A good shot could place ten rounds into an 8in (20cm) bull at 200yd (180m) and it had a maximum effective range of around 500yd (460m). In total, some 22,500 were manufactured but it simply didn't catch the public imagination.

Another player in this mechanical merry-go-round was the Remington-Keene that was manufactured on the basis of three patents granted to James Keene of New Jersey, on a bolt-action tube magazine rifle. It was introduced purely as a sporting rifle and had a curiously hybrid look, something between a Winchester and a needlefire Dreyse. It was first produced in 1877 and had several unique features. It used both a turning bolt and separate hammer, the hammer only being set to half-cock when the action was cycled; it had to be manually hand-cocked before firing. This, at a stroke, did away with one of the main advantages of the bolt rifle, the ability to chamber a round and instantly fire it, but Keene had thought of this and each rifle could have the half-cock disengaged by means of a slider let into the tumbler. The disadvantages of tube magazines were well known, so the Model 1877 could also be loaded from either below or above the receiver and the cartridges could only be placed on the magazine carrier when the breech was opened. In fact it could even be loaded when the rifle was inverted, not something that the average Winchester owner could do, even if he wanted to. Like the Lee, it was chambered for the popular .45 Government round as well as commercial .44-calibre ammunition, but it proved a little too expensive at $35 and only 5,000 were manufactured before the company ceased offering it in 1885. One of its disadvantages, common to many of its contemporaries, was that the Remington-Keene was not easily adapted to use the high-velocity smokeless ammunition that was becoming popular.

Hotchkiss and Remington had not been alone in attempting to create the perfect bolt-action gun, for another maker, James Paris Lee, had also been working on similar designs. Lee was a Scot who had emigrated in 1831 and in his early years had designed several rifle actions, most notably a promising single shot in 1874. He had examined the early needle-fire rifles and set out to produce his own, which he did with the assistance of the manufacturing expertise of the Remington Company. His first bolt-action rifle had locking lugs on the shoulder of the bolt handle and an opposing lug that engaged on a seat machined into the inner wall of the receiver. It used a rotating extractor and had the sensible addition of a detachable five-shot box magazine. In 1879, he formed his own company in Bridgeport, Connecticut, coincidentally in the same building where the Sharps Company was on the verge of bankruptcy. Lee did not repeat the mistake of Hotchkiss, and produced his rifles in .45 Government calibre but also .44 and .43 calibre as well, using bottlenecked cartridges. A number of rifles were supplied to the Navy, but despite the efficiency of the design and the improved velocity of the bottlenecked cartridges, the rifle's action was not deemed fast enough to operate and it did not have a sufficient magazine capacity. The Model 1882 Remington-Lee proved to be a commercial success outside the United States, but was not viable within the country and production ceased in about 1896. But unlike many other rifles, the Lee action went on to have a long and distinguished history as a military rifle with the British Army in the guise of the Lee-Enfield, although that, as they say, is another story.

5 Military Muzzle-Loading Longarms

The story of the American military longarm is a fascinating one, for although the US Board of Ordnance was as staid and conservative as their British counterparts, they did not suffer quite so badly from the 'tradition' syndrome where firearms were concerned. As a result, they were more open to technical innovation and more likely to embrace new ideas, many of which were, of course, to originate from their own gunmaking industry. In fact, the US Army adopted a bewildering number of firearms over a comparatively short period of time. To give one example, during the four years of the Civil War, some nineteen different types of carbines were put into service. In comparison, Britain had but three service carbines in use for its entire artillery and cavalry, and two of those were virtually identical.

One of the problems that beset early attempts at standardization of military weapons was the means by which the muskets were supplied. For while Congress authorized the Federal government to supply each of the states with muskets for issue to their Volunteer or Militia units, the major arsenals, such as Harper's Ferry, were already working flat-out to provide enough service muskets to supply the regular army. There was simply no spare capacity for supplying state units, so private contractors were employed to manufacture the necessary longarms for the state militias, ostensibly to a standard pattern. This simply led to a situation of little real standardization or control over the type of guns issued, except to the regular army, and even here, there was considerable latitude. For the volunteers and militia units the situation was chaotic, with a plethora of different models being issued and little standardization even between the same types of musket.

The longarms used against the native Indians and during the early days of the Revolutionary War were mostly carried by Militia units who were little more than loosely organized armed civilians. As a result, their weapons mirrored those carried by all civilians of the mid- to late eighteenth century, namely smoothbore and some rifled flintlocks. Despite the fact that history would now have us believe that every militiaman was a crack shot, capable of felling a running man at 200yd (180m), the truth, as is so often the case, was somewhat different. Many of the early militia units were not in the least adept with their muskets; in 1775, Captain Johnson of the New Hampshire Militia informed Congress that less than half of his men actually possessed a gun, and even then they had 'only one pound of powder to twenty men', and this situation was by no means unique. Yet it is a fact that the rumblings of discontent that were to result in the outbreak of war against the British were to lead eventually to the formation of what was to become the best armed professional army in the Western world. Although there was no centrally co-ordinated organization for issuing muskets to the American militia and army units at this time, there were faint signs of standardization beginning to show, for in most states Committees of Safety had been appointed who were responsible for ensuring that the men were adequately armed.

In the East, where a suitably large number of gunsmiths could be found, muskets were ordered to be manufactured to patterns similar to either the British Land Pattern issue or the French infantry muskets. The bulk of these muskets were built along very similar lines, having 43in pin-fastened barrels and being about .73 bore. On average they weighed 9lb (4kg) and were as good as any other longarm of the period. However, it was not until some twenty years after the War of Independence that the US army eventually settled on a standardized pattern of military musket and this was the US Musket Model 1795. It was manufactured at what was to become America's premier arsenal, the Springfield Armory in Massachusetts, which had also been established in 1795, although some were later produced at Harper's Ferry in Virginia. The musket was more than loosely based on the French Model 1763 Charleville that had seen so much use during the Revolutionary War, and some 9,000 were produced. It had a distinctive 'U.S.' marked lock, 44½ in barrel, a calibre of .69in and weighed

A Militiaman of the Revolutionary War, carrying an early Pennsylvania rifle, powder horn, and pigskin bullet and patch bag. Photo courtesy of Christine L. Malson-Ruckman.

9lb (4kg). In total, it was almost 60in long and could fire accurately out to about 80yd (75m), that put it on a par with just about every other smoothbore musket in use. It had provision for a simple triangular socket bayonet that was held in place by a Z slot in the socket that rotated around a stud at the muzzle. Like all of its type, this was prone to unlocking and falling off at inopportune moments, but the cold steel of the socket bayonet had always proved for the Americans to be very much a last resort and little attention was given to its development. The Model 1795 was not particularly well-made or finished and went through a number of variants, becoming the Models 1812, 1816, 1821 and 1840, some even seeing use during the Civil War of 1861–65. Confusingly, there was also a near identical 1795 pattern produced for issue to the militias, but this was known as the 1808.

Increasingly beset by supply and manufacturing problems, the Ordnance Department decided to create a new pattern of musket, the Model 1812. Uniformity of construction was not its strong point, however, as models made at Springfield had different stocks from those from Harper's Ferry and to add to the confusion contract muskets were also being simultaneously produced by commercial makers such as Eli Whitney. They were constructed just in time to be used in anger, for the war of 1812 created a huge demand for muskets and some 55,000 were produced up to 1815. Improvements, such as a heavier 42in barrel and altered lock, resulted in the Model 1816, many of which were shipped west and were to see hard frontier service. Some of these Revolutionary War muskets were still issue weapons to the frontier army as late as the mid-1820s and many of these early guns were found in Indian hands as late as the 1880s. In a report on Indian weapons captured after the disastrous Battle of the Little Big Horn in 1876, of the 13 muzzle-loaders found, there were among them '1 old Musket marked U.S., and 1 Harpers Ferry musket.'[1]

Quality was still variable, with few parts being interchangeable even when produced by the same factory and fitted by the same worker. Development continued apace and yet again a new pattern was produced, this time the Model 1822, whose main claim to fame was that it was the first military musket that was not supplied with bright steelwork. The 1822 had a browned barrel that did not reflect the light, but aside from that it was not exactly a quantum technological leap forwards. It was rather prone to having its barrel bent because the steel was too thin and soft, and was disparagingly referred to in an inspector's report as 'defective and coarse' in manufacture. Ordnance did their best to rectify the problems and over a ten-year period the Model 1822 was eventually to become the most reliable and best made of all the issue flintlock muskets, which was just in time for it to change once again.

In the 1830s, many sporting guns were being manufactured with the new efficient percussion

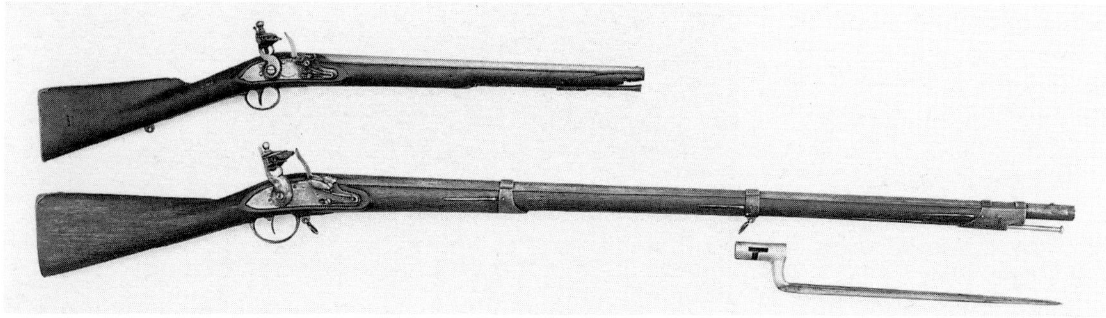

Two early American military longarms. Top is a Model 1807 Carbine, below is an Eli Whitney Model 1812 musket with its socket bayonet. Private collection.

locks and in 1833 the Ordnance Department had agreed, in theory at least, to the adoption of the percussion system. So in 1839, the US Ordnance Department showed that it was not lagging behind by instigating the manufacture of yet another flintlock musket that was obsolete even before it was made. Ironically, the new Model 1840 was arguably the best designed and manufactured of any flintlock military longarm to date. It retained the now standard 42in barrel, that was manufactured of thicker section steel but had an improved, faster acting lock and even sported a longer 18in bayonet that incorporated a simple swivel collar that locked it firmly in place and prevented it from falling off. By the time the Model 1840 was in full production, even the most wooden-headed Ordnance officers had realized that it had to be converted to percussion, so a simple series of modifications were undertaken. The old lock was removed and a new lockplate was substituted with a hammer replacing the cock. A steel bolster or 'snail' with a percussion nipple fitted into it was screwed to the breech over the old vent hole. The big problem lay in the sheer cost of converting the 1840 as well as all of the old muskets to percussion ignition, as some 375,000 muskets were in store. Besides, regardless of how easy they were to convert and while there were undoubtedly great benefits to percussion ignition, the fact was that new smoothbore muskets were no more accurate than the old ones they replaced.

The production of these Springfield and Harper's Ferry Model 1840 muskets is worth lingering over a little, for their manufacture was to revolutionize production techniques. Traditionally, all firearms were hand assembled, which gave rise to all manner of problems when it came to field repairing a damaged or broken gun. Makers such as Eli Whitney had begun, in the late eighteenth century, to pioneer new manufacturing techniques that were to become the cornerstone of what is understood today as modern mass production. Whereas traditional gunmaking in Europe had hitherto relied on taught skills, learned over a long period of time, the new armouries used highly skilled fitters to assemble all of the required parts that had been made to very precise patterns. These were rigorously checked against dimensional drawings and these first, or 'pattern' models became the standard by which all subsequent rifles or pistols were then produced. In addition, the increased use of machines to cut stocks, bore barrels, machine breeches and do a hundred other tasks meant that a very high standard of uniformity could be maintained. In practical terms this meant that, with a minimum of hand finishing, one assembler could put a musket together without having to undergo the long years of apprenticeship that were accepted as the normal process for gunsmiths. Firearms could be produced in numbers hitherto unattainable by a semi-skilled workforce at very competitive prices. It was the first truly workable form of mass production that men like Samuel Colt were subsequently to hone to a fine art, and that every major industrial power in the world would copy. To give some idea of just how great the improvements were that had been wrought since 1803, a report on the huge flood that swamped Harper's Ferry in the spring of 1852 concluded that, although some 30,000 muskets had been badly damaged, after they were stripped and the component parts thrown into boxes

> [after] … cleaning these arms – 9,000 percussion muskets have been stripped and completely dismantled, their parts being thrown into great masses, and after repolishing they were reassembled from these lots of 9,000 components, having no distinguishing marks, every limb filling and fitting its appropriate place with perfect exactness.[2]

The phoenix that was to rise from the ashes of the Model 1840 was the Model 1842 Percussion Musket, which was manufactured using full mechanization and production-line techniques wherever possible and was, for the first time, assembled with fully interchangeable parts. Even the Chief of Ordnance was pleased with the musket, stating it to be '… as nearly perfect as can be attained'.[3] Production of the Model 1842 actually continued until

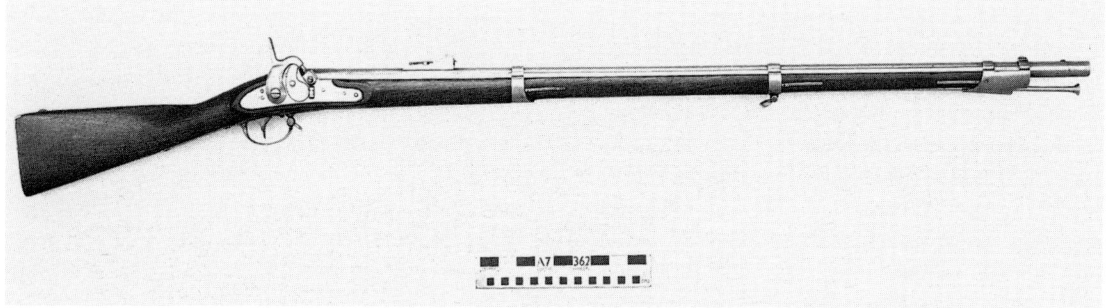

US Model 1842 Springfield Armory conversion to percussion. Courtesy of the Trustees of the Royal Armouries.

1855 and they were manufactured in very large numbers, some 106,800 being made at Harper's Ferry and 172,000 at Springfield, as well as several thousand more by private contractors, but it was to be the last of the .69-calibre smoothbores. In practical terms, this meant that the infantry were at last armed with a dependable musket that could easily be repaired in a remote Western fort that may be a hundred miles or more from the nearest gunsmith.

This was becoming increasingly important as the demands upon the army were growing with the swelling numbers of pioneers and settlers who were heading west. They demanded protection against the marauding bands of Indians who resented the white man's intrusion and regarded the lumbering wagon trains as a mobile fancy goods store, to be plundered whenever the opportunity arose. The problem for the army was simply one of logistics. The distances involved were vast and railroads had yet to make any significant inroad into the West. New recruits who needed to reach the more distant forts would travel by rail as far as possible, often for several days, then transfer to a wagon train at the railhead or even walk. One infantry draft sent to Montana detrained at Corinne, Utah then walked the 600 miles to Helena, taking a month to do so.

Getting the new percussion muskets to these outposts was just as difficult and many garrisons, even in the early 1840s, were equipped with a mix of obsolete old pattern flintlock muskets of varying makes including, as one inspector noted, 'Model 1822s and Whitney made flintlocks'. In 1842, the Ordnance Department inspected all of the muskets held in government stores with a view to converting them to percussion use. It was eventually decided that those made from 1812 to 1820 were to be held in their original condition for emergency issue to infantry or militia units. Those made from 1821 to 1831 were to be examined for condition and suitable examples sent for conversion. Any made after 1831 were authorized for immediate conversion, the quality being generally regarded as better than those of the early examples. For the most part, the old locks were replaced by the new percussion lock incorporating a Maynard tape primer.

This was a simple device that used a wheel to rotate a roll of percussion caps, strongly resembling those used in modern toy cap-guns. Dabs of fulminate were placed along a strip of paper which was folded over, glued and varnished. One problem with this system was that the varnish did not always waterproof the primers properly and many guns failed to fire when required. This was not a disaster, as a standard percussion cap could still be used, and generally the new conversion muskets were regarded as a great improvement over the old flintlocks. In a report of the military units in Texas in 1853, the performance of the Maynard percussion muskets was specifically commented upon by an officer stationed in Fort McKavett:

The soldier on the extreme right holds an obsolete M1842 .69 calibre musket, probably converted to percussion. The four civilians on the right are federal surveyors. All four were subsequently killed and scalped by Indians. Photo courtesy of Oklahoma Historical Society.

I have never known them [the muskets] to be damaged from firing nor do they miss oftener in firing than the common percussion musket. The great advantage the Maynard possesses over the others is the rapidity with which they can be fired, at least two or three shots to two of any other musket … in making this report I have … taken the experience of my Sergeants who have been using them constantly for nearly two years. [4]

Clearly, conversions could not continue to be undertaken forever, particularly in view of the increasingly prevalent use of the rifled musket. Britain had adopted the rifled musket in 1853, following the lead of many other European powers. The Unites States was lagging behind, and their experiences in the war against Mexico in 1846 led many to believe that the rifle was the only logical way forwards. Until the mid-1840s, the problems

A roll of Maynard tape primers inserted into the mechanism of a Sharps rifle. Author's photo.

with windage and its resultant lack of accuracy meant that most US military units were issued with a curious but effective cartridge that contained both a musket ball and three large lead buckshot. These were universally known as 'buck n' ball' and they made up by far the largest proportion of musket ammunition supplied, the Ordnance Department issuing some 2,700,000 buck and ball cartridges, about three times the number of standard ball cartridges. The reason was very simple; buck and ball was more lethal than a musket ball because the multiple projectiles stood a far better chance of hitting something.

With the adoption of the percussion musket, scientific tests were carried out, probably for the first time, to look closely at the actual performance of the smoothbore musket. This was partly due to the geography of the country and the nature of fighting in it. The close-packed firefights that characterized linear warfare in the seventeenth and eighteenth centuries had given way in America to fighting in an altogether different environment that can best be summed up as open warfare. The conflict with Mexico and the continual need for defence against Indian depredations meant that the musket was often found to be a less than useful weapon against an enemy who refused to come very close and stand still while he was shot at, generally a prerequisite for hitting anything with a smoothbore musket. Ordnance Captain B. Huger, who conducted accuracy tests with the issue muskets, reached some unsurprising conclusions, namely that manufacturing the lead balls so that they were actually spherical and reducing the windage by increasing ball size helped considerably (a fact well known to every hunter and trapper who used carefully sized patched balls) as did regularly cleaning out the barrel. The problems of accuracy could have been much alleviated, though not solved, if soldiers could have taken the time and care in loading that a buffalo hunter did. But in combat, time was of the essence and informing an infantryman during a fierce fight that he must wash out his barrel and carefully patch his musket ball was hardly practical. The solution to the prayers of almost every musket and rifle owner was to come in 1844 in the shape of a French Captain called Claude-Etienne Minié.

His simple idea, based on earlier but less efficient designs by two other Frenchmen, Delvigne and de Thouvenin, was simply to make a conical bullet with a deep concave recess in its base, into which he fitted an iron cup. The pressure generated on discharge forced the cup into the base of the bullet, expanding its skirt and causing it to tightly grip the bore of the musket. The exterior of this new self-expanding bullet was also ribbed, and these ribs were filled with lubricant to aid loading and help reduce fouling. At a stroke, the problem of windage was solved, and the new Minié bullet had the added benefit of helping to clear the barrel of fouling.

Despite the rapidly increasing use of this new system in Europe in the late 1840s and the understanding by the Ordnance Department of the pressing need for the introduction of a rifle, this did not, however, lead to a wholesale adoption of a new percussion rifled musket in the US. The army was not going to be rushed, for the Ordnance Committee was not entirely happy with the Minié bullet, believing that it did not meet all of the requirements for a military projectile. In particular, they felt with some justification that the use of the inserted metal cup was detrimental. Early use of these bullets had shown that upon firing the cup had an unfortunate tendency to be blown completely through the lead bullet, leaving its remains firmly stuck to the bore of the rifle. So they embarked on a four-year series of tests at Springfield and Harper's Ferry to determine whether the new bullet was actually superior to carefully made, patched balls. It was, but a number of improvements were recommended, the most important being the adoption of a bullet designed by James Burton of Harper's Ferry. It was of the Minié type, but with a much deeper concave base that did away with the need for a separate cup, and Burtons' bullet was to become the standard for the new military rifle. In 1854 the tests eventually led the Board to conclude, perhaps with tinge of regret that:

> The results stated to have been achieved in foreign services, and those derived from our own limited experiments, indicate so great a superiority of the rifled bore with the elongated expanding ball that it seems the use of smoothbored arms and spherical balls may be entirely superseded.[5]

The benefit of the new bullet was, of course, that it could be fired from any rifled or smoothbore arm with a resultant improvement in performance. Many of the older muskets that had been issued to soldiers on the frontier were given a new lease of life with the fairly rapid introduction of these new 'rifle expanding bullet cartridges'. This was only a stop-gap measure, for what the army really needed now was the large-scale adoption of a rifle. In fact, despite the proliferation of the smoothbore musket, the rifle had already seen a considerable amount of service in the army.

Percussion cartridges: .58 musket, .60 musket, .52 Sharps linen, .36 Adams, Patched ball. Photo courtesy of B. Lees.

MILITARY RIFLES

Despite the image of rifle-equipped colonists hiding behind every tree waiting to ambush the English, in truth the number of militia riflemen in America in the late eighteenth century was actually quite small, although when encountered they were certainly dangerous. Major George Hanger, himself a shooter of no mean ability, recalled being spotted by an American rifleman while observing enemy troop positions during the Revolutionary War.

> Colonel, now General Tarleton and myself were standing a few yards out of a wood observing the situation of a part of the enemy which we intended to attack … our orderly bugler stood behind us about three yards, but with his horse's side to our horses' tails. A rifleman passed over the mill dam, evidently observing two officers, and laid himself down on his belly; for in such positions they always lie, to take a good shot at long distance. He took a deliberate and cool shot at my friend, at me and at the bugle-horn man. Colonel Tarleton's horse and mine, I am certain were not anything like two feet apart … a rifle ball passed him and me; looking directly at the mill I observed the flash of the powder. I directly said to my friend 'I think we had better move, or we shall shortly have two or three of these gentlemen amusing themselves at our expense.' The words were hardly out of my mouth when the bugle-horn man behind me, and directly central jumped off his horse and said, 'Sir my horse is shot'. Now speaking of this rifleman's shooting, nothing could be better … I have passed several times over this ground and … I can positively assert that the distance he fired at was a full 400 yards.[6]

So taken aback were the British at the ability of the American riflemen that when one Corporal Walter Crouse of York County, Pennsylvania was captured both he and his rifle were sent to the Tower of London. Cpl Crouse was quite convinced he was to suffer a grisly public execution but, to his great relief, was asked instead to demonstrate his shooting skills to King George III, which he did. Interestingly, although Crouse was allowed to return to America, his rifle is still preserved in England, being now a part of the Armoury at Warwick Castle. His accuracy at 200yd (180m) was said to have so shocked the King that it prompted him to hire German riflemen from the Hessian States to fight alongside the British troops. While this may be a slight exaggeration, it is certainly true that some 4,000 riflemen were employed by the British in America. The nearest that His Majesty's army ever came to meeting the colonial riflemen on equal terms was in the short-lived formation of a British rifle company of 100 men commanded by Captain Patrick Ferguson, of the 70th Foot, who in 1776 had adopted and improved an earlier French breech-loading musket, the Chaumette patent. His small company were hastily armed with Ferguson's rifle, made by the English gunmaker Durs Egg, and acquitted themselves well against the colonists. Unfortunately, Ferguson was himself killed by a rifleman in 1780 at King's Mountain and the whereabouts of his 100 rifles has remained an enduring mystery.

In 1803, the first rifle ever made at a government arsenal was produced at Harper's Ferry. It had an iron flintlock of very standard pattern and a 33in, 54-calibre half octagonal, half round barrel. In other respects though, it was quite different from any other military musket of the period. For a start it was half-stocked, with the fore-end woodwork only reaching to the first barrel band. The barrel itself was held in place by easily removable wedges not pins, and its calibre was, by military standards, a fairly minuscule .54in. In addition, the butt had a raised cheek-piece on the left to give a more comfortable rest for the face and a traditional Kentucky-type brass patchbox was inlet into the right side of the stock. Like the Tower muskets produced at the same time in England, these rifles were virtually hand-made, for mass-production was yet to reach its zenith. Although pre-formed parts were supplied in bulk, each rifle had to be laboriously hand-fitted by skilled journeymen, which was time-consuming and inefficient. It also meant that there was virtually no interchangeability between muskets, every repair having to be undertaken on an individual basis, and in the course of service, the 1803 proved to be less than robust.

The first real trial of the new musket was in the hands of the redoubtable Captain Meriwether Lewis and his Corps of Discovery, who set out on a daunting expedition with William Clark westward from Missouri in May 1804 to explore nearly 800,000sq mi (2,072,000sq km) of new territory purchased from the French. The party mostly carried Model 1803s that were continually in need of repair and replacement, as Lewis noted in his diary 'But for our precaution in bringing extra locks and parts of locks, most of our guns would be now useless'.[7]

The party was fortunate in having a skilled metalworker with them, John Shields, who was able to repair almost any damage or mechanical failure, but even his improvisational skills were defeated by the constant breakages on the rifles. Zebulon Pike, who was also leading a party on a similar voyage of discovery on the northern reaches of the Mississippi had also experienced problems with the Model 1803. The stocks were prone to breaking and he also noted that: 'We … bursted one of our rifles, which was a great loss, as it made three guns which had bursted … and one of my men was now armed but with my sword and pistols'.[8]

The experience that these expeditions gained from their odyssey across America armed with the Harper's Ferry guns had probably placed more strain on the rifles than they would ever have received in five years in the hands of militia or regular troops, but it was experience put to good use. The Ordnance Department instigated some changes and the barrels were lengthened to 36in, and improvements were made to the tempering of the iron of the springs and cocks. Plans were made to produce an improved rifled musket. There was a growing need for it, for the number of emigrants and hunters heading west of the Mississippi was growing annually and more military forts were being constructed to provide protection for them.

The size of the regular army was still comparatively small, around 7,800 men, but the area they had to police was vast, and to be poorly armed in such a land was to invite trouble. Work continued apace to produce an improved model 1803 and the Model 1814 rifle was eventually introduced, having the suggested improvements incorporated in it. It was certainly stronger than the earlier model and soon became more generally known as the Model of 1817, or the Common Rifle. Few of these rifles were actually made by Harper's Ferry, most being produced by commercial contractors, such as North, Deringer and Johnson, leading them to be referred to quite often as 'contract rifles.' It was manufactured pretty much to the accepted standards of the day for a commercial flintlock, having a browned, seven-grooved rifled barrel of 36in in length with iron mounts and it fired a .54-calibre ball. In common with sporting guns, a patchbox was set into the stock, although it too was of iron rather than brass. The Model 1817 was capable of an aimed shot out to about 300yd (275m), although it took a good deal of skill to hit a target at that range. What it could do, unlike its musket equivalent, was repeatedly hit a man at 100yd (90m) whereas the smoothbore only stood a 40 per cent chance of a hit at that range.

Target shooting by the riflemen equipped with the Model 1817 was a popular pastime, and many soldiers prided themselves on their marksmanship. The expectation was that those who could put half of their bullets into a 3in (7.5cm) bull offhand at 50yd (46m) were considered second-class shots while those who could do the same at 100yd (90m) were first-class shots. Some idea of the benefits of a rifled musket can be gleaned from contemporary accuracy tests undertaken at 50, 100 and 400yd (46m, 90m and 365m). A .69 calibre Model 1808 flintlock musket was able to group five shots in 12¾in (32cm) at 50yd (46m), 42in (107cm) at 100yd (90m) and could not even hit the target at 400yd (365m). At the same ranges, a US Model 1841 Mississippi rifle, firing a .53-calibre ball achieved groups of 5¼in (13cm), 9¾in (24.8cm) and was certainly able to strike the target at 400yd (365m), but with no discernible grouping.[9]

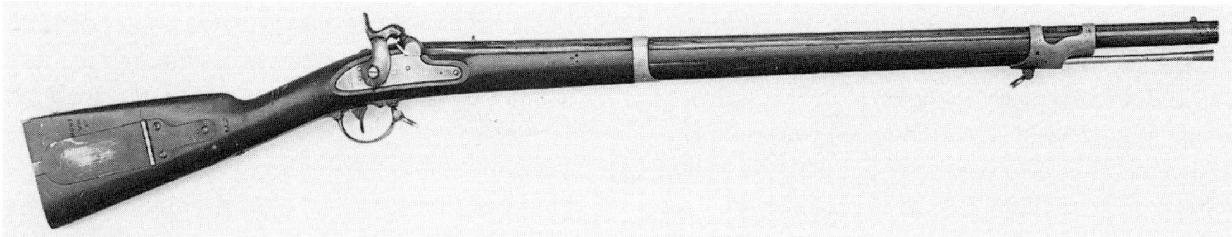

US Model 1841 Mississippi or 'Yager' rifle. Courtesy of the Trustees of the Royal Armouries.

However, the issue of rifles to the infantry was not widespread, in part because of their cost and because of the slowness of loading a rifled long gun. At this time, the Military still considered the rate of fire to be more important than long-range accuracy and the rifle could not compete. Tests undertaken in 1826 showed that a company of men armed with muskets could fire 845 shots in ten minutes compared to a rifle's 494.[10] As had been discovered by the riflemen of the British Army fighting Napoleon some two decades earlier, there were other problems associated with the rifled arm in combat. A rifle cannot easily be loaded unless a soldier is standing still and vertical and for a rifle to work efficiently the bore must be kept clean of fouling. This was a near impossible task on the frontier, where the dry atmosphere turned the burnt powder residue to the consistency of concrete. This fouling made loading a carefully sized, patched bullet almost physically impossible; indeed during the Napoleonic Wars the British 60th Rifles had to have small mallets issued to them to assist with loading their Baker rifles. The end result of pounding a soft lead bullet was to cause deformation to it, which inevitably destroyed the rifle's main advantage – accuracy. To combat this, riflemen invariably carried undersized, standard issue musket balls to enable them to continue loading and firing, which rather defeated the purpose of issuing expensive rifles. Indeed the US Army actually had no formally raised rifle regiments until 1846. Some rifles were issued to regiments piecemeal, a few were retained by quartermasters and issued to the best shots in each company and many simply languished in armouries, becoming unserviceable or simply unwanted. In the mid-1830s, an Ordnance audit was carried out to see exactly what was on hand in the Government armouries, showing some 5,000 rifles compared to over 73,000 muskets.[11]

As part of a continuing programme of development, the Ordnance Department were keen to see improvements in the quality of longarms issued and, because such considerable effort had been expended to improve the ordinary musket, the rifle had, out of necessity, been sidelined. This was to change with the adoption of the Model 1841 percussion rifle, sometimes called the 'Whitney' or 'Windsor', though its more popular name was the 'Mississippi.' This had nothing to do with place of manufacture or its style, but was due to Jefferson

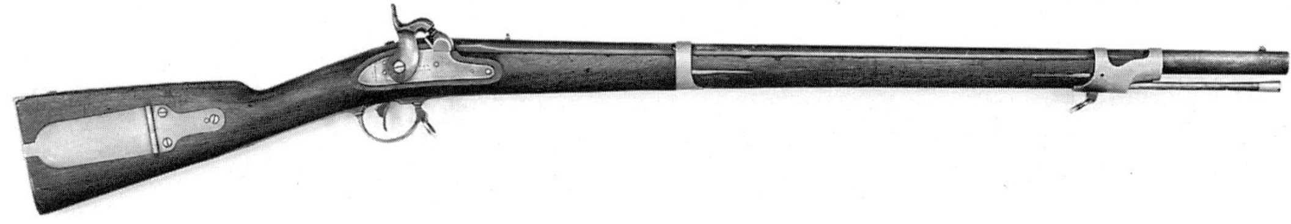

Model 1841 Mississippi rifle, made by Robbins and Lawrence. Photo courtesy of G.Williams.

Davis's Mississippi Volunteers carrying them during the Mexican War. It was purpose-designed for the task and it was a compact and handsome weapon, fully stocked and in its original form still with a patchbox in the butt. Its 33in browned barrel was in .54-calibre with seven-groove rifling and fired its Burton bullet at a healthy 1,500fps. In line with its practice of issuing contracts to commercial gunmaking companies, for the first five years of production the government had the Model 1841 made by Eli Whitney and Robbins and Lawrence, before Harper's Ferry began production in 1846. The model 1841 was still only issued in comparatively limited numbers to some infantry, dragoons and mounted riflemen, but it quickly became a popular weapon and many were to see long service. They were used in quantity during the Civil War and after the war were sold off as surplus, many being used on the frontier for years afterwards. There had been one other rifle adopted by the Army, that deserves a closer look, for in form and function it was like no other. It was patented by John Hall, a native of Maine and it was not only a rifled arm, but also a breech-loader.

It first made an appearance in flintlock form in 1811, probably its main attraction being the simplicity of its mechanism, that used a solid breechblock that was held in place by a rear-mounted pivot pin. To load, the front of the block was unlocked by a spring catch and it swung upwards, exposing the open chamber for loading. This was easily accomplished with either a paper cartridge of loose powder and ball, the bullet being seated with no more than thumb pressure and the block then pushed down, being locked into place by the spring catch. Two recoil lugs on either side of the block rested against the shoulders of two metal supporting straps between which the breechblock lay. These took the strain of the recoil on firing, preventing the possibility of a dangerous failure of the pivot pin. The entire mechanism of the lock, cock, springs, priming pan and frizzen, even the trigger, was fitted internally into the block making it entirely self-contained. What was more, the Hall had total interchangeability of parts, one breechblock being able to be fitted into any other rifle. This required very accurate machining, but was something of a landmark in production techniques. It was chambered for a .53in ball and had an unusual 16-groove barrel.

The Ordnance Board tested it favourably in 1813 commenting particularly on the advantage of its speed of reloading over other rifles. But they then failed to do anything about it until in early 1817, when 100 were ordered at a total cost of $2,500. These were immediately sent west for field trials on the frontier, which proved quite satisfactory apart from a tendency for gas leakage to occur between the mating surface of the breech-face and the barrel, though this was not considered serious enough to warrant rectification. The Hall was accurate enough by the standards of the day, achieving 7¼in (18.5cm) groups at 50yd (46m) and 16in (40cm) groups at 100yd (90m) and even exhibiting some ability to hit a target at 400yd (365m). At least one dragoon recorded how his officer with a Hall's rifle shot a Mexican officer who was observing him at that distance through field glasses. By 1817, the Hall was being adopted in small numbers into US service and by 1826 both rifles and carbines were being produced at Harper's Ferry, with Hall himself supervising their manufacture.

The design was to see a surprising length of service, for it remained in use with mounted units into the late 1830s, when Hall redesigned the lock to convert it to percussion, and a number of mechanical improvements were made as a result of experience gained in service. The barrels were seven-grooved, and the release catch was improved to ease opening of the block, and some 3,000 percussion rifles were made between 1842 and 1844. It saw considerable use with the Dragoons in the war against Mexico, which saw it figure in one of the more unusual incidents of the conflict. A Dragoon named Sam Chamberlain, enjoying a quiet drink in a small saloon, noticed that he was slowly being surrounded by Mexican guerrillas, none of whom were taking kindly to the gringo soldier drinking at their bar. He decided on prompt action and:

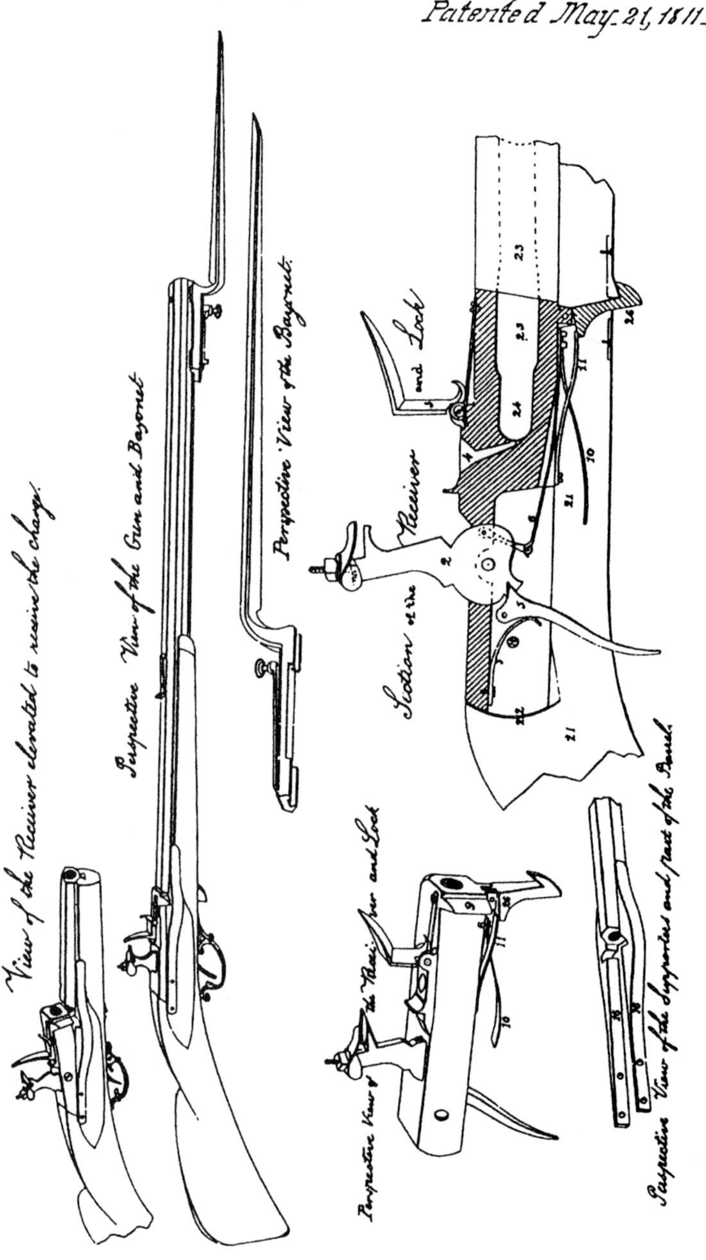

Hall's 1811 Patent for his breech-loading rifle, with the screw-attached bayonet.

> … sprang behind a large table used for a bar, drew the chamber of my Halls carbine (that I always carried in my pocket) said a short prayer, and stood cool and collected, at bay before those human Tigers, guerrillars. There was one grizzled old fellow who seem'd more ferocious than the others, he had but one eye … he rushed for the table as if he would spring over, when the sight of the little iron tube pointing right for his solitary optic, caused him to pause … twenty brigands were held at bay by the strange weapon I held, they seemed to know it was sure death to one, and none seemed willing to be that one.[12]

The issue of the Hall in carbine form in 1833 was significant for it was the first purpose-designed short rifle to be issued to mounted units, in this case the Regiment of Dragoons. Mounted soldiers had always carried short rifles wherever possible, but the percussion Model of 1833 was specifically produced to meet the needs of a soldier who may have to fight on horseback or on foot and it was unusually equipped with a bayonet. It was 8in shorter than the rifle and, like all carbines, it had to use a smaller powder charge to prevent the recoil being unmanageable; so to compensate, its bore was enlarged to .58in, then still further to .62in on the Model 1836. This proved to be a handful even for the hard-bitten Dragoons, one of whom pronounced the recoil 'quite excessive and most unpleasant'. Most of these carbines were produced by Simeon North, who modified the recoil lugs and improved the action of the loading lever, and they were produced in rifled and smoothbore versions until 1843. Although it was a competent firearm, all Halls suffered to a greater or lesser extent from gas leakage, which as the mating surfaces wore, became progressively worse. It was also comparatively expensive to make compared to other models of flintlock rifle, and production of it ceased in late 1844 as it became clear that its expense did not warrant its further manufacture. It simply could not compete with the new rifled muskets coming into service.

THE NEW RIFLED MUSKET

Meanwhile, extensive trials had been going on for several years to find a suitable rifled musket for general issue to the Infantry to replace the old smoothbores, and in 1855 a new rifle was introduced. The US Model 1855 was a purpose-designed percussion rifled musket that still used the Maynard priming system but was manufactured in a new calibre of .58in to fire the Burton expanding bullet, and this was to become the standard for all US muskets until the eventual adoption of the breech-loader. It had a 40in barrel, a three-grooved bore with gain twist rifling that was markedly easier to keep clean than a five-groove rifle, and it was capable of accurate shooting out to 400 or 500yd (365m or 460m). Such was the improvement wrought in manufacturing techniques and machine tolerances that the new rifle had a barrel that could only pass inspection if the

A Model 1819 Hall rifle. Courtesy of the Trustees of the Royal Armouries.

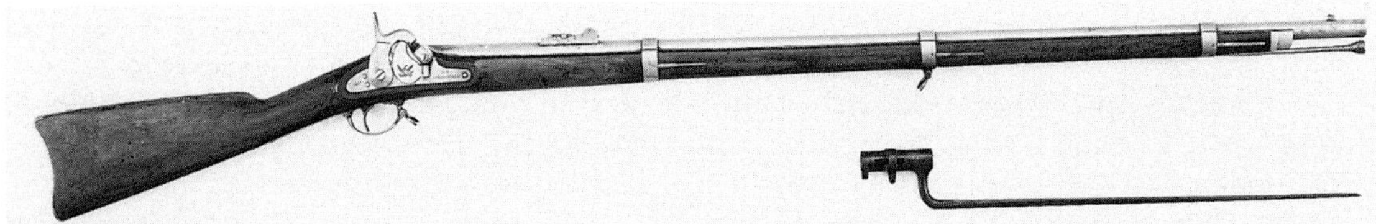

(Above) Model 1855 Springfield rifle musket with Maynard primer and socket bayonet. Courtesy of the Trustees of the Royal Armouries.

(Below) US Harper's Ferry Model 1855 .58-calibre rifle and bayonet. Courtesy of the Trustees of the Royal Armouries.

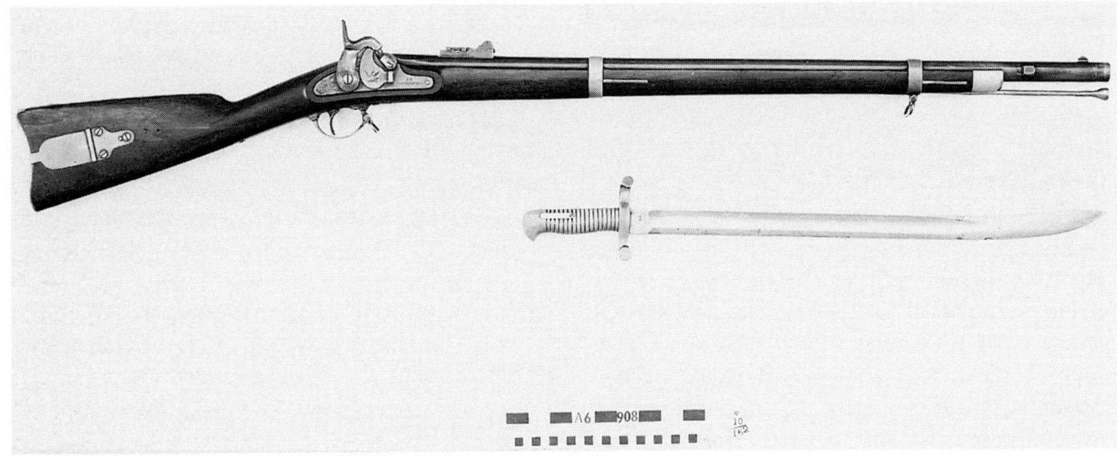

bore size did not deviate by more than .00025in, a level of accuracy that would have been impossible to attain in mass-produced weapons just a decade before. One inevitable problem facing the Army were the thousands of old-pattern muskets still in stores, and the Ordnance Department embarked on a mammoth conversion programme with some 20,000 Model 1822 and 1842 muskets being converted at the Springfield, Harper's Ferry and Frankford arsenals. Field tests showed that both the Model 1855 and the converted Model 1822 and 1842 rifles were very serviceable arms, reliable and capable of good accuracy at 500yd (460m). That the conversion work was worthwhile was not doubted by the Ordnance Department, who reported that the conversion of these muskets was:

> ... favorable, and there seems no doubt that all serviceable flint-lock muskets may, by rifling and percussioning, be converted into good and efficient long-range arms such as are commonly called 'Minnie rifles'.[13]

The new rifles began to find their way west in the early part of 1856 and some were unofficially 'improved' by the addition of long-range sights by soldiers and officers who took a more than keen interest in shooting. Even in standard form, the Model 1855 was a match for any other rifle and it was certainly a far better infantry weapon than anything issued before, as Gen George Crook proved when his men arrived at a post in the mid-west. Advised by the Captain of the incumbent garrison that his men's old-model rifles were far better than the new ones, Crook took his men onto the target range with their new model 1855s to watch the target practice: '... after seeing them shoot ... I took out ... an equal number of my men. Not a man of their guard hit the bull's-eye, while there was not a man of mine missed it'.[14]

There was nothing wrong with the converted muskets, but they were really only a stopgap measure and gradually the new rifle began to replace the old patterns. Soldiers on the lonely frontier outposts who were armed with them found them a great improvement over the older models, not least because they were at last able actually to hit their targets. One officer of the Sixth Infantry recounted how an Indian warrior rode past a line of soldiers at 300yd (275m) distance, normally well beyond practical musket range, only to be met with '… the Hundred minnies levelled at him. Did he die? … we poured a plunging fire … with our long range rifles'.[15]

THE RIFLE MUSKET IN THE CIVIL WAR

By 1860, some 60,000 had been manufactured, and many were seeing hard service on the frontier, where they were proving their worth in the increasingly frequent clashes with the Indians. The Ordnance were still unhappy with the tape primer system, which was unreliable and made the locks difficult to manufacture, so in 1861 yet another model was introduced that completely omitted the Maynard primer mechanism. But by this time, an event had occurred that was to change forever the role of the military musket, and this was the outbreak of the war between North and South. It was technologically to prove one of the most fruitful periods in firearms' history, taking the United States from the era of the flintlock musket through to the breech-loading cartridge repeating rifle in a matter of four years. That this should have been accompanied by such a wanton loss of life was in itself a tragedy, but throughout history wars have always been something of a proving ground for weaponry, and the test material is inevitably human.

To give some idea of the scale of development that occurred in those short years, there were no less than twenty-six new rifles and carbines introduced during the war, as well as three major models of US rifled muskets, each of which pattern can be subdivided into its own variations. In addition, Austria, Germany, France, Belgium and England supplied tens of thousands of rifles and muskets to both sides – profit showing no favouritism. It would not be possible to give a comprehensive list of every model that saw use during the war, so the most influential will be looked at as well as a sprinkling of those that were, if not the most sophisticated, at least interesting.

Undoubtedly the most widely used longarms were the infantry muskets. The Model 1855 was slightly revamped as the model 1861, with the removal of the characteristic humped lockplate that had been required for the Maynard system, an improved rear sight and 40in, .58-calibre barrel. Most of these were made at Springfield or by contractors, as the Harper's Ferry arsenal had been burned by Federal troops in April 1861 to keep its production facility out of Confederate hands. A vari-

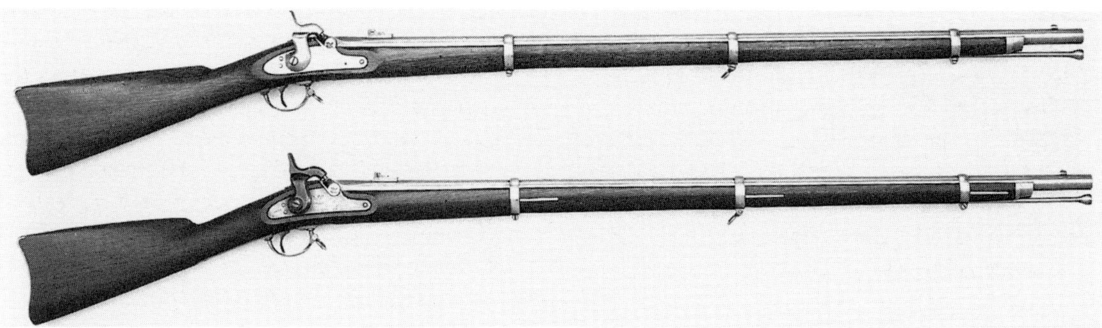

A Colt contract Model 1861 rifle musket and (below) the later Model 1863. Courtesy of the Trustees of the Royal Armouries.

ation on the Model 1861 were the contract rifles made initially by the Colt company, which varied from the standard pattern in fit and were not interchangeable with the issue Model 1861.

Some 180,000 of these rifles were made by contractors and most were issued to individual state militia and infantry units. The Model 1863 that followed was virtually identical apart from some small details that eased production difficulties, and included the abandonment of browned barrels, the issued rifles simply having polished surfaces that reflected like mirrors in sunlight. Some 794,000 rifled muskets were manufactured by Springfield alone throughout the war years. If this seems a large number, some idea of the scale of the war can be understood from the fact that the Federal Army raised 1,966 infantry regiments and independent companies. Indeed, so huge was the Springfield production facility that when the poet Henry Wadsworth Longfellow visited, he was moved to compose a poem about the Armory, probably the only such poem ever dedicated to the manufacture of firearms.

The British-made 'three-band' Enfields costing $26 each, were generally regarded as the best made and most accurate rifles to be had during the war and they were at a premium on both sides of the conflict. Second to the Springfield, the P53 saw more use than any other rifle musket, and was used by both sides, in every battle from 1861 to the last of the fighting in 1865. It is estimated that some 900,000 Enfield pattern rifles were imported during the war, with some 428,000 of these going to the Federal forces. It is a little appreciated fact that the Enfield factory output of Pattern 1853 rifles did not go to the Federal government, for virtually all Enfield-made rifles were used to meet government contracts for supplying the British army. The vast bulk of the rifles supplied to the United States were produced by private contractors such as Ward & Sons or the London Armoury Company who, in truly impartial fashion, supplied absolutely identical weapons to both Union and Confederate. A useful benefit for the armies involved was that as long as the bore was clean, the .577-calibre Enfield could be loaded and fired with the US .58-calibre bullet, which most other foreign rifles would not do, providing a logistical nightmare for Quartermasters. In trained hands, the accurate P53 could be a formidable weapon. During the Battle of Gettysburg, Maj-Gen George Pickett led a doomed charge towards the Union lines. At a distance of 200yd (180m) some 1,700 rifles were aimed at the advancing Confederates and the command 'Fire' was given. One eyewitness described the effect:

> The lines underwent an instantaneous transformation. They were at once enveloped in a dense cloud of dust. Arms, heads, blankets, guns and knapsacks were tossed into the clear air. A moan went up from the field distinctly to be heard amid the storm of battle.[16]

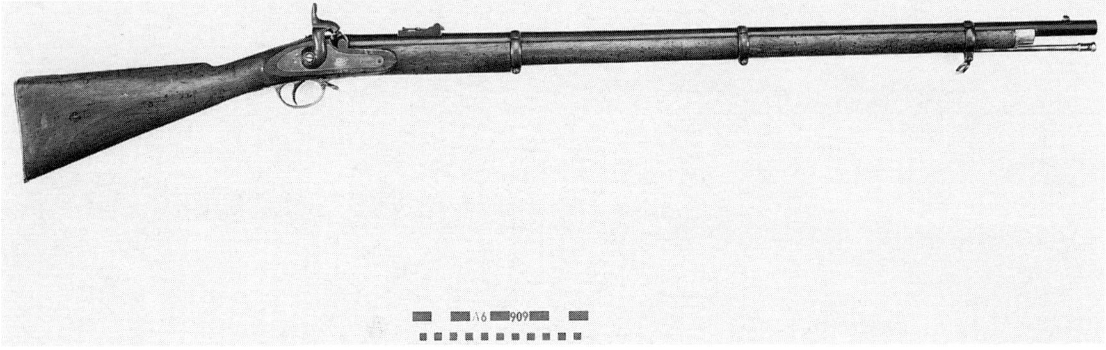

An American copy of an Enfield Pattern 1853 rifle musket, by Ezra Millward. Courtesy of the Trustees of the Royal Armouries.

The soft lead bullets did terrible damage to the human body, deforming wickedly as they struck, shattering bone beyond repair and severing limbs. Such was the volume of fire delivered during some of these battles that accounts talk of fields of corn being utterly razed to the ground by the bullets that littered the landscape like lead hailstones.

A quantity of surplus Tower-manufactured Pattern 1841/42 and 1851 converted rifle-muskets was also sold to the Federal army. These were early percussion conversions of the old flintlock India Pattern muskets, commonly known as the 'Brown Bess', that had been an interim measure to arm the British army with a rifle prior to the adoption of the P53. Of large calibre, they were well made and reliable enough, but not exactly at the cutting edge of firearms' technology and their heavy bullets lacked range, although they were certainly damaging enough at close range.

If the Federal forces suffered from a lack of suitable rifles, it was nothing compared to the South, who not only had little ability to acquire raw materials or manufacture on home territory but also had to pay a premium for its imported firearms, all of which had to be sailed through the Federal naval blockade. A $26 Enfield cost the South around $100 and the troops lucky enough to have them guarded them like gold.

Still more precious were the much coveted Whitworth rifles, similar in appearance to the Enfield, but firing a hexagonal .45-calibre bullet with extraordinary accuracy. The favourite of long-distance target shooters in England, the Whitworth has developed almost mythical status as the Civil War's premier long-range sharpshooting rifle. In skilled hands, the Whitworth was perfectly capable of felling a man at over 1,000yd (915m), but they were so phenomenally expensive ($1,000 each or $1,500 with optical sights) that the South probably imported less than 170 in total, and these were only issued to men whose shooting prowess, even among so many good shots, was nothing short of extraordinary, and most of the accurate shooting on the battlefield was done with Enfields or Springfields.

If the Whitworths were the pinnacle of muzzle-loading technology, there were plenty of rifles that were at quite the opposite end of the scale. Many thousands of poor-quality muskets were supplied to the South, in the knowledge that any substandard

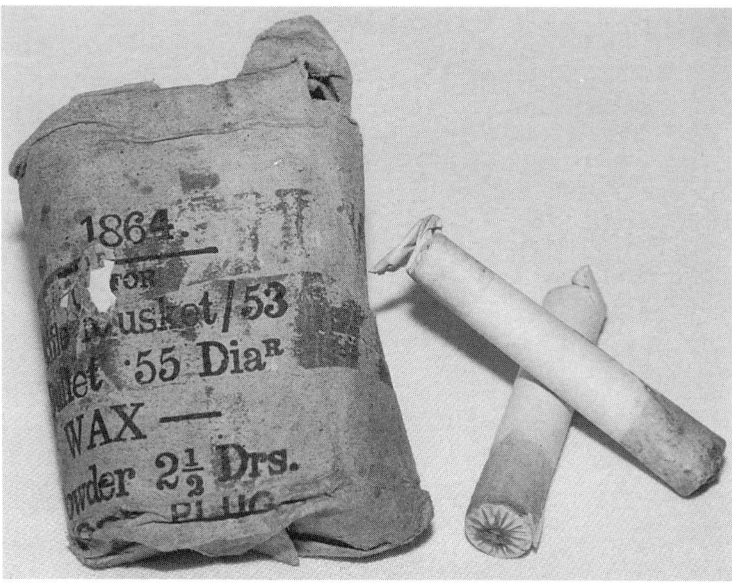

A pack of Civil War period cartridges for a .577 musket.

arms that were received were almost impossible to return because of the blockade. It is to their credit that the Confederates managed to produce a very reasonable number of rifles and pistols for themselves from their arsenals at Fayetteville and Richmond, which were the primary manufacturing centres for the south. Made in the largest quantities were the Richmond rifle and rifle muskets that were very close copies of the US M1855/61 rifle muskets, which is hardly surprising as much of the machinery used had been at Harper's Ferry and was simply relocated to Richmond, Virginia in early 1861. They were made and supplied to the South until the fall of Richmond in 1865. The Richmond rifle was chambered for the standard .58-calibre bullet but was never made to accept the Maynard primer system, although the rifles still had the familiar humped lockplate seen on the Springfield. The Confederate Ordnance also simplified production by using brass furniture instead of iron and the elimination of the largely useless patchbox.

The other rifles to see service with the South were also clones of US weapons, these being the Fayetteville and Palmetto rifles. The arsenal at Fayetteville in North Carolina also used Harper's Ferry machinery to re-create an almost identical copy of the US Model 1855 rifle, and the locks bear the 'Fayetteville' stamp. Fayetteville was not the only arsenal capable of producing the Model 1855 copies, for D.C. Hodgkins and Sons in Macon, Georgia also made Springfield M1855s. The Palmettos were made under contract by William Glaze and Company of Columbia, South Carolina and comprised two models, being exact copies of the US .69-calibre Model 1842 Musket and the .54-calibre M1841 Mississippi rifle. So exact were these copies that parts could be swapped between the US and Confederate rifles. Mostly supplied to the South Carolina Militia, they were never made in large numbers (probably no more than 6,000 muskets and 1,000 rifles), were highly prized for their workmanship and saw widespread service. But there were other manufacturers who also helped supply the South's war effort; two expatriate English brothers named Cook had a small manufacturing company in New Orleans and, not surprisingly, made reproductions of the Enfield rifle-musket, as did the Asheville Armory in North Carolina who made copies of the short two-band Enfield rifle-musket. After the war, many disillusioned Confederates who headed West to a new life carried these 'rebel guns' with them and they turned up in unexpected places on the Frontier and East coast for many years afterwards.

The products of the Federal and Confederate arsenals were by no means the only rifled muskets in service throughout the war years. The demand for weapons from the two opposing forces was so great that by 1862 almost any country with the desire to get rid of its surplus or obsolete arms could find a ready market with the warring factions. Tens of thousands of foreign manufactured rifles and muskets were to see service; in fact, in 1862, the Federal government had listed an impressive range of longarms in their arsenals that included: 170,255 Austrian rifles and muskets, 57,194 Belgian rifles and muskets, 8,999 British 'Tower' muskets, 116,740 British Enfield rifles, 52,959 French rifles and muskets, 111,549 Prussian rifles and muskets, 5,179 Minié rifles and 203,801 miscellaneous foreign rifles and muskets.[17] The majority of these foreign arms were of a fairly standard military service percussion type, being a mix of rifled and smoothbore, but the variance in quality could be very marked. In the main these were imported by the Confederate states who did not have the manufacturing resources of the North and were heavily reliant upon foreign imports for almost all of the material required to fight a war.

Many of the 'Enfields' that were sold during the war were actually foreign copies supplied by gunmakers from Belgium and elsewhere in Europe, who frequently produced rifles with spurious 'Tower' marked locks. In fairness, many were perfectly serviceable weapons, albeit lacking the quality of their British-made counterparts. However, some Belgian Enfield copies received by the Ordnance Department were so poor that after testing they were deemed 'not even third-class quality' and immediately re-packed, to be returned to the maker. Some P53 copies were also produced by French companies, but the French

An interesting converted Model 1842 type, possibly of Confederate manufacture. Photo courtesy of B. Lees.

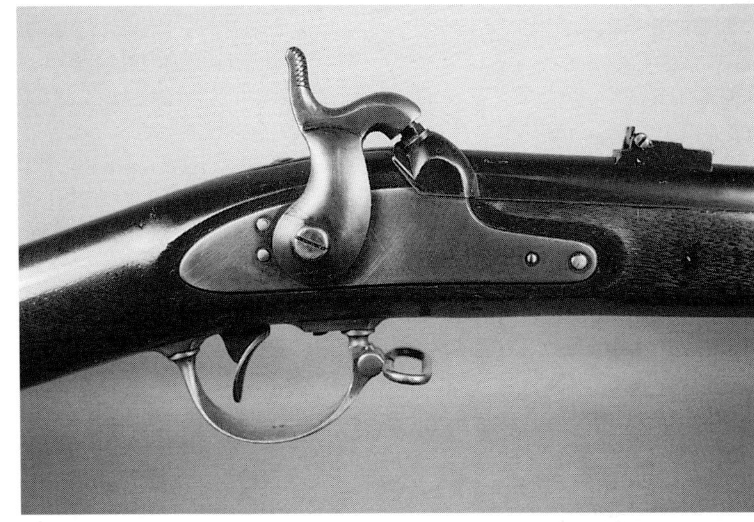

(Right) A Belgian copy of the US Model 1862 Zouave rifle. This example has been modified for the commercial market as a smoothbore musket. Courtesy of the Trustees of the Royal Armouries.

mainly sold off some of their huge stocks of surplus rifles and muskets from their own arsenals and supplied a very broad cross-section of different models, from old converted flintlock models dating anywhere from 1816 to 1842, to relatively new percussion rifles. One problem for the Confederates who purchased these guns was the number of different calibres in which they were produced. Some were in their original .69-calibre, but others, although identical models, had subsequently been bored out by the French to .71-calibre and both were often packed together in a single shipment. As if that was not confusing enough, the same problem bedevilled the Federal government who purchased large numbers of the popular Model 1846 T *carbine à tige*, which was the French equivalent of the Mississippi rifle. With its 34in barrel and .69-calibre it was a well-made and very useful weapon that was later slightly modified by the French to become the standard 1853T. These were also closely copied by the Belgians in .71 calibre and all models of the *tige* rifle were referred to as 'Vincennes' rifles and ammunition of the wrong calibre was frequently supplied to the hapless troops. One officer whose men were equipped with .58-calibre Model 1848 Jägers, gave his impressions of being at the sharp end of a pitched battle with Sioux Indians:

> ... by noon we had ourselves pretty well intrenched, using our dead soldiers and horses to help our breastworks. About this time my men commenced to say 'This is my last cartridge.' I then had 3,000 extra ones brought from the wagon and commenced distributing them, when we discovered that the ordnance officer had given us 62 caliber for 58 caliber rifles. Immediately I put the men to whittling [with knives] down the balls to the size of our rifles, and now gave orders not to fire except when necessary ... when relieved next day we did not have five rounds to the man left.[18]

Nor were all of these rifles in the first flush of youth, for thousands of old .71-calibre Austrian made Jäger smoothbore muskets also saw service, many of which used a primitive, and by then outdated, percussion system known as the 'tube-lock', that required a thin cylindrical percussion cap. The major benefit was their price, for at $6 each they were virtually disposable and hundreds were subsequently, and quite successfully, rifled for a fraction of the cost of buying a new factory-made weapon, but hundreds were of very questionable quality. One inspector reporting on a Union regiment that it had '... the Austrian rifle, made of poor materials and badly constructed. I examined eight hundred ... and I do not consider one hundred to be serviceable'.[19]

Surprisingly, Austria came second only to England as the biggest supplier of longarms to the North and South, principally selling its Model 1854 rifle to the Confederacy. This was universally

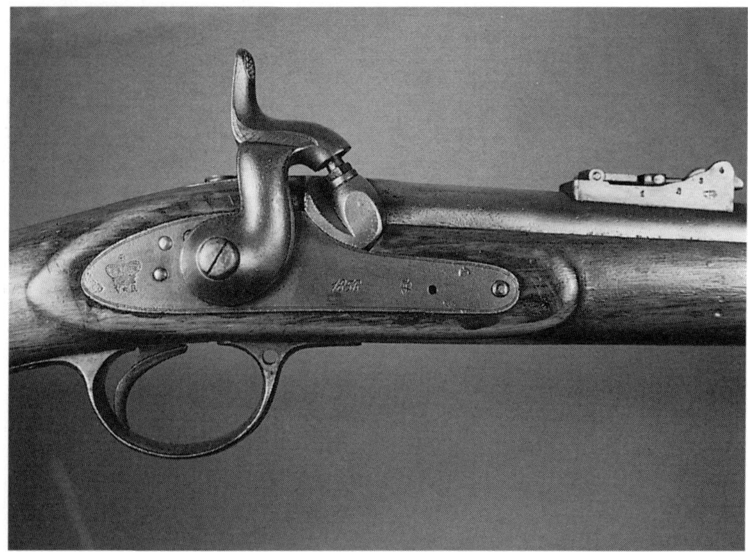

Counterfeit Belgian-made Enfield P53 rifle musket, with spurious Tower lock marks. Courtesy of the Trustees of the Royal Armouries.

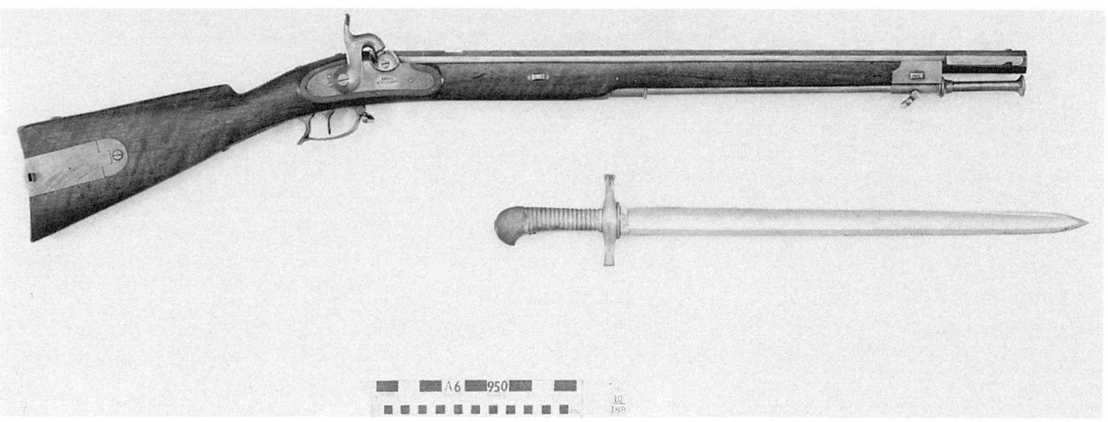

A German .67-calibre Jäger flintlock rifle, converted to percussion, with bayonet. Thousands of similar surplus rifles were sold to the US during the Civil War. Courtesy of the Trustees of the Royal Armouries.

known as the 'Lorenz' rifle and it was manufactured in several calibres, the primary one being .54. The Lorenz was used by large numbers of Confederate units fighting in the western theatre of the war, but several other more unusual Austrian patterns also made an appearance. Fort Lyon in Colorado reported to the Ordnance that in 1864 it held some 326 'Rifles, Austrian, sabre or sword bayonet, Calibre .625 inch'.[20] Curiously, it seemed that nobody at the Fort knew exactly what model of musket it was that they had in store.

The German states were also a major supplier of longarms; in three weeks alone some 25,000 Prussian muskets were shipped to the depot at St Louis for issue to infantry units. Several models saw service but the two most numerous were the Saxon Model 1851/57 rifle muskets, commonly known as 'Dresden' muskets, and the Model 1848 Prussian Jäger rifle. Early in the war over 27,000 Dresden muskets were shipped to the Union and some idea of their quality can be judged by the fact that the Ordnance Department always referred to them as 'first-class arms', an accolade reserved mainly for Springfields and Enfields. The Models were identical apart from the barrel lengths, the 1857 being 3in shorter at 37in. Otherwise, both fired the standard .58-calibre conical bullet and proved as reliable as any rifle-musket used in the war. The design of the Prussian Model 1848 Jäger rifle harked back to the early target rifles of the eighteenth century, with its short, heavy 27½in octagonal barrel retained by wedges, not barrel bands, full-length stock and a patchbox with sliding wooden cover. It had double-set triggers and was supplied, almost inevitably, in both .576 (.58) and .62-calibres, and many of these European rifles and rifle-muskets were sent to the garrisons of the western forts.

During the Civil War, Indians continued to fight unabated in the West and most units stationed in the far-flung forts were forced to use whatever weapons they had been supplied with. Seldom were they given the most recent Springfields, but more often a miscellaneous mixture of imported and surplus weapons, of varying calibres and condition. Conflict with the Indians grew more frequent and the old muzzle-loaders simply proved too slow and cumbersome to beat back the lightning attacks of the native tribes, but fortunately for the troops garrisoned there, by the mid-1860s the days of the muzzle-loader were numbered.

6 Military Breech-Loaders

By the end of the war, the majority of the infantry and cavalry units stationed in the Western outposts were still armed with old pattern rifle-muskets, but gradually supplies of the new Springfield were finding their way to the frontier, and by 1867 and early 1868 they were being issued. While both sides certainly had more than their fair share of outdated and often dubious quality weaponry in service, the war had led to a great burgeoning in firearms' development and nowhere is this better illustrated than in the rapid rise in popularity of the breech-loading rifle. The conflict was to see the introduction of a number of historic 'firsts'. The first bolt-action rifle, the first breech-loading repeating rifle and the first metallic cartridge rifles were all adopted into service, paving the way for the eventual introduction of the modern service rifle as we know it today. It is worth remembering, however, that to a great extent it was the demands of the civilian shooters that did much to create the wide range of firearms that appeared in military hands during the war. Much of the development work for these guns had been undertaken by commercial gunsmiths and inventors pre-war, but such were the demands for rifles and carbines throughout the war years, that the majority actually began their lives as service rifles in military hands.

The Army's adoption of the breech-loading rifle was undoubtedly hastened by the exigencies of the war, for good as the best rifled muskets were, they did not encourage efficient use among troops who were scared or panicked, which most soldiers on the battlefield were. To give some idea of the difficulties of using the musket efficiently in war, of the 27,000 abandoned muzzle-loading longarms recovered from the battlefield after the Battle of Gettysburg, 24,000 were still loaded. If the reader thinks this is a figure to conjure with, then consider too that of those 24,000 some 13,000 were *double* charged and almost 6,000 had *multiple* charges in them, one Springfield having an extraordinary twenty-three loads rammed into its barrel. The fact it did not fire is probably just as well, as the resulting barrel explosion would have sent the hapless soldier into orbit. The reason for this was simple: frightened soldiers would load, cap the gun and fire, firing off the cap but not necessarily igniting the charge. In the smoke and confusion of the battle, they would reload, and recap what was probably a thoroughly fouled and blocked nipple, and go through the same procedure again, with the gun repeatedly misfiring (although managing this twenty-three times in one musket takes some doing). With a breech-loader, performing these sort of mechanical gymnastics was not possible. If the rifle failed to fire, it could not be reloaded until the original cartridge or charge was removed. Ergo … no more useless misfires and a much quicker rate of fire. As one Civil War veteran rightly commented:

> the objection has been urged that we fire too many shots with our present muzzle-loaders and consequently it would be folly to add to the waste of ammunition by affording us greater ease or facility in loading. Do our good friends ever reflect that the loss of time in loading is the great cause of haste, and consequently inaccuracy in firing?[1]

It is not possible to look at all of these breech-loaders in detail; many models have entire books devoted to the story of their development. This chapter will concentrate on a select few that subsequently became the most widely used.

While development of both the Henry Rifle and the Spencer have been covered in Chapter 3, their use during the war is worthy of a little more comment. Without doubt the most significant of the earliest American breech-loaders of the nineteenth century were the products of three of the larger manufacturers, Henry, Spencer and Sharps. Their later importance on the frontier and their impact on American history cannot be ignored, although strangely two of them, the Henry and Spencer, got off to a very shaky start. Both failed to gain any acceptance for military use having been summarily rejected by Brig-Gen Ripley, Chief of the Ordnance, when they were tested in 1861. Ripley was not one of the North's mental giants where technology was concerned and could see no possible use for repeating rifles, although to give him his due he eventually changed his mind as the war progressed. Initially the New Haven Arms Company who manufactured the Henry, were informed in all seriousness by the Ordnance Department that if they wanted to see their gun in use they would have to arm a regiment at their own expense as well as keeping it supplied with ammunition and spares! It is true that the Henry was very expensive at $50 but that did not stop the men of the 66th Illinois Infantry from purchasing their own, and other regiments, impressed by its performance, followed suit. As production numbers rose, the cost dropped and an order from Ripley himself, in 1863, was to firmly establish the repeating rifle as a part of US military history. He requested that New Haven Arms '... furnish immediately one hundred and twenty Henry rifles at $36 each, also two hundred cartridges for each rifle'.[2]

The frames of wartime Henrys were made of wrought iron, but it proved problematic to manufacture, being prone to cracking, and later models had brass receivers. There was also no means of securing the combined trigger-guard/ loading lever in the closed position, and it would drop open, sometimes allowing a cartridge to slip out of the chamber. A small latch was subsequently added to hold the lever closed, a feature that was to be carried over to later models. The 24in, .44-calibre barrel was considered to be an ideal compromise for infantry and cavalry use, and the Henry's 15-shot firepower was unmatched in combat, even if the 200 grain bullet was underpowered. With a 28 grain black-powder charge (roughly the same as a Colt revolver used) it could reach a modest 1250 fps which was certainly on the slow side for a small projectile. Nevertheless, the fact that they were considered effective enough was proven by accounts of their use in combat. In March 1864 the 1st District of Columbia Cavalry was equipped with them and used them in August in a skirmish at Ream's station.

> Our regiment of cavalry was dismounted ... to build light breastworks for the moment. There were received a most desperate charge from the enemy. We used the Henry rifles and easily repulsed the foe, while the infantry (around us) were broken and swept from their well-constructed breastworks. Our Regiment with the Henry rifle stood like veterans ... and as the men often said, and I concur in the opinion, that with this rifle and plenty of ammunition they could safely meet four to one men than with any other arm.[3]

The Henry was never to see the sort of widespread use that Springfields or Enfields enjoyed during the war, and only around 10,000 were manufactured, of which a mere 1,731 were actually purchased by the US government. The majority of the rest were private purchases, but its use during the war earned it the respect of all who came into contact with it. Probably the highest praise came from the Confederate General Mosby, who after an encounter with Union troops armed with the Henry remarked of it that '... he did not care for the common gun or the Spencer's seven shooter, but as for these guns they could wind up on Sunday and shoot all the week, it was useless to fight against them.'[4]

Next to the Henry, the Spencer was the most important repeating rifle to emerge, the mechanics of which have already been covered, but unlike the Henry, it was purchased in large numbers by the Federal Government, some 10,000 rifles being ordered in 1861 alone, at the comparatively high price of $40 each. Included in this price, however, was a very attractive socket bayonet. The signal honour of probably being the first man to ever use a government issue repeating rifle in battle actually goes to Sergeant Francis O. Lombard of the First Massachusetts Cavalry who took his privately acquired Spencer into action with him on 16 October 1862. The rifles proved an immediate success, being reliable and accurate, and the shorter carbines proved an ideal combination of size and weight for

Rimfire: .44 Henry, .43, .44, .56/52 Spencer, .56/56 Spencer, .52/70. Photo courtesy of B. Lees.

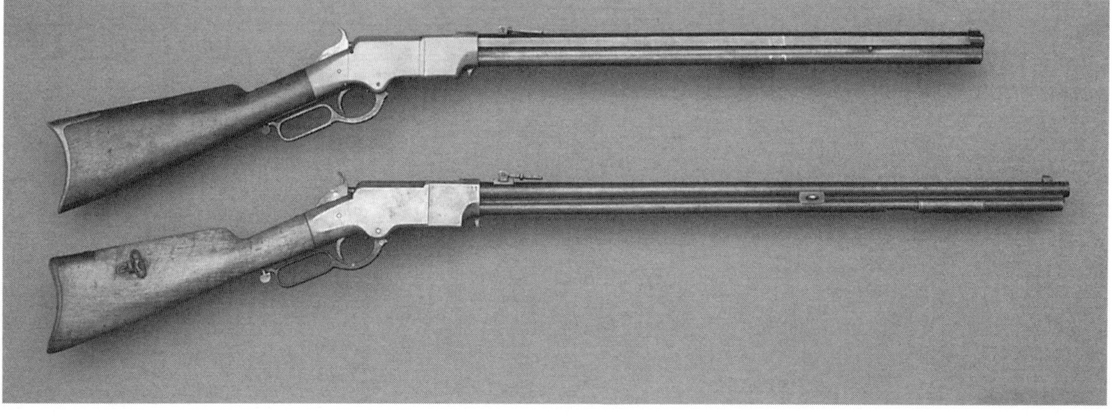

The .44 calibre rimfire Henry rifle and an excellent German-made copy beneath. Courtesy of the Trustees of the Royal Armouries.

mounted use. Many found their way out west and were much sought after by the infantry and cavalry units stationed there. Unlike many other better quality arms made during the war, the Spencers were manufactured in larger numbers than the Army actually ordered – some 11,500 Model 1860 rifles and 95,000 carbines were supplied to the Ordnance. As a result, by 1864 both models were available commercially from dealers in St Louis, Texas and California. The Spencer was to see far more service in military hands post-1865 than the Henry, mainly because its 350 grain bullet and 45 grain charge made it a far more potent weapon than the puny bullet and powder combination of the Henry. In the Indian Wars that ranged across the West from the end of the Civil War to the late 1870s, the Spencer proved its worth, remaining in service until the eventual adoption of the new Springfield rifle in 1873. However, it was the venerable Sharps that had originally been issued as the Model 1859, and subsequently modified, that proved to have the greatest longevity of all of the single-shot rifles. Both sides had used it throughout the war, the Confederates even making their own identical copy. Postwar, many of the carbines were converted to accept the government .50-70in carbine cartridge, and the Sharps long rifles had the distinction of being one of the few military weapons to be used as a true sniping rifle.

The Union forces were the first army to ever raise specialist regiments of sharpshooters. Formed by Colonel Hiram Berdan and eventually equipped with the Sharps, they proved that well-trained men with accurate rifles could wreak havoc on the battlefield. The requirements of a man wishing to enlist in one of Berdan's sharpshooter regiments were stiff indeed, each man being required to place ten consecutive shots into a 5in (12.5cm) bull offhand at 300yd (275m). Amazingly, many men were able to do even better than that.

CIVIL WAR CARBINES

There was no shortage of ingenious new breech-loading weapons issued to the hapless cavalrymen during the war, which was to prove something of a tough proving ground for some of the less robust designs. Many were well designed and technically innovative, while others, as one disgusted Cavalry trooper commented, 'was barely adequate for a row-boat paddle'.

The list of beech-loading carbines and rifles produced between the late 1850s and 1865 makes impressive reading, even though the names of many now have little significance to any but the most dedicated firearms' enthusiasts. Ballard, Ball, Palmer,

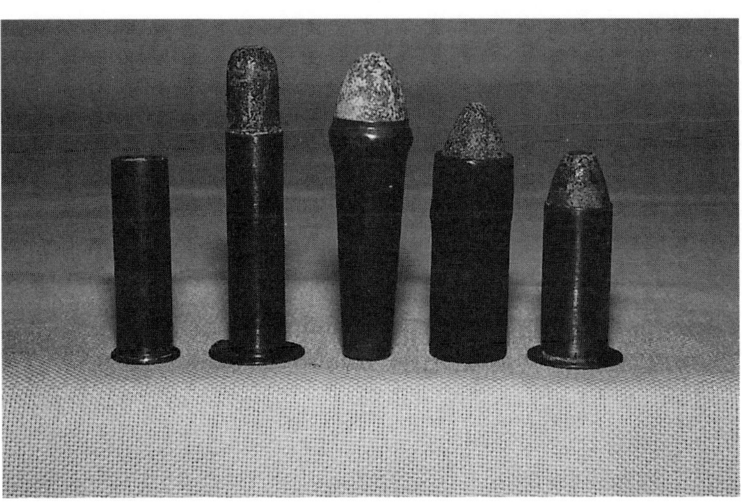

Civil War: .44 Ballard, .40 Maynard, .56 Burnside, .50 Smith rubber, .50 Maynard. Photo courtesy of B. Lees.

Burnside, Gallagher, Gibbs, Greene, Jenks, Joslyn, Lindner, Maynard, Merril, Remington, Sharps, Sharps and Hankin, Springfield/Joslyn, Smith, Starr, Warner and Wesson were just a few of the designs that saw action during the war and, as cheap surplus arms, were to see further hard use in the west post-1865. Almost all were percussion breech-loaders, using pre-prepared combustible cartridges and a standard percussion cap, although some, such as the Ballard, Maynard and Burnside used proprietary metallic cartridges, although they still relied on percussion ignition. The Ballard was one of the better designs to come out of the war and used an internally primed metallic cartridge. The falling-block breech design of the 44-calibre carbine overcame one of the great failings of early metallic breech-loaders, efficient ejection of the spent case, by using a spring-loaded rod under the breech. Once fired, the action was opened and the rod used to knock the empty case out; its breech mechanism was quite simple, operated by a pivoted lever/trigger-guard, and closing it automatically put the hammer on half-cock.

Another good rifle that avoided the pitfalls of many of the single-shot breech-loaders was the Joslyn and it was certainly one of the more interesting designs to come out of the war. Benjamin Joslyn had patented a breechloader early in 1855 and the following year it had the minor distinction of becoming the first breech-loading gun to be manufactured at the Springfield arsenal. The action was worked by means of a locking lever actuated by a large finger ring that lay on the wrist of the stock. Lifting it up exposed the chamber, that

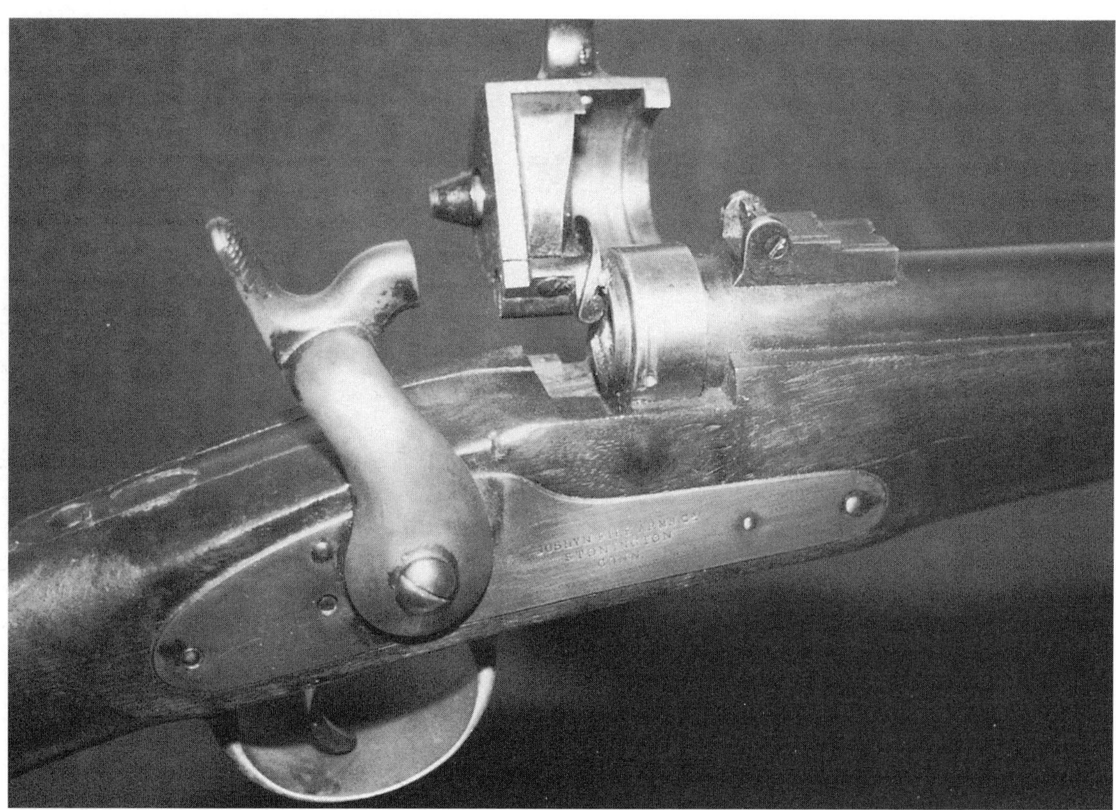

The complex breech mechanism of the Joslyn carbine. Photo courtesy of B. Lees.

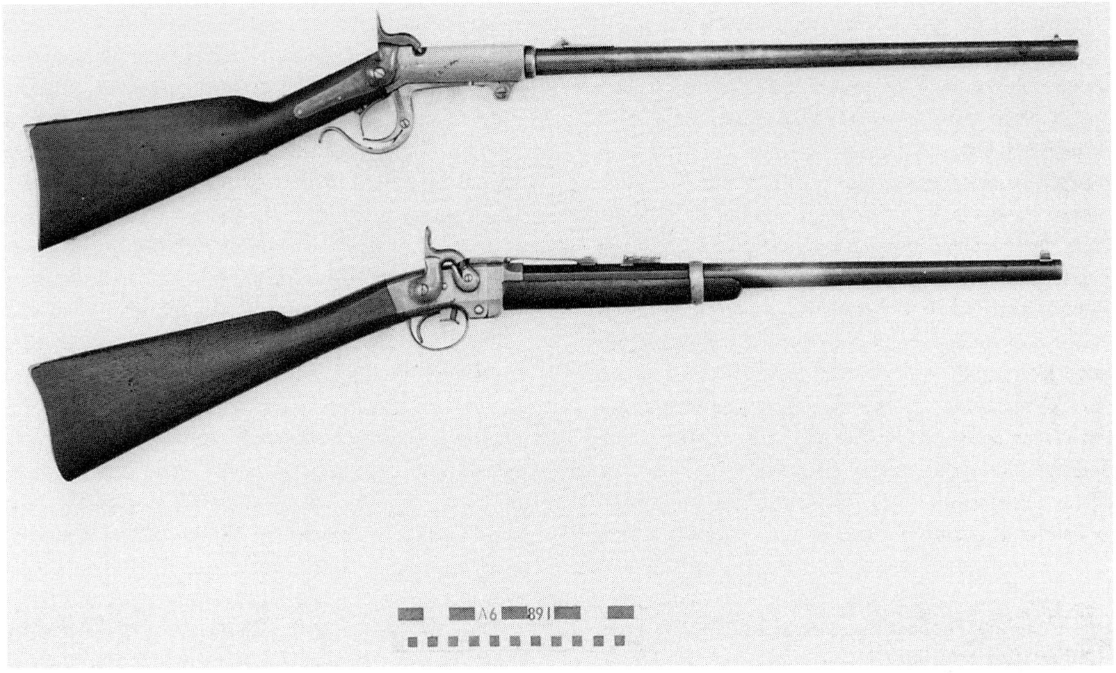

The .56-calibre Burnside and (below) .52-calibre Smith carbines. Both used cartridges that were unique to their weapons. Courtesy of the Trustees of the Royal Armouries.

accepted a .54-calibre paper cartridge. The breech used steel rings to form a gas seal when the gun was fired, but although the Army were not overly impressed, the Navy ordered a small number. Joslyn was aware of the limitations of the paper cartridge so in 1861 redesigned the breech to accept the new .56-calibre Spencer rimfire ammunition. The new Model 1862 used a hinged breechblock that unlatched and swung to the left and some 20,000 were ordered. Improvements continued throughout the war but when only about half had been supplied hostilities ceased and the government promptly cancelled the contract.

Another clever design that also used a metallic cartridge was the Burnside, some 50,000 being manufactured. This, too, used a combined trigger-guard/ loading lever, but the breech mechanism tilted upwards at the front exposing a cone-shaped breech that accepted, unsurprisingly, a cone-shaped brass cartridge. This had a tiny hole in the base through which the flash of the cap could pass to ignite the charge. However, it too suffered from the problem of difficult extraction after firing, the cases sometimes having to be dug out with a knife blade, a problem that also seriously affected the Gallagher that used a similar tilting breech mechanism. Both sides used Burnsides during the war but by 1865 the company had ceased manufacture of the carbine and were manufacturing Spencer rifles under contract. This was partly because of demand, and partly because the externally primed Burnside cartridge simply proved too unreliable. Before long the Burnside rifle was to fall by the wayside, although many found their way west as surplus arms.

Another carbine to see widespread use was the Smith, which had an unremarkable but efficient pivoting barrel, which utilized a brass release catch in front of the trigger that released a spring steel strap on top of the barrel. This, in turn, released the barrel, which pivoted downwards to expose the chamber. What was very unusual about the Smith was its ammunition, for it used a rubber cartridge case. Although the concept of rubber ammunition sounds unlikely, it did in fact work tolerably well, the soft cases being easy to reload and, like the Burnside, they were ignited by means of a small hole in the base. Their shortcoming was that after half a dozen firings the rubber hardened to the point that it became embrittled and would break, and naturally it suffered from the inevitable problems with extraction, despite its ingenious mechanism. It ranked fourth during the war in terms of the numbers manufactured and issued, some 31,000 being supplied, and many found their way into the hands of Confederate cavalrymen.

Probably the least known and quirkiest carbine to see service was the Greene, which had the doubtful distinction of being the only underhammer percussion bolt-action rifle ever produced. It was invented by an aspiring military student, James Greene, whose mother subsequently refused to let him join West Point Academy. Greene was apparently determined to exact revenge in some form, so in 1857 patented a .54-calibre rifle with a 36in barrel and a hexagonal bore similar to that of the Whitworth. It had a breech design of mind-numbing complexity that required a single bullet to be seated by pushing forward the bolt handle; the bolt then had to be pulled back to allow a combustible cartridge that had its bullet at the base, to be inserted into the breech, whereupon the bolt was again pushed forward, rotating and locking it by means of lugs behind the chamber, which meant that the breech had one bullet ahead of the charge and another behind it, acting as a gas seal. The cap then had to be placed on the nipple *underneath* the chamber and the hammer cocked. Once fired, the rear bullet had to be pushed forwards into the chamber and the whole laborious process repeated. Not surprisingly, it failed dismally in military tests but Greene, who was by then Colonel of the Massachusetts Volunteer Militia, still managed to sell his own regiment several hundred rifles, although what they had done to deserve this is not recorded. It says something about their desirability that at the end of the war most of these rifles were still held, unissued, in stores.

A Greene's Patent underhammer bolt-action rifle. Courtesy of the Trustees of the Royal Armouries.

POSTWAR BREECH-LOADERS

Even before the end of the war there had been a general consensus of agreement within the Ordnance Department that breech-loading would ultimately prove to be vital technology for both cavalry and infantry weapons. This was reinforced by their experiences during a war that proved to be the biggest field test of military armaments the world had ever seen. The experience gained with some of the carbines and rifles that had been issued proved that even a poorly designed breech-loader was in most respects a better arm than a well-designed muzzle-loader. There was also a broad acceptance that the large calibres used were not entirely necessary, and smaller calibres such as .50 or even .45in had proven to be more than adequate for military use. Gen Dyer, Chief of Ordnance throughout the war years, had been looking for a means of replacing the rifled musket since the late 1850s, and experience gleaned during the conflict served to reinforce his view that they should be replaced by breech-loaders '... as soon as the best model ... can be established ... the alteration of our present model of muzzle-loading arms is also a very desirable measure.'[5]

Gen Dyer also wisely held the opinion that having in service over thirty different types of rifled muskets, smoothbores and breech-loading rifles and carbines, in a plethora of calibres, was both inefficient and impractical. It was proposed that a standard rifle should be adopted for issue to all army units. The problem facing the Ordnance postwar was the resultant cost of attempting to introduce a new rifle on the scale required. The answer seemed to lie in adopting a workable system for converting the large numbers of Springfields still in service to centrefire ammunition, but finding a mechanism that was cheap, efficient and easy to install seemed beyond their powers. True, there were designs that could have been used, the Joslyn for one and the Mont-Storm conversion of the Pattern 1853 Enfield rifle that used a hinged breechblock for another, but there were serious mechanical shortcomings with both systems that would not suit the hard life that a service rifle could expect, particularly in the Frontier. The problem was solved by an armourer at Springfield, Erskine S. Allin, who patented an improved breechblock mechanism that could be fitted to modified rifle muskets by cutting away the top of the breech, machining a recess in the breech screw and modifying the hammer.

The idea was not in itself new, but incorporated two vital features, an efficient ejector mechanism and a locking system that securely held the block and prevented accidental discharge. These Allin conversions were first tried on Model 1865 Springfields, 5,000 of which were modified to use a copper cased, internally primed .58-calibre cartridge. In trials this calibre proved unsatisfactory, with heavy recoil from the 500 grain bullet and poor accuracy. The following year, the calibre was reduced to .50in, an improved breechblock and thumb latch were introduced and a positive lock safety was introduced that prevented the hammer from striking the firing pin unless the breech was firmly locked. In tests against other rifles, such as the Remington Rolling Block, Ward-Burton and Peabody, the Allin proved only average, but it was saved from a plunge into obscurity by the fact that, despite the Board's recommendation that .45-calibre be universally

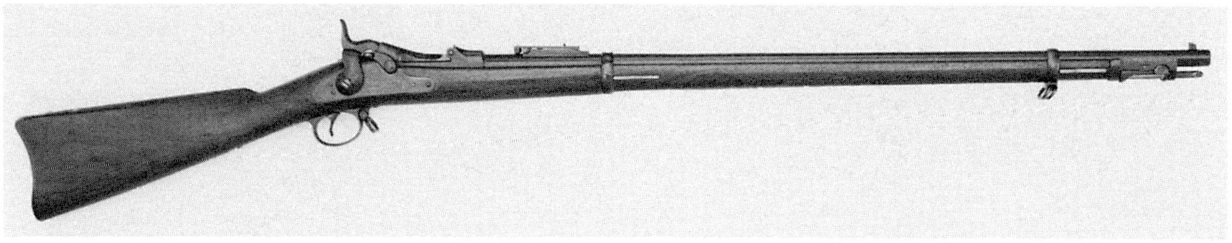

A .45-70 calibre 'Trapdoor' Springfield rifle. Courtesy of the Trustees of the Royal Armouries.

adopted, it could be easily (and more importantly, cheaply) converted to accept the new .50-70 centre-fire cartridge then being introduced. As a result, over 50,000 M1866 conversions were done, many of which were promptly issued to the units stationed in the forts in the Departments of Missouri and Platte, hotbeds of Indian fighting. Just what a difference these new rifles could make in combat was soon shown when in the summer of 1867 several hundred Sioux under Red Cloud attacked a small detachment of soldiers and woodcutters in what was to become known as the Wagon Box fight, near Fort Phil Kearny in Wyoming. The twenty-six infantrymen who accompanied the civilian woodcutters were equipped with the new Allin conversion Springfields. While the larger body waited, a small party of Indians attacked, the main war party anticipating the inevitable lull as the white men frantically reloaded their muskets. Instead, they were met with an unbroken fusillade of shots, as Sgt Gibson of the Twenty-Seventh Infantry recounted:

> … instead of drawing ramrods and thus losing precious time we simply threw open the breech-blocks of our new rifles to eject the empty shell and slapped in fresh ones.[6]

After three hours of attack the confused Indians were forced to withdraw, having, as Red Cloud later admitted, lost some of the finest of his warriors. Certainly, the 'Trapdoor' Springfield as it rapidly became known, proved to be an ideal compromise, but in much the same manner as the British used the Snider Enfield conversion, it had only ever been adopted as a temporary measure until a properly designed rifle could be found. Trials in early 1870 tested a number of longarms, including some with an excellent pedigree. The Remington Rolling Block, Sharps, Springfield, Martini-Henry, and the bolt-action Ward-Burton were all examined.

The Ward-Burton is worthy of a closer look, for although it was never adopted, its performance was to profoundly influence the Ordnance Department in the future. It was a good example of an early bolt-action design that actually had its antecedents in an 1859 patent by Bethel Burton. In many respects, it was a very advanced rifle and the 1871 trials model incorporated a rotating bolt that used interrupted threads at its rear, enabling it to lock securely with corresponding threads machined in the receiver walls. When opened, the bolt completely exposed the chamber, and it also incorporated a longitudinally sliding, sprung firing pin that remained to the rear once the bolt was locked home. This was to become the norm on all later bolt-actions but at the time was regarded as a poor feature, one Officer commenting that it made the Ward a 'dangerous rifle in the hands of green troops'. Where untrained soldiers were concerned the same criticism could probably be made about a knife and fork, but it was sufficient to prevent the .50-calibre Model 1871 from being accepted as a service arm, which was unfortunate for the only real defect the Ward-Burton had was that it was twenty years ahead of its time.

The Remington may have won the trials by a whisker, but it did not remain the winner for long,

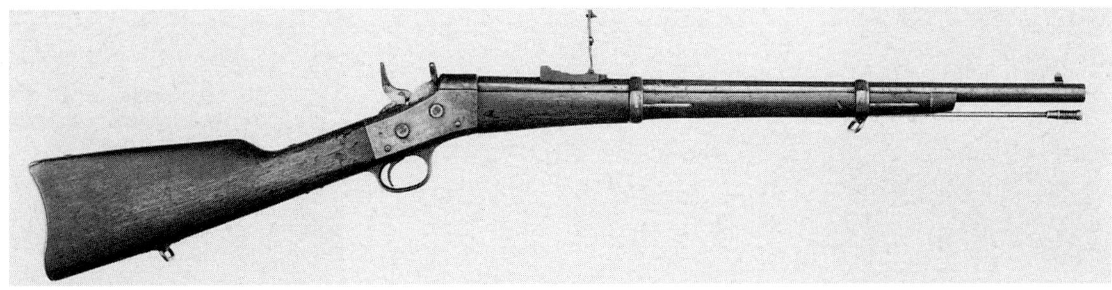

Remington Rolling-Block carbine. Courtesy of the Trustees of the Royal Armouries.

as field trials exposed a number of weaknesses, some of which were slowness of operation compared to the Springfield, the inevitable ejection problems and most worryingly, an action that meant that the rifle had to be loaded at full cock, resulting in a number of accidents. Still, the Springfield Armory manufactured some 10,000 and from 1872 a newly devised hammer-locking system was added that incorporated a half-cock safety. Tests also continued on cavalry carbines, where the Ward-Burton again surfaced, but without success.

Meanwhile, heedless of the work of the Ordnance Department, the cavalry units on the frontier, who were becoming embroiled in ever more frequent fighting with the Indians, were still using the carbines that they had fought with during the Civil War. These were mostly .56-calibre Spencers and .50-calibre Sharps, of which some 30,000 had been converted to accept the .50-70 centrefire cartridge which gave a far better performance than the rimfires of the Spencer. In fact, almost obsolete though it may have been, the old Spencer was to prove a vital weapon during the Indian wars, but by the end of 1871 new carbine versions of the Trapdoor Springfield, Sharps and Remington had been produced and with some reluctance, the Board selected the Springfield. Interestingly, in its report the Board made a recommendation that seemed to show it was uneasy with its decision to adopt yet another single-shot rifle:

> That in the opinion of the Board the adoption of magazine-guns for the military service by all nations, is only a question of time ... that whenever an arm shall be devised which shall be as effective as the best of the existing single breech- loading arms ... every consideration of public policy will require its adoption.[7]

10th US Cavalrymen 1894, armed with Trapdoor Springfields and .38 Colt double-action revolvers. Photo courtesy Montana Historical Society.

The problem was that after examining some eighty different commercial and military designs, there was not yet a breech-loading magazine rifle that the Ordnance felt inclined to adopt. As a result the Trapdoor rifle continued in service, being converted in 1873 to fire the new copper-cased .45-70 government cartridge that was to cause unforeseen problems. The 32 ⅝in barrel of the rifle could propel the new 405 grain bullet at 1,500fps, the 22in carbine managing a tolerably good 1,200fps from a reduced load .45-55 cartridge. Externally the two cartridges were identical enabling many soldiers to play painful practical jokes on their carbine shooting friends. One trooper, the butt of such a joke, commented that on firing the rifle cartridge from his carbine '... you thought the sky fell in'. Accuracy was tolerably good, with the rifle having a maximum range of 1,100yd (1,006m), and in the hands of a good shot it was quite capable of felling a standing man at 1,000yd (915m). By mid-1875, most army units had the Model 1873 and sporting versions were proving popular with officers who could afford them, costing as they did up to $80, about four times the cost of the issue rifle. George Custer was particularly fond of his, but many troopers paid with their lives because of the Springfield's idiosyncrasies where cartridge ejection was concerned. In fairness, it was a problem that bedevilled all single-shot rifles of this period, for the thin copper deformed easily and any man whose cartridges had been carried in leather loops or pouches for any length of time soon found that the harsh climate in the West caused verdigris to form. When the cartridge was inserted into a hot chamber and fired, it set like cement and as if that were not problem enough, the primers also suffered from corrosion, frequently misfiring. When the breech was opened the ejector would simply rip off the thin base of the jammed cartridge leaving the case stuck in the chamber. Most troopers who arrived in the frontier posts immediately purchased thin-bladed knives to deal with the problem, sensibly choosing to ignore the official remedy as carefully laid out in the National Armory manual:

> The best method of extracting the shell is to take out the ball from a cartridge and reduce it with a knife ... so that it can be inserted into the muzzle or the barrel. Ram the ball hard with a ramrod when the breech is closed; this will upset the ball and fill the headless shell. Open the breechblock and the ball and shell can be easily pushed out with a ramrod.[8]

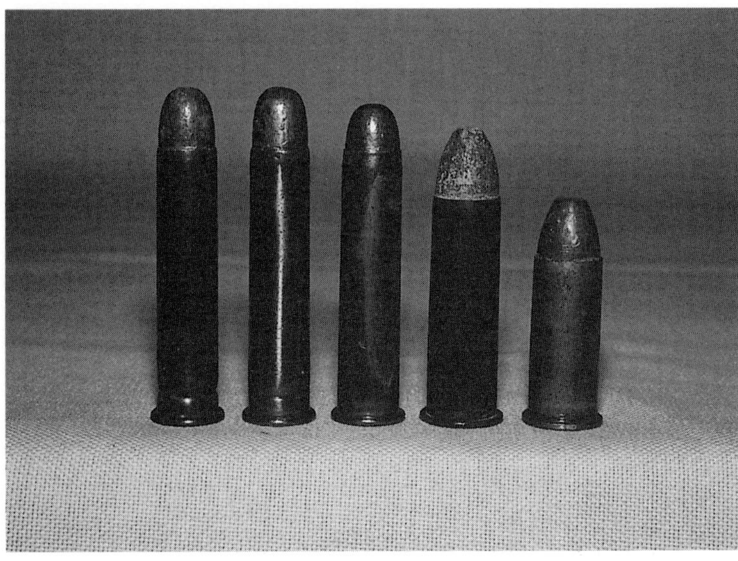

Military rifle: .50 Springfield, .45-70, .45-55, .50-70, .50 US Carbine. Photo courtesy of B. Lees.

Clearly many 7th Cavalry troopers also failed to adhere to the guidelines carefully laid out in the manual, for there is evidence to show that jammed carbines may well have contributed significantly to the defeat of Custer's force on the Little Big Horn in 1876. Examples of cases with their bases ripped off have subsequently been found during archaeological work undertaken on the battlefield site.[9]

THE BOLT-ACTION RIFLE

Clearly such a situation was not acceptable so, in 1878, yet another new round of tests began to find a replacement repeating rifle for the army. Ironically, one of the biggest problems in finding a suitable weapon lay in the .45-70 cartridge adopted by the Ordnance. It proved very difficult for existing designs of repeater such as the Winchester to accommodate its long case and it was left to the new breed of bolt-action rifles to prove their worth. Several were tested, including the Burgess, Chaffee-Reese, Ward-Burton, Remington-Keene, Colt-Franklin, Lee and Sharps-Vetterli, but of these it was the Winchester-Hotchkiss, Remington-Keene and Lee that were to prove the best designs. Aside from the Trapdoor Springfield that was still soldiering on, the four main contenders were whittled down to the lever-action Remington, the Lee with its unique box magazine, the Chaffee-Reese and the Hotchkiss, all of which are deserving of a closer look. The Remington-Keene has already been briefly described in the chapter covering sporting repeaters, for, like the Lee and Hotchkiss, it was to have far greater commercial success abroad than it ever achieved in the United States. From the Ordnance point of view, its greatest asset, aside from its nine-round magazine, was the necessity for it to be manually cocked after loading and its light weight, the rifle being just over 8lb (3.6kg). The Lee was to prove one of the most successful rifles never to be adopted by the United States, who initially refused even to test it because of a misunderstanding about the chambering due to an error on a dimensional drawing. During tests, this resulted in a bolt lug failure, subsequently corrected with the addition of a second opposed lug that engaged on the inner wall of the receiver. The Lee rifles were actually made by Remington and had five-groove 33½in barrels and were sighted up to 1,200yd (1,097m), at which range they proved quite accurate. Up to the end of production in the

The Remington-Lee bolt-action magazine rifle. This example is dated 1887. Courtesy of the Trustees of the Royal Armouries.

early 1890s the US Navy had ordered some 4,000, but the US Army proved to be completely indifferent to the Lee, despite the fact that it proved it could be fired up to thirty times a minute without misfire or failure. It was on the battlefields of twentieth-century Europe that the Lee design was to prove its worth.

The Hotchkiss was actually the result of a joint venture, the design originating from the quiet genius of Benjamin Hotchkiss and the supply of the actions undertaken by Winchester, while the other rifle parts were supplied by Springfield. The rifle had a 28⅝in barrel, the carbine 24in, and it used one-piece government stock, through which ran a tubular magazine. Five cartridges were loaded through a butt-trap and a sixth could be loaded straight into the chamber. To ensure positive cartridge feed, a stop was connected to the trigger so that when the trigger was pulled a single round moved forward under spring pressure and stopped when it reached the underside of the bolt. Raising the bolt handle unlocked the action and cammed back the firing pin, but did not fully compress the spring until the bolt was pushed forwards and locked down. This prevented accidental discharge, one of the great concerns of the Ordnance Department. The Hotchkiss was made in fairly small numbers up to 1883, only some 22,500, when the design was significantly improved by doing away with the butt-trap and producing a rifle that could now be loaded through the top of the action. Mass-production techniques meant that it was very competitively priced at $15, but there was still great scepticism about the practicality of the bolt-action rifle for military use. That the Chief of Ordnance, Brig Benét, recognized this can be seen in his report of the test, when he said that:

> ... the principle of the Hotchkiss is a good one, but there seems to be some prejudice existing in our service against the bolt system and its awkward handle, that time and custom may overcome.[10]

The Chaffee-Reese was also manufactured at Springfield and used a tube magazine, but had one slightly unusual design feature. It employed two ratchet bars on either side of the magazine, with carefully spaced internal teeth that rested on the base of the forward cartridge in the tube. Opening the bolt, then closing it, slid the right bar forwards, pushing the cartridge into the chamber, while the

Model 1883 Hotchkiss rifle, manufactured by Winchester, showing the open bolt and cartridge-loading ramp. Courtesy of the Trustees of the Royal Armouries.

left bar prevented the cartridges still in the magazine from sliding backwards. This ingenious system prevented the bugbear of tube magazine rifles, the detonation of one cartridge by the nose of another striking its primer, but the design was prone to mechanical failure and malfunction if it became dirty. It was also considered a difficult rifle to field repair. Some soldiers disliked the feel of this action, believing it to be too heavy, although in practice it worked quite well. The Chaffee-Reese was to fade swiftly from sight, not even managing to raise any commercial interest in the burgeoning sporting rifle markets. If the tests undertaken between 1872 and 1887 had proven anything, it was that for military use the single-shot rifle was outmoded and close to the end of its practical working life and that the way forward was with the new magazine rifles. The faithful Trapdoor had staggered on in various guises through no less than five models, the last being introduced in 1890, but in terms of development, it had run its course.

Then, in one of those curious cases of serendipity that seem to happen from time to time, two events coincided that were to have a profound effect on the course of rifle technology in the USA. Firstly in 1888, the thin-walled copper-cased .45-70 ammunition manufactured by the Frankford Arsenal and supplied to all military units was phased out. Production began of a heavier, stronger brass-cased ammunition that eliminated many of the extraction problems in the army's rifles but, more importantly, it enabled the second development to be fully utilized. The French developed a new nitrocellulose-based powder that was virtually smokeless and developed far higher breech pressures than could ever have been achieved with black powder. Successful experiments were made in the USA to duplicate the properties of the new propellant, using a new small-bore .30-calibre, high-velocity cartridge. Unfortunately, this had the effect of showing up fundamental flaws in the design of many of the older rifles, namely the inability of their breeches to cope with the higher chamber pressures. The new ammunition effectively spelled the death of the old Trapdoor, for the angle of the breech-block made it prone to bursting open when fired. When the block was modified, the opposite occurred, and in tests some breeches were found to have solidly jammed closed.

So once again, the Ordnance embarked on a search for a replacement rifle, this time looking predominantly at the new bolt-action designs. From Europe, Mauser, Schmidt-Rubin, Mannlicher, Kroptschek, Lee-Speed, and Krag-Jorgensen were tested, as well as home-grown designs like Chaffee-Reese, Savage, Lee, Bruce and Durst.

In 1890, exhaustive trials were again begun that continued for two years, which, by military standards, was quite rapid. The Board of Ordnance had by now had more experience in conducting weapons' trials than probably any other military board. The demands on the rifles selected were heavy. They had to pass stringent tests including dust, rusting, 500-round rapid fire, high-pressure cartridges and defective ammunition. Some of the cartridges used for pressure testing quite literally blew the rifles apart. One by one the contenders were eliminated, until only the Lee, Krag and Mauser were left. Although in terms of design and construction there was little to choose between them, it was the Danish Krag that eventually triumphed. In construction it was reasonably strong, having a locking lug on the head of the bolt, as well as a long guide rib that bore on a shoulder of the receiver, a positive point in view of the power of the .30-40in smokeless cartridge that the army was to adopt. The strength of the locking system was to prove questionable later on, but at the time its strength was regarded as satisfactory and the action of the bolt was regarded as particularly good, being smoother than that of the other rifles tested. It was the Krag's most unusual feature, its magazine, that particularly endeared it to the test board. The Ordnance officers conducting the trials were very keen to ensure that a rifle was adopted that did not encourage troops to waste ammunition by blazing away needlessly, which they were sure would be the result of issuing a bolt-action rifle with a magazine. It had an unusual side-mounted pivoting box magazine that swung open to the right to act as a loading platform into which the ammunition could be dropped one round at a time. Additionally it could also be isolated by means of a cut-off, enabling the shooter to load directly into the breech in the manner of a single-shot rifle. In this they were mirrored by the British Board of Ordnance, who until 1916 insisted that all Enfield rifles were equipped with magazine cut-offs for the same reason. By the start of 1892, the first Model 1892 Krags were being issued and in its short life it was to go through a large number of improvements, being issued in modified form as the Model 1896 then the Model 1898. Despite the improvements, the Army were still not happy, particularly as experiments with a new .236in (6mm) high-velocity cartridge showed up inherent defects in the strength of the Krag's bolt-locking system. Impressed by the .236 ammunition, a number of straight-pull designed Lee rifles chambered for it were adopted by the Navy, but the army did not waver and the hunt was on again for a replacement for the Krag.

By this time, the Western epoch had come to an end. The Indians, after a final attempt at asserting their traditional ways at Wounded Knee in 1891, had been bullied into submission, the buffalo had gone and settlements dotted the prairies and hills of the old frontier. For the Army there was little to occupy them at home whereas political events occurring elsewhere, in particular the Philippines, were calling them. It was extraordinary that in such an incredibly short time period – little more than eighty years – the US military had taken firearms' technology, that had remained fairly static in development terms for 400 years, from the smoothbore flintlock to the high-velocity, bolt-action rifle. They had used, field-tested and rejected more types of longarm than any other nation in history.

Krag rifle, with the magazine open for loading. Courtesy of the Trustees of the Royal Armouries.

7 Civilian Pistols

If the rifle has become synonymous with the American struggle for freedom from what was widely regarded as British tyranny, then without a doubt the revolver, or more specifically the 'six-shooter', has become the most universally and instantly recognizable icon of the American West. Much of the cause of this has been the prominence of the revolver in films and TV over the last few decades, where every US cavalryman, lawman, gunfighter, cowboy and Indian appears to be armed with a .45 Colt. The reality was, of course, somewhat different, for historically the pistol had quite a slow start and its lineage does not stretch as far back as that of the musket due mainly to the practical constraints of early technology. The sixteenth- and seventeenth-century matchlock mechanisms were not practical for a firearm that was to be carried next to the body or concealed under clothing. It was only the advent of the wheel-lock mechanism in the early half of the sixteenth century that first enabled gunsmiths to consider miniaturizing a firearm to the extent that it became portable. Even so, the first handguns were heavy, cumbersome and awkward to use, but very gradually they became more compact, to the extent that by the mid-sixteenth century they attracted the attention of the authorities in England and Europe who had begun to see them as an insidious threat. In 1579, a proclamation was made by Queen Elizabeth I that is reminiscent of modern legislation, when she made it illegal for concealed pistols to be carried in towns or cities on pain of imprisonment and also forbade the commercial sale of 'dags' as they were known. In fact, most early snaphaunce or flintlock pistols were anything but portable and quite unsuited to being carried, being heavy, long-barrelled guns primarily designed to be carried in pairs in saddle-mounted holsters, a method that was to continue unchanged until the mid-nineteenth century.

The advent of the flintlock had certainly been a boon for gunmakers, as the mechanism was simpler and lighter than the wheel lock, and could be miniaturized still further. A number of different types of flintlock pistol had found their way into the colonies by the late seventeenth century, mostly of simple military flintlock type, but no true American style was to appear until the Revolutionary War. The reason was quite simply that there was little demand for the pistol. It had almost no use for hunting, lacking range and power and was in essence nothing more than a back-up weapon to the musket. Most were imported from Europe, in particular from France and Britain and these were to satisfy the modest home market until after the Revolutionary War. The most useful pistols were of the larger horse or holster type, and having 10 to 12in smoothbore barrels, and fairly large calibres commonly between .50 and .70in. The specifications of these pistols was to remain fairly standard throughout the eighteenth century and well into the nineteenth. Inevitably, many were supplied by the English commercial gun trade, but there was also a sprinkling of ex-military Tower-made flintlocks of various patterns such as Sea Service and Dragoons that had found their way to the shores of the East coast with settlers and some made their way across the continent, while the more elegant pistols by makers such as Durs Egg were carried by those whose status demanded such a costly accessory, although the likelihood of their ever being used was remote. The men who carried and used pistols were the explorers, trappers and mountain men, for in an emergency their comparatively large bullet, fired from close range, could make the difference between life and death. Washington Irving commented on the increasing frequency with which the pistol was being carried on the frontier, describing a typical trapper as being

> dressed in a blanket of scarlet or some other bright color … where around his waist he wears...a red sash, in which he bestows his pistols, knife and the stem of his Indian pipe.[1]

Any experienced frontiersman would have at least one single- or double-barrelled pistol on him at all times. These large pistols even proved adequate for killing buffalo from horseback, although it took considerable skill at horsemanship and good shooting skills to achieve it. In his book on early Frontier life, Washington Irving commented on the dangers of using a pair of elderly flintlocks to hunt buffalo.

> Pistols are very effective … as the hunter can ride up close to the animal, and fire at it while at full speed, whereas the long heavy rifles … cannot be easily managed. My object, therefore, was to get within pistol shot of the buffalo … I urged my horse sufficiently near, when, taking aim, to my chagrin, both pistols missed-fire. Unfortunately … in the gallop, the priming had been shaken out of the pans.[2]

However, in common with the musket, it was not long before American gunsmiths on the east coast began to adopt their own particular style of pistol, generally known as Kentuckies. In form, these early pistols were of a more delicate style than some of their European counterparts, typically stocked with fine striped maple or burr walnut, with a fairly short iron barrel of perhaps 6 to 10in and calibres from .30 to .50in, although larger were not unknown. Most were fitted with front and rear sights, and about half of those manufactured had a rifled barrel that in the right hands made them quite formidable guns, generally reckoned to be as accurate as a rifle out to 50yd (46m). One unnamed diarist recorded how he and his brother would astonish Indians by shooting candles out of each other's hands using what he described as 'large duelling pistols'. By the late 1790s, several makers began to earn a solid reputation for the quality of their pistols, and names such as Moll, Golcher, Creamer and Constable became synonymous with these new pistols although many of them were, like the makers of the Kentucky rifles, actually Pennsylvania-based gunsmiths. Even the famed Hawken brothers began to manufacture Kentucky pistols.

The finer quality pistols could command quite large sums of money, a plain pair costing around $40–50. These paired pistols are sometimes incorrectly referred to as duelling pistols, and most paired pistols were simply high-quality travelling or horse pistols, supplied in a stout wooden box

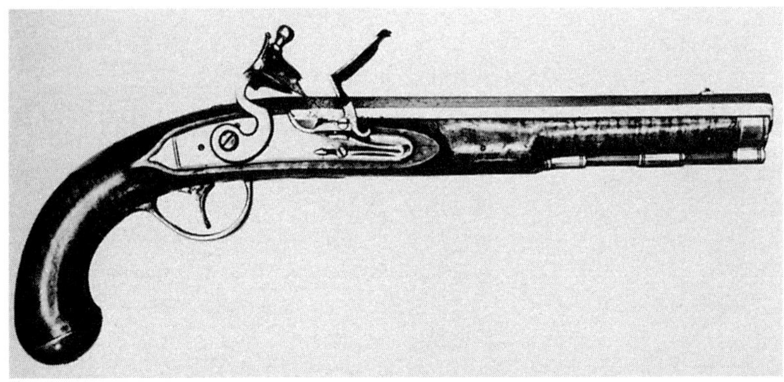

A typical Kentucky-style pistol of about 1800. It is maple stocked and in .52 calibre.

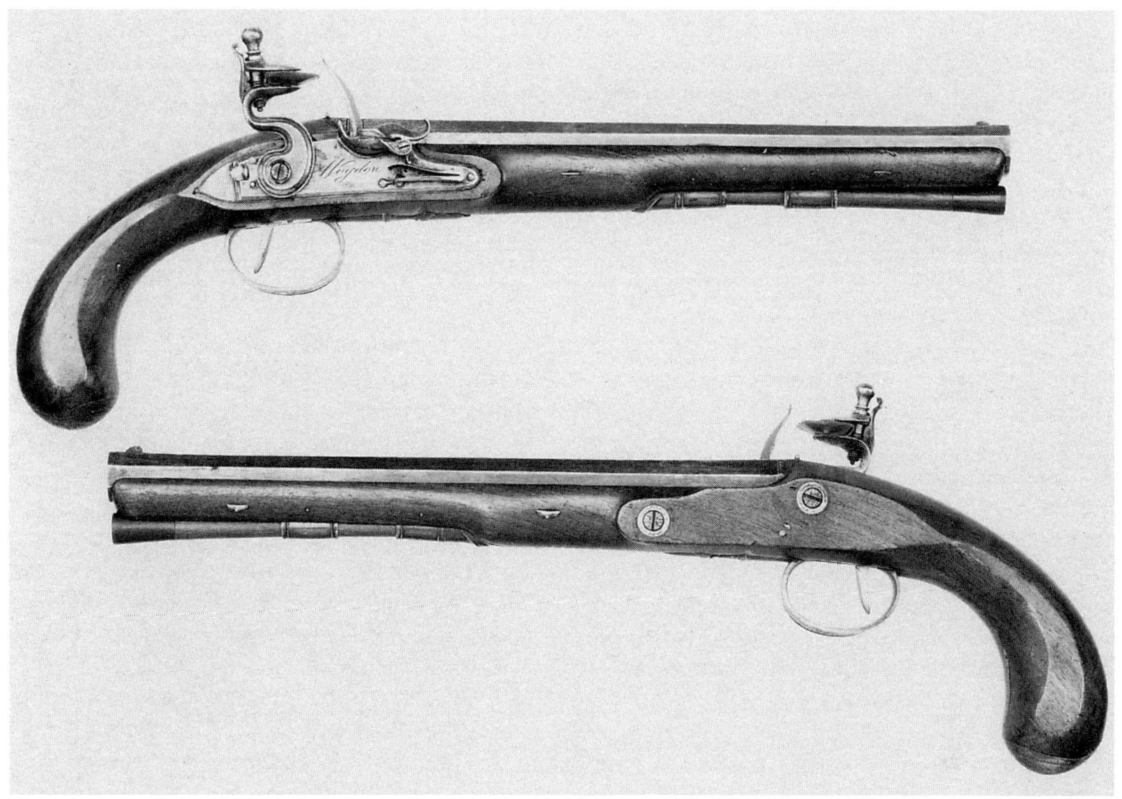

Duelling pistols by Wogdon of London, circa *1780. Similar in style to holster pistols of the period, these have hair triggers and weigh a mere 1½lb (0.7kg) each. Courtesy of the Trustees of the Royal Armouries.*

with all the necessary accessories for the traveller to be self-sufficient. Although there is little doubt that, during the years in the late eighteenth century when duelling was popular in both Europe and America, such pistols could be pressed into service to settle a dispute, they were not specifically constructed for the purpose.

True duelling pistols were very finely balanced with lightweight barrels fitted into ergonomically shaped stocks, that permitted instant pick-up and sighting, with no time wasted attempting to balance the gun in the hand. Some were 'saw-butt' in shape giving a very positive grip, others more rounded but well shaped to the hand. The barrels were octagonal and calibres were quite large, anywhere between .45 to .65in with smoothbore barrels, for at the range of most duels, around 20yd, this was perfectly adequate. As the muzzle energy of a .45-calibre pistol at that range, nearly 300 foot pounds, is roughly equivalent to that of a modern .44 Special, even being winged by a bullet at that distance would certainly cause an alteration to one's plans for the rest of the day. Duelling pistols were equipped with a foresight but rarely a rear sight – too much time could be wasted attempting to line the sights up – and there were no decorations such as silver mounts or escutcheons to catch the light or distract the shooter. By 1800, frictionless locks for faster ignition were used and duelling pistols by Patrick, Egg and Manton as well as American makers such as Creamer have become almost an art form, with a commensurate price tag. In 1809, a pair of duelling pistols by Creamer fetched an incredible $250, the equivalent of an annual wage for many, and some of the designs had begun to be copied on more mundane commercial pistols.

Meanwhile, at the other end of the spectrum, it was not unknown for a worn or damaged musket to be converted to a pistol, with a cut-down barrel and replacement stock but retaining its original lock. These were generally recognizable by the heavy nature of the barrel and larger calibre, but many were very nicely converted indeed and would have given sterling service. Double-barrelled flintlock pistols were also used, although they were comparatively rare and many were English imports, as they were a popular sidearm for hunting in India or the Colonies. The weight penalty made a double-barrel an uncomfortable choice for a sidearm, but many explorers relished their hitting power and carried them in improvised holsters on pack mules, horses or even slung on leather straps over their backs.

Not all of the early flintlocks were large, heavy guns, for there had long been a demand in the east for small pistols for personal protection and in this marketplace the English trade thrived, for pocket pistols of every shape and type abounded. Most common in America were the little canon-barrelled turn-off pistols. These were small-framed, boxlock pistols, with an internal flintlock mechanism mounted centrally behind the smoothbored barrel that could be unscrewed to enable the powder and ball to be loaded directly into the firing chamber. This method of loading meant that the ball was a tight fit in the barrel, eliminating windage and providing surprisingly good accuracy and range for their small calibres. A typical turn-off pistol could place a .36 or .40-calibre ball into a palm-sized bull at 25ft (7.6m), more than adequate for self-defence. Some pistols were actually small enough to be easily concealed in the palm of the hand and probably gave the impetus for the subsequent manufacture of the famous Derringer pocket pistols. Although Derringer had primarily been a rifle maker, he had also been manufacturing pistols since the early 1820s. Within a decade, however, the era of the flintlock pistol would be in rapid decline as percussion ignition took over.

PERCUSSION PISTOLS

If percussion had been an important technological advance for longarms, then it was doubly so for the pistol. The more enclosed mechanism of the percussion pistol lent itself well to use in a handgun and it could be miniaturized without all the complications of requiring flint and a frizzen, with its associated snagging in clothing. More importantly, the flat percussion lock and simple hammer could be easily fitted to a flintlock pistol. The addition of a simple 'snail' on the side of the breech required no more than a couple of hours' work for a skilled gunsmith to convert the old technology to the new. Many old flintlocks were thus given a new lease of life in this manner, but percussion ignition was to bring about far more radical changes in pistol design.

Most single-shot pistols were carried in pairs, which was at best inconvenient as they were heavy and unwieldy, and the hunt had been on for many decades for an effective multi-shot pistol. Some material advances had been made, such as the revolving flintlock designed in 1818 by Artemus Wheeler of Concord, Massachusetts and patented in England by his friend Elisha Collier, but the big problem was always in producing a reliable and uncomplicated means of ignition that did not require each cylinder to be individually primed before each shot. At a stroke, percussion solved the problem, enabling a barrel, or several barrels, to be loaded, capped and kept in instant readiness for almost as long as the shooter deemed necessary.

In the mid-1830s a number of good single-shot percussion pistols were being produced by American makers of whom Henry Derringer was prominent. Other makers included Young of New York, Revol of New Orleans, and Ethan Allen of Grafton, Massachusetts. Allen had begun to make pistols around 1833, initially using an underhammer

A Collier flintlock revolving pistol, circa *1825. It has a self-priming pan but had to be manually rotated. Courtesy of the Trustees of the Royal Armouries.*

design. Crucially, he used a cast-steel rifled barrel that was almost indestructible regardless of how large a black-powder charge was used and they provided excellent accuracy out to 50yd (46m) and often beyond, well beyond the capabilities of a smoothbore. In 1835, when challenged about the accuracy of his rifled pistol, Col Randolph Marcy proved his point by splitting in two the handle of his opponent's expensive new knife at 50yd (46m).

Underhammers proved to be quite popular pistols in the West, a phenomenon that occurred almost nowhere else, and the number of makers were legion: Davis, Cooper, Gibbs-Tiffany, Leman, Chase, Billinghurst, Hale, Spies, the list goes on and on. These curious single-shot pistols were identical in mechanical function form to the rifles, with an under-barrel hammer that struck a downward-pointing nipple. Their slim lines made them excellent boot or pocket pistols, as their hammers were not prone to catching on clothing, but as with the rifles, their ability to function properly relied on having a very close-fitting percussion cap on the nipple. Asking a drunken, fighting-mad assailant to wait a minute while a dropped cap was retrieved from the floor, was not generally an option. Interesting as these were, more firepower was still the goal of pistol makers, and a number of double-barrelled percussion pistols made an appearance, most of which were English imports. The problem, as always, was that of weight, an 8in barrelled, 50-calibre double pistol could weigh 5lb (2.3kg) and was not the sort of pistol to carry nonchalantly in a coat pocket, unless the owner did not mind walking with a distinct list to one side.

The solution was to come in two forms, the first and initially the most successful, was paradoxically to fail, while the second, that originally failed financially, was to prove the most enduring. The mention of the word 'revolver' now invariably conjures up images of six-gun-toting screen heroes, but the six-shot revolver actually evolved from a quite different form of revolver, the pepperbox. The basic design of these pistols was European, where they had proved popular in Britain, France and Belgium since their introduction in the late 1820s. A pepperbox comprised a cluster of full-length barrels of any number between four and seven, rotating around a central axis pin, each with a percussion nipple at the breech end. To shoot, the long spur

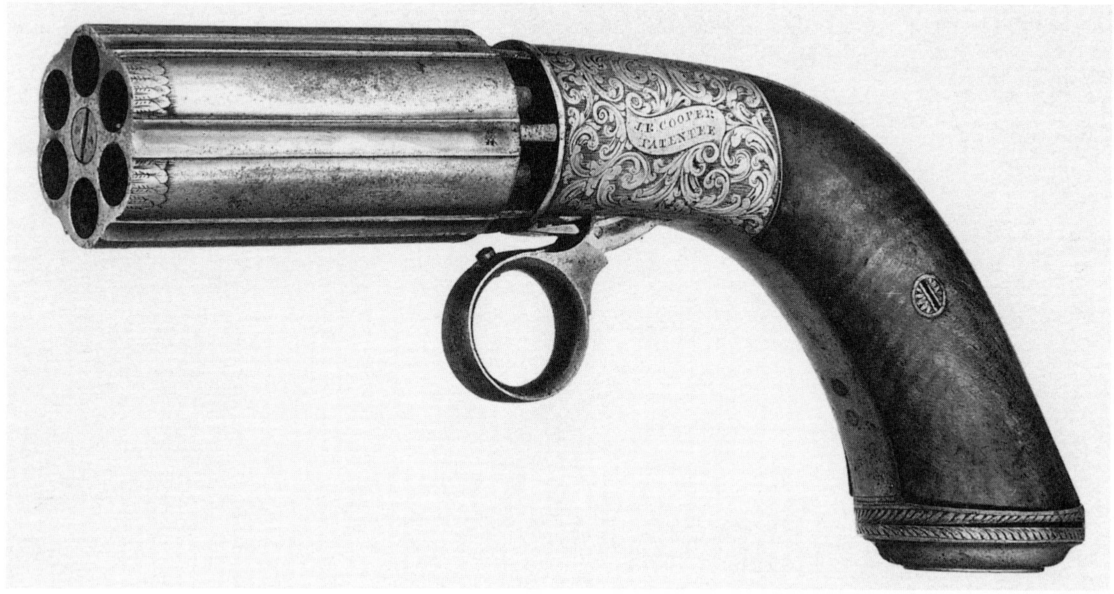

A fine quality Cooper Patent ring trigger pepperbox pistol, with internal hammer, of the 1840s. Courtesy of the Trustees of the Royal Armouries.

hammer was cocked by pulling on the trigger. Early examples had internal mechanisms that were simple in the extreme, and there was initially no means of linking the barrels to the trigger, so in practice this meant that the barrels had to be hand-rotated after each shot which, although slow, was reasonably effective. There were other drawbacks, for their weight and size meant that any but the most modest of calibres, of between .28 and .31in, simply made the pistols too heavy to hold and too bulky to carry. As if that were not enough, they were also prone to suffering from chain-fire, when all the barrels would ignite following the first shot. Although it was not as dangerous to the shooter as chain ignition on a revolving rifle, it was frightening to behold and invariably led to any onlookers caught in the line of fire heading for the hills. Chaplain White, who was accompanying some cavalrymen through Indian territory in 1866 pulled out a seven-barrelled English pepperbox when the party were ambushed by Sioux. All seven ignited simultaneously, killing one Indian and frightening the others so much that they fled and while it may have saved the Chaplain's life, it must have done little to help his nerves.

In an attempt to prevent this problem, some makers put metal shields around the nipples and very careful loading was heartily recommended. If this seems to be a crude and inefficient system, it must be remembered that the only alternative to the pepperbox were single-shot pistols and that any advance in portable firepower was regarded as an improvement. Most pepperboxes were sensibly priced at between $10–15 and while many were imported, considerable numbers were made by American manufacturers. Some of the earliest were made from around 1834 by Barton Darling of Massachusetts. Blunt and Syms of New York also produced popular models, using such novelties as concealed hammers and mechanisms that fired the bottom barrel of the cluster, rather than the top, lessening the recoil and making sighting for further shots easier. They also sensibly used horizontally mounted nipples, that faced towards the shooter, rather than vertical nipples that had a tendency to lose their caps. Other makers also produced pepperboxes, but the most significant was undoubtedly the design patented by Ethan Allen in 1837, that utilized a self-cocking action that rotated the barrels after each shot.

As with most pepperboxes, the pistols made by Allen and Thurber were smoothbores of .31 or .36 calibre in five- or six-shot configuration but they were quite refined, with double-action triggers. This meant that they were faster firing than the new single-action revolvers beginning to appear and did not suffer from the problems of most early revolvers, that of barrel alignment. In a pepperbox, as long as the nipple was in line with the hammer, the gun would fire. In an advert for Allen's revolvers in 1842, it was claimed with some honesty that:

> The chamber and barrels are in one piece, and therefore cannot blow apart like some repeating pistols … they can be drawn from the pocket and used with one hand … six shots can be fired as fast as a man can crook his finger.[3]

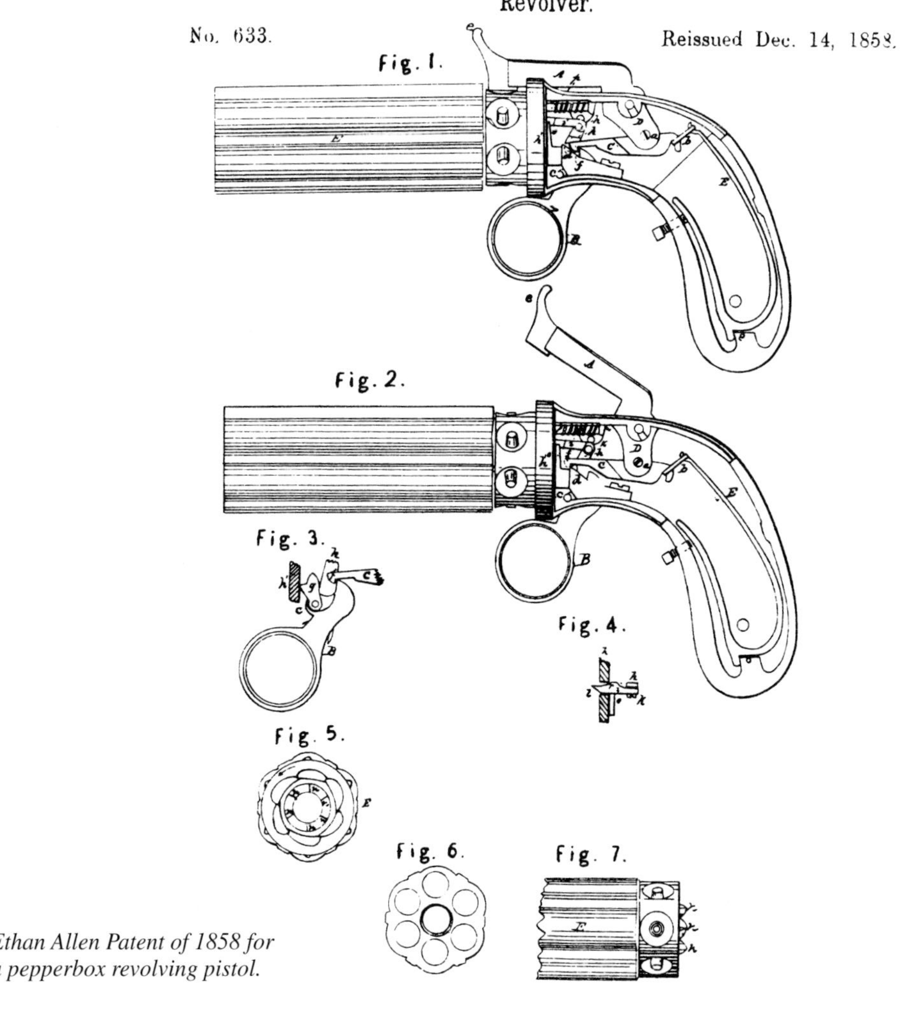

Ethan Allen Patent of 1858 for a pepperbox revolving pistol.

Their accuracy was poor, good only for 10 or 15yd, but few pistols were used at any ranges beyond this and what the Allens lost in accuracy they made up for in firepower. Pepperboxes outsold every other type of pistol on the frontier up to the start of the Civil War. However, by then the age of the multiple-barrel handgun had pretty much drawn to a close, although few would have forecast it a decade before.

In late 1836, Samuel Colt, inventor, entrepreneur, businessman and salesman *par excellence* patented a design for a revolving cylinder repeating pistol. Made by Colts Patent Arms Manufacturing Company in Paterson, New Jersey, the design actually incorporated nothing that was radical. This was hardly surprising, as revolving cylinder pistols had been in existence since the eighteenth century, and Colt had examined a number of early examples at the Tower of London during an earlier visit to England.

His patent covered a five-cylinder revolver in .28 or .36 calibre with a sprung trigger that dropped down when the gun was cocked and, more importantly, had a pawl and ratchet system that automatically turned the cylinder each time the hammer was cocked, aligning a fresh chamber with the barrel. It was also easily stripped, with a wedge holding the barrel to the frame. The tendency of the Paterson to jam because of percussion caps catching in the frame in front of the hammer, and its less than amusing trick of losing its barrel wedge, allowing the barrel to drop off, did not earn it as many fans as Colt would have liked. The basic design of his revolver was a sound one, but in practice the pistols did not live up to their promise.

For a short while it appeared that the disappointing commercial sales might be alleviated by orders; the 'Paterson' revolvers were a novel and reasonably efficient means of producing a multi-shot handgun, but there was quite literally a price to pay. The Colt was costly, between $40–50 in 1839, a quite substantial amount of money for a longarm, let alone a handgun. Even orders from the US Navy and the Texas Rangers' purchase of 180 pistols were not enough to make a difference and the company closed in 1842, but wisely, Colt retained his patent rights.

As is so often the case, matters may have rested there had not a war broken out with Mexico in 1846 creating a sudden demand for serviceable firearms. As a direct result, an officer of the US Mounted Rifles, Captain Samuel Walker, was given a brief to find serviceable firearms for the army and this brought him into contact with Sam Colt. Walker had used an early Paterson revolver during his service with the Texas Rangers and well understood its benefits as well as its shortcomings. Between them, he and Colt created a replacement for the Paterson that was to become the nineteenth-century equivalent of the .44 Magnum, the 1847 Walker Colt. It was a technically significant pistol for several

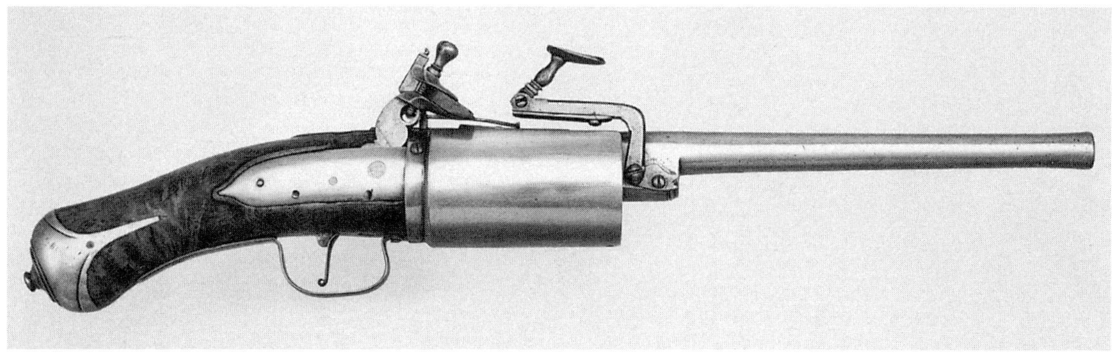

An early English snaphaunce revolver, of about 1660. Samuel Colt examined this pistol in detail when visiting London in 1851. Courtesy of the Trustees of the Royal Armouries.

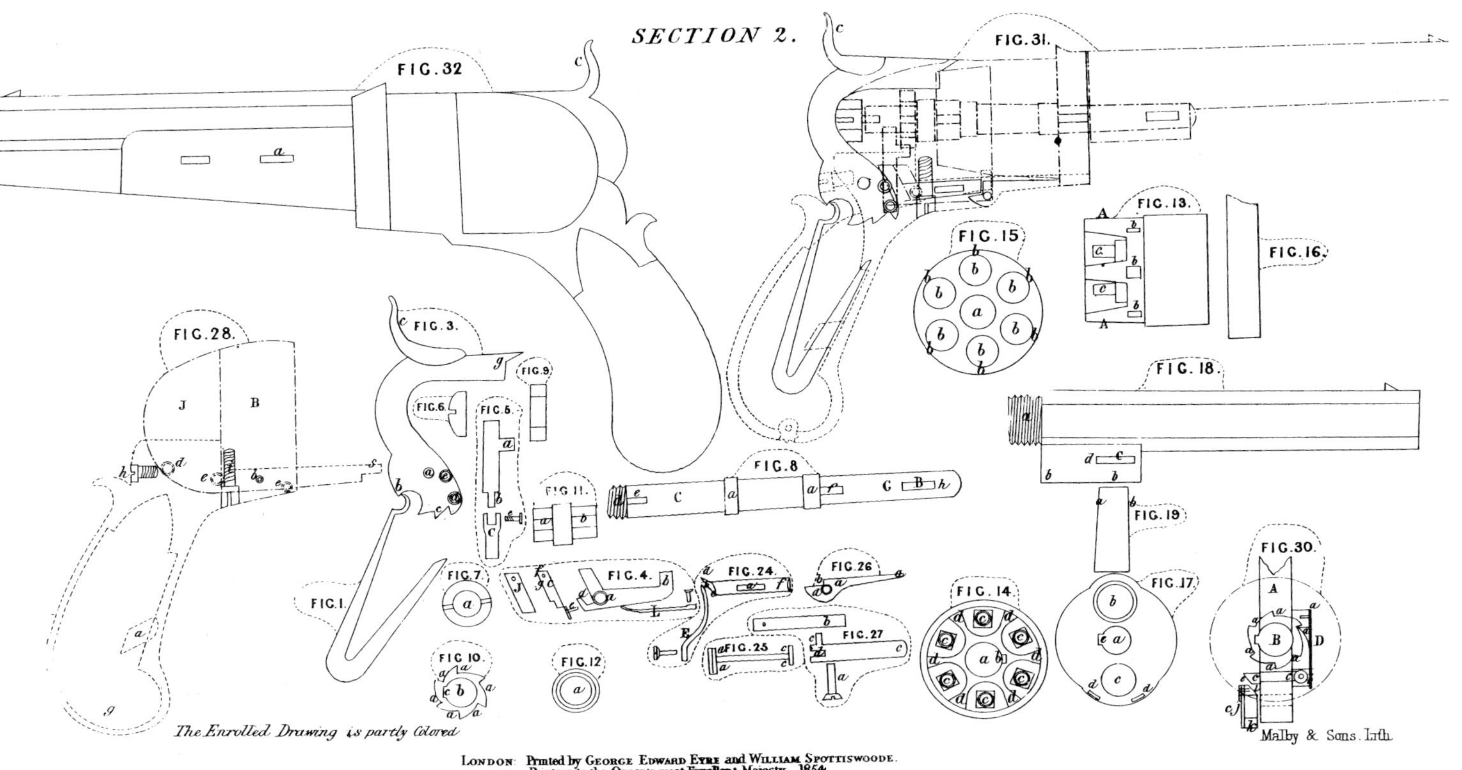

Colt's 1835 Patent for the Paterson revolver.

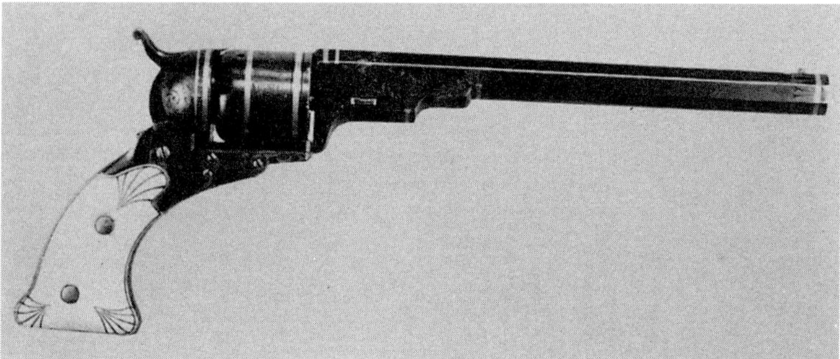

A Paterson revolver, made for Colt by the Patent Arms Manufacturing Company of Paterson, New Jersey about 1839. This fine example has a 9in barrel and is in .36 calibre. Courtesy of Wadsworth Athenium, Hartford, Connecticut.

reasons, not the least because the design was to provide the blueprint upon which an entire generation of single-action revolvers was based. It was, even by modern standards, a massive revolver, 15in long, weighing 4½lb (2kg) and firing a .44-calibre ball with up to 57 grains of powder behind it, equivalent to a carbine load. It was basically the same mechanism as used in the Paterson, and early models were manufactured by Eli Whitney. They were known as Whitneyville-Hartford Dragoons, but to cope with the demand for it a new Colt factory was built in Hartford, Connecticut. Here Colt used the most advanced production techniques anywhere in the world, and he ensured company loyalty by making sure his employees were both well paid and well looked after. The popularity of the Colts, and indeed every other sort of revolver, was fuelled by the Californian Gold Rush of 1849 when demand for firearms exceeded supply, a Colt Paterson fetching $150 or more. One newly arrived prospector, armed with his new Walker Colt, had not unpacked before he became the centre of a crowd of men all outbidding each other for his revolver, the price eventually reaching an astronomical $500.

The Walker and its improved successor, the 1848 Dragoons, were not immune from problems, one of the most serious being a tendency to burst their cylinders. Nevertheless, some 20,000 Dragoons were sold up to 1855, when production of the big pistol ceased. Despite Colt's success, his pistols were by no means the only ones being manufactured, for the pepperbox was still in great demand throughout the Frontier and there was hot debate between the two marques' owners as to which were the more effective, one miner writing home that he had bought a Colt as

> One of Colt's large pistols is sufficient for each man to protect him from either marauding Mexicans or Indians. No man who values his life should carry Allen's revolvers, for they are more to hurt the person who fires them than the person fired at.[4]

The insurmountable problem for potential revolver manufacturers was that Colt held the patents for the mechanism, making it impossible to produce copies without the threat of serious legal action, so many makers continued to persevere with the old designs. Indeed, despite the new revolvers, manufacture of the pepperbox was not slowing down, as some ingenious new models were being introduced by makers like Robbins and Lawrence, who were better known for their work manufacturing the Sharps rifle. Their neat five-shot pistol, introduced in 1851, had a screwed-on barrel cluster as well as being hinged underneath, forward of the frame. This unique design allowed the barrels to be unscrewed so powder and ball could be inserted into the rear section of the breech, the barrels then being screwed back into place on top. A latch on top of the frame was then lifted, so the entire barrel and breech assembly dropped down exposing the nipples set into a backplate. Once capped, these were fired by means of a longitudinal striker cocked by a ring trigger. It was a very advanced design and was

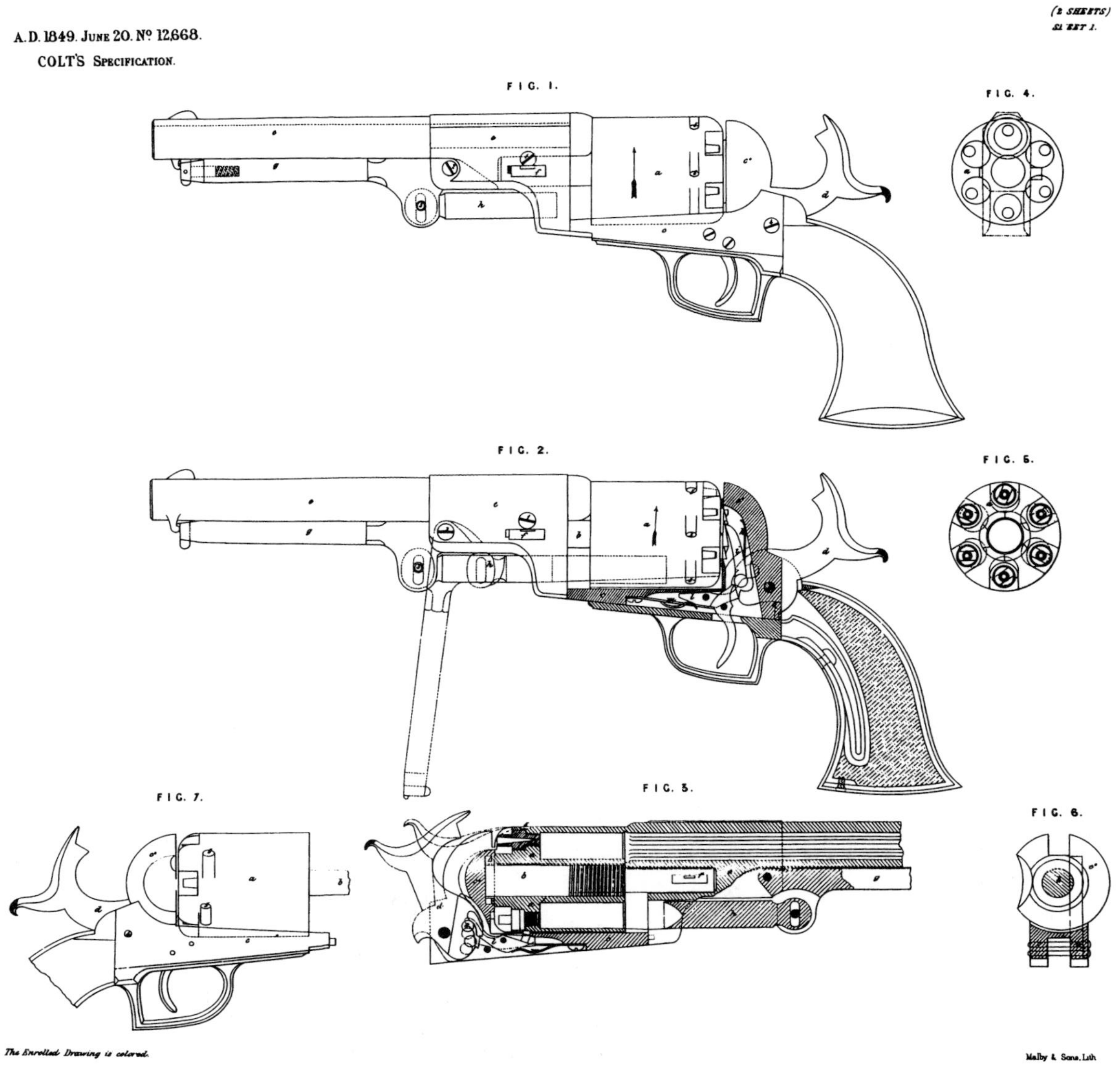

(2 SHEETS)
SHEET 1.

A.D. 1849. JUNE 20. Nº 12,668.
COLT'S SPECIFICATION.

FIG. 1.

FIG. 4.

FIG. 2.

FIG. 5.

FIG. 7.

FIG. 3.

FIG. 6.

The Enrolled Drawing is colored.

Malby & Sons, Lith

The Colt Patent for the Dragoon revolver.

actually the first breech-loading percussion pepperbox to come onto the market. Other makers also produced variations on a theme, the theme really being any form of workable multi-shot revolver.

In 1837 Wesson and Levitt had manufactured a true revolver, its revolving cylinder designed by Daniel Levitt, that was worked by bevel gears, the concept of which came from the agile brain of Edwin Wesson, later to move on to greater things with Smith and Wesson. The pistol had a fixed .31-calibre barrel of between 3 and 7in and the large 'Army' model was produced in .40 calibre, physically being about the same size and weight as the Colt Dragoon. Springfield Arms also made a very similar revolver to the Levitt, but with a hammer-actuated cylinder. It was known as the Warner and was produced in .28, .31 and .40-calibres, but had a complicated actuating system with two-trigger mechanism, one of which indexed the cylinder, the other working the hammer. As if things were not complicated enough, Massachusetts Arms made a revolver in .28 and .31 calibres utilizing the Maynard tape priming system and incorporating a Joshua Stevens Patent that relied on some interesting mechanical gymnastics to avoid infringing the Colt Patent. The revolver worked by thumb-cocking the hammer in the normal manner, an action that also rotated the Maynard primer. Squeezing the trigger unlocked, revolved and locked the cylinder, eventually allowing the hammer to drop onto the percussion cap. Although the action was later simplified, it never became a runaway success, and under 1,600 were manufactured.

DERRINGERS AND POCKET PISTOLS

By the late 1840s, one specific type of pistol was beginning to carve a significant niche in its own particular sector of the market and that was the Derringer. Although he had been manufacturing handsome, large-calibre holster pistols since the 1830s, at around the time of the Californian Gold Rush Henry Derringer had begun to produce distinctive small-framed single-shot percussion pocket pistols, of comparatively large calibre, between .36 and .54in, with back-action locks and short barrels, usually just 4½in long. This was in response to demand for a compact but

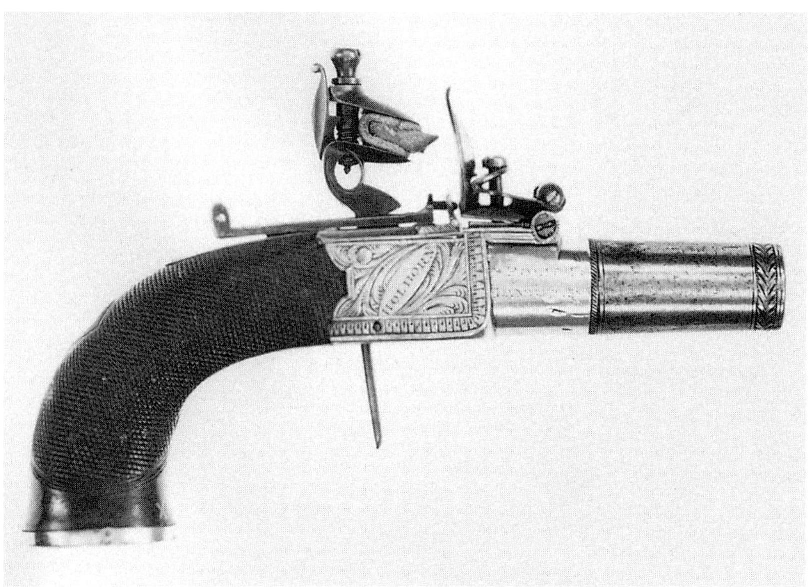

The forerunner of the derringer, a London-made Parker turn-off pocket pistol. Although only 5in (13cm) long, its .45-calibre ball made it a formidable close-range weapon. Courtesy of the Trustees of the Royal Armouries.

powerful pistol that could be easily carried and was not bulky. The nature of these pistols made them an immediate success with men who did not necessarily want to advertise the fact that they were armed, and at close range they were deadly. Henry Derringer unwillingly lent his name to an entire manufacturing industry of pocket pistol that are universally known today as 'derringers'. In fact so much in demand were his pistols that a tailor in Philadelphia named Jacob Derringer made his fortune by licensing his name to gunmakers to put on counterfeit pistols, and Derringer himself was forced to complain in the press about the '… dishonest persons [who] have manufactured and offered for sale a counterfeit or imitation … fraudulently stamping them with my name'.[5]

In the mining camps, virtually everyone, male or female, was armed, frequently with a revolver in a holster and a Deringer as a concealed weapon, and they proved immensely popular. It is some measure of the popularity of his pistols that both Colt and Remington were to make their own 'derringers' [sic], Colt producing their own range of pocket pistols starting in 1870 with the single-shot swivelling-barrelled No. 1 National Derringer in .41 rimfire followed by the very similar, but no more sophisticated, Thuer Derringer. This was rapidly followed by the unusual House Pistol in 1871. This revolver, with a four-shot cloverleaf cylinder and 3in barrel, but with a more conventional round cylinder, grew to become the Police and House pistol that became popular as 'backup' guns for the Police, Peace Officers and others who were somewhat less concerned with the law.

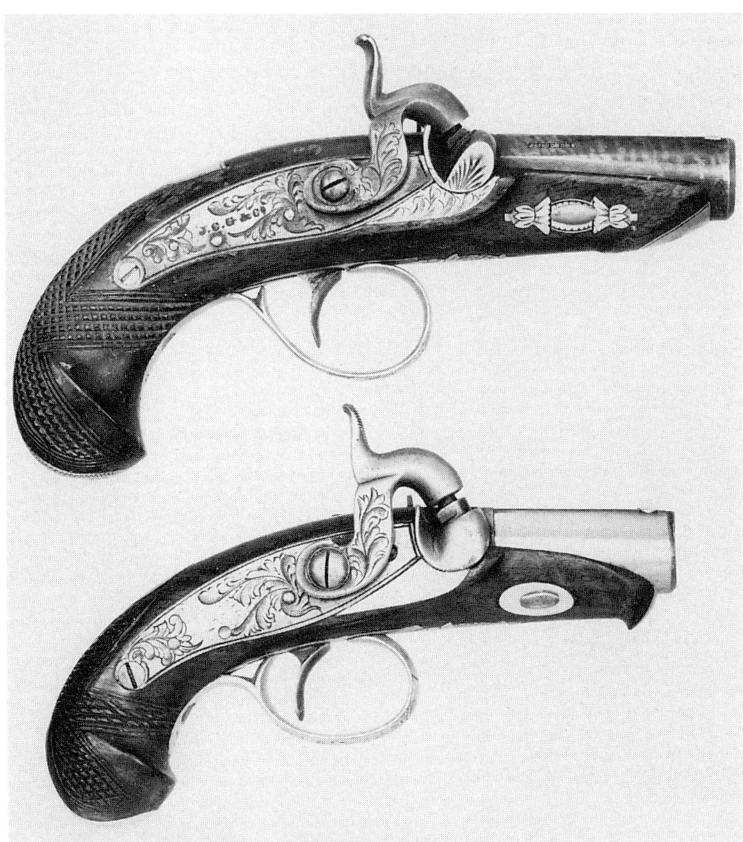

Two percussion 'derringers'. The top one is a Belgian-made copy of circa *1860, the lower one is an American 'derringer' of unknown make. Courtesy of the Trustees of the Royal Armouries.*

Colt also produced thousands of tiny Pocket .22 revolvers, chambering seven long or short .22 rimfires. However, it was Remington of New York, who were, ironically, to produce the best, and most profitable lines of 'derringers'. One of the very longest established names in the firearms' manufacturing business, they had traditionally been reliant on the rifle and shotgun trade for their reputation, but they too were enticed into the pistol market by the ever increasing demand. In 1860, they brought out the Remington-Elliott, a six-barrelled .22 with revolving barrel and ring trigger, but a year later this was replaced by the Elliot's Pocket or Vest Derringer, with fixed four- or five-shot barrel clusters in .22 or .32 calibres, fired by a revolving striker and with a special nickel-plated finish at no extra cost as well as mother-of-pearl grips. Although they sold some 50,000, this paled in comparison to the sales of their next pocket pistol, the double-barrelled 'Double Repeating Derringer Pistol.' Introduced in 1865, it was to remain in production for an extraordinary seventy years. It comprised a pair of 3in .41-calibre rimfire barrels, one on top of the other, that were latched underneath and could be pivoted upwards for reloading. The Vest pistol retailed at a miserly $3.75 and $8 for the Double Derringer. Remington even produced a magazine derringer, the Remington-Rider, that had a tube magazine underneath the

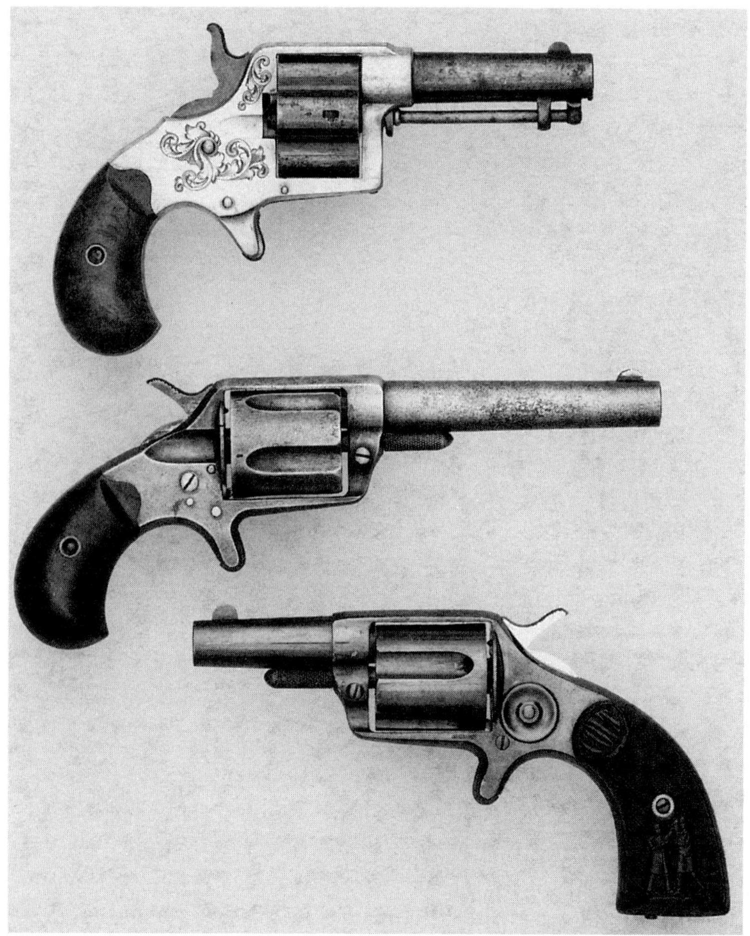

Colt small-frame revolvers, the .41-calibre 'Cloverleaf' or House pistol (top), a 'New Line' seven-shot, of 1873 (middle) and a 'New Police' .38 five-shot of 1885 (bottom). Courtesy of the Trustees of the Royal Armouries.

barrel, arguably making it one of the earliest forerunners of the modern semi-automatic pistol. At $10 it was cheap, light, fast to shoot and easily concealed, but like many new ideas, it was never the success that it deserved to be.

Nor were Remington the only rifle manufacturer to enter the handgun market, for the nimble mind of Christian Sharps had been working on a four barrel tip-up pistol that he patented in 1859. Small framed and weighing a modest 7oz (200g), they were chambered for .22, .30 and .33in rimfire. The entire barrel assembly slid forward on a brass or steel frame to expose the breech and they were fired by a rotating striker. Most of these pistols were manufactured in America by Sharps and Hankins, but in England they were made under licence in considerable numbers by Tipping and Lawden. Not everyone found the derringer rimfires adequate for their purpose though. Sheriff Frank Canton always carried a .41 rimfire derringer but changed his opinion of their usefulness after he shot an escaping prisoner at point-blank range with it.

> [I] drew my derringer and fired at his head. The bullet struck him in the forehead just over the left eye … when the doctor examined the wound he found that the bullet had not penetrated the head, but had glanced round the skull under the skin and come out at the back of his head. He was unconscious for twelve hours … I threw away this derringer … and have never carried one since.[6]

Three derringers. Top is a National Arms Company .41 calibre of about 1868, later becoming the Colt No 1. Centre is a Colt Thuer with a horizontally pivoting barrel, and bottom is the popular Remington Double Derringer. Courtesy of the Trustees of the Royal Armouries.

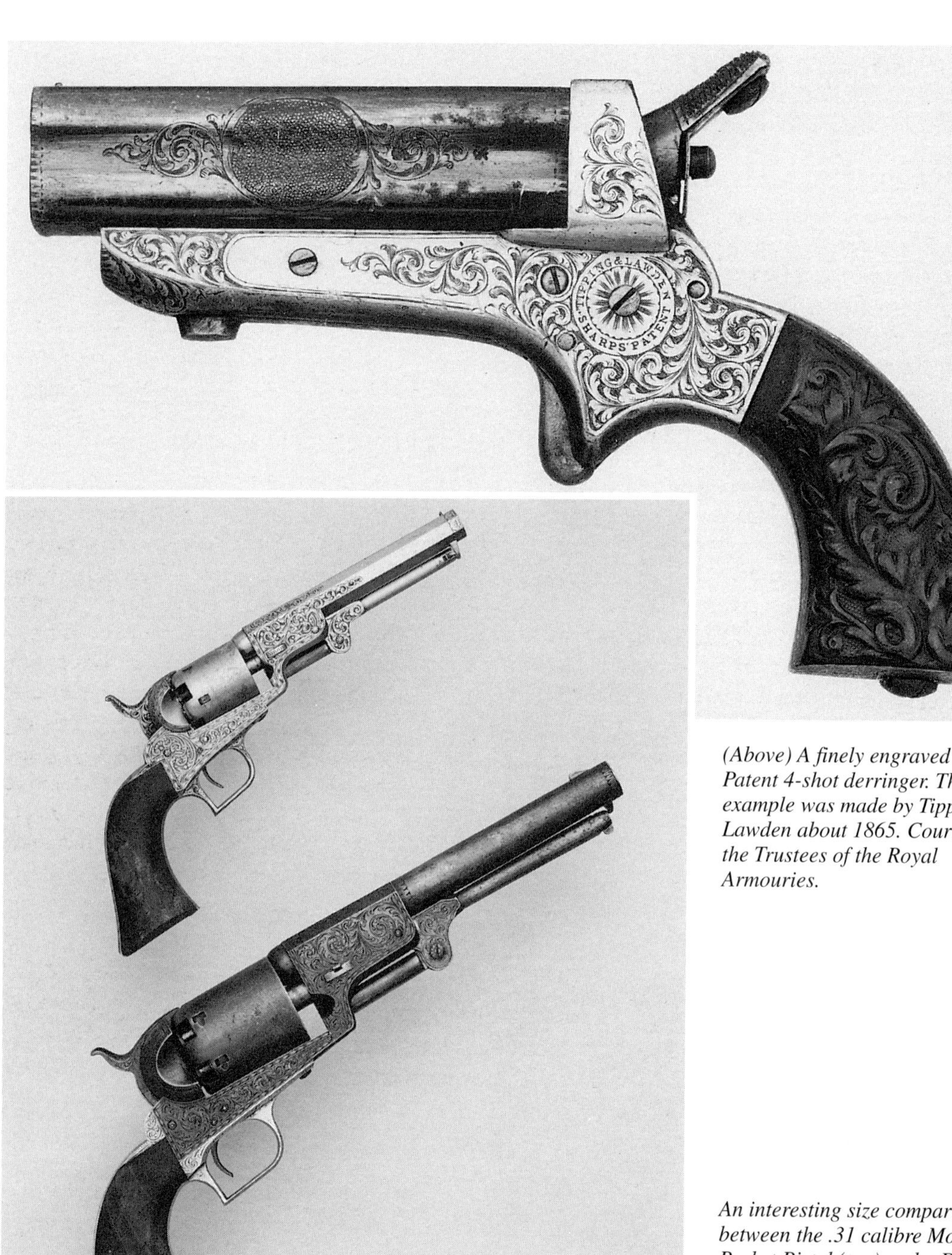

(Above) A finely engraved Sharps Patent 4-shot derringer. This example was made by Tipping and Lawden about 1865. Courtesy of the Trustees of the Royal Armouries.

An interesting size comparison between the .31 calibre Model 1848 Pocket Pistol (top) and a Dragoon (bottom). The engraving on both pistols is typical of the American style popular in the 1850s. Courtesy of the Trustees of the Royal Armouries.

Although Henry Derringer died in 1867, the concept of his pistols continued, and today is still embodied in a wide number of small-framed pocket pistols.

Inevitably, the products of the Colt company come to the fore again for, spurred on by the success of the Dragoons, Colt produced a more manageable sized revolver in 1848, the .31-calibre Baby, or Little Dragoon. This was simply a scaled-down small-framed .44 with octagonal barrel of 3, 4, 5 or 6in in length. It was simple in the extreme, lacking a loading lever although a spare loaded cylinder could be substituted in seconds, and in two years some 15,000 were sold.

This was followed with yet another small-framed .31 Pocket Model but this benefited from a pivoting loading lever, but the real gem of the Colt Company was the Navy model, manufactured in 1851. A medium-framed revolver, it was light, at 2½lb (1.1kg), very well balanced, and although its .36-calibre ball did not have the weight to carry to extreme ranges, it was a more comfortable pistol to carry, adapting well to a holster, and its grip shape and modest power made it easy to shoot. In his book on early frontier life, Frederick Olmstead made some pertinent comments about the Navy he carried that he regarded as one of the very finest contemporary revolvers.

> Though subjected for six or eight months to rough use, damp grass … not once did a ball fail … nothing got out of order, nothing required care; not once though carried at random … was there an accidental discharge. Before taking them from home we gave them a trial alongside every rival we could … but for practical purposes one Colt was worth a dozen of all others. After a little practice we could surely chop off a snake's head from the saddle at any reasonable distance, and across a fixed rest could hit … a man at ordinary rifle range. One of our pistols was … submerged in a bog for some minutes, but on trial though dripping wet, not a single barrel missed fire.[7]

Colt did not have things entirely his own way though, for in 1851 Massachusetts Arms obtained the rights to manufacture the British Adams, the design of which was protected under English patents, and there was little argument that it was a better designed revolver than the Colt. Available in .31, .44 and .50 calibres, it had an octagonal barrel forged as one with the solid frame, and even the big .50-calibre pistol was some 1¼lb (0.57kg) lighter than the Colt Dragoon. In the event of having to use the pistol as a club (once a handgun was empty this was a more frequent occurrence than one would believe) the Colt's fragile barrel-to-frame

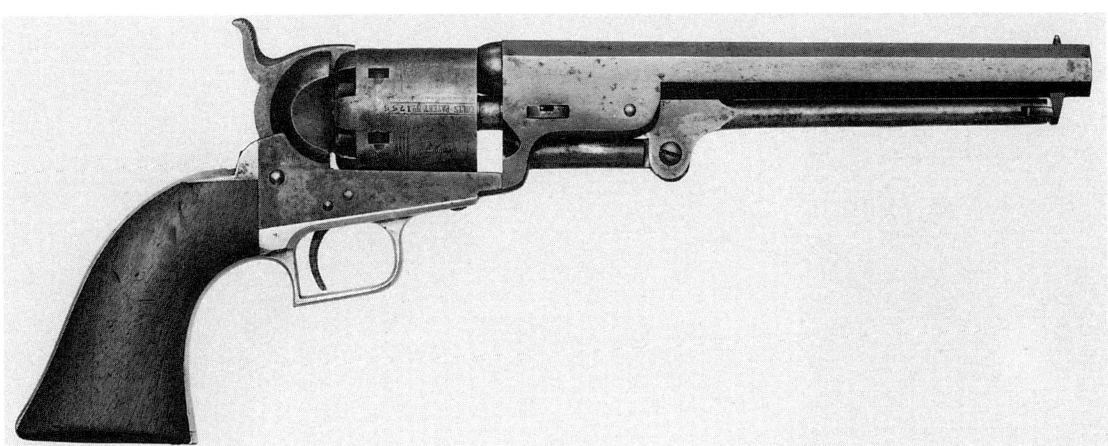

The 1851 .36-calibre Colt Navy, Second Model. Courtesy of the Trustees of the Royal Armouries.

locking wedge could cause the cylinder axis pin to bend slightly under any impact, rendering the pistol useless.

The Adams, on the other hand, could probably have been used to batter a buffalo into unconsciousness without damaging the gun structurally. It also had an effective self-cocking action, which was just as well for the original design had no spur on the hammer to permit manual cocking. It did suffer from some defects though, holding only five shots, and having no loading rammer or recoil shield behind the cylinder. This led to a tendency for the percussion caps to become vulnerable to displacement and accidental discharge.

Nor was the Adams the only challenger from England, for the Tranter, a similar design, was available in five barrel lengths, six calibres and had a unique double trigger permitting single- or double-action shooting. Although not manufactured in the US, it attracted considerable interest as did the unusual sidehammer Kerr, designed by the Superintendent of the London Armoury Company. It was a fine quality, well-made pistol, with the advantage of easy access to the hammer without having to strip down the revolver should it suffer a mechanical problem.

Between them, the English designs were in time to help topple the Colt from the advantageous position it held. By the 1850s, revolvers were becoming widely available across the Frontier, through Colorado, Denver, Kansas, Arizona, Texas and California. Many dealers such as Kernahan of New Orleans, Freide of St Louis, Parker of Achison, and Whites of Arizona, were offering a wide choice of pistols from Derringers, to Adams and Colt as well as numbers of cheap imports that, like their long-arm counterparts, circumvented many US patents and were, if not of the finest quality, at least serviceable weapons. Belgian copies of British revolvers were popular, retailing at $10–12, which was more than enough for a sidearm that was

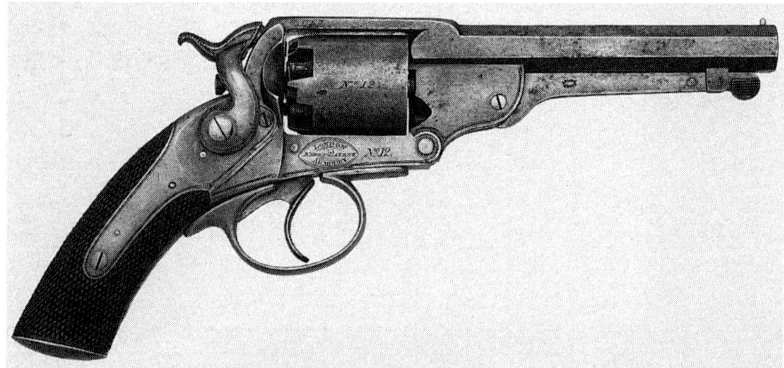

(Left) The sidehammer Kerr revolver, patented in 1859, that saw much use by the Confederacy during the American Civil War. Courtesy of the Trustees of the Royal Armouries.

(Below) The unusual LeMat revolver, its smoothbore barrel clearly visible beneath the rifled barrel. Above it, is a very rare example of the revolving rifle. Courtesy of the Trustees of the Royal Armouries.

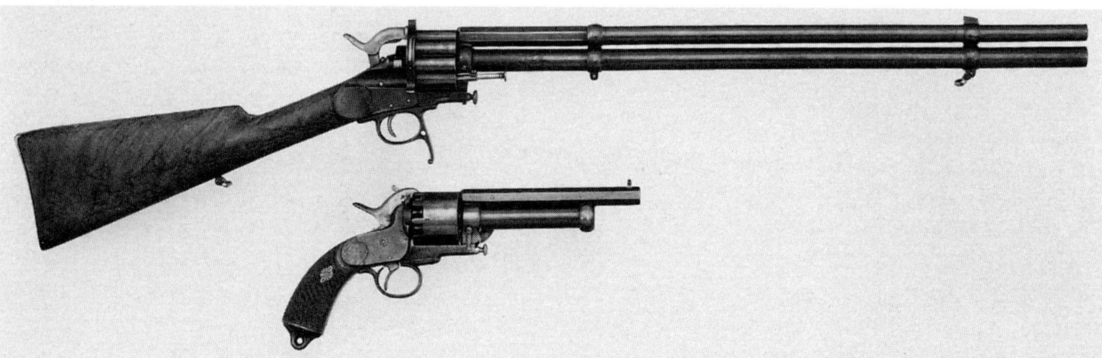

unlikely to ever see much use beyond a little target shooting. Better quality Belgian-made pistols did have some popularity, particularly during the turbulent war years, Lefaucheux and LeMat being two of the better known.

Surprisingly, many purchasers of revolvers actually had no means of reloading them, for rammers were not fitted as a matter of course to all revolvers, and pepperboxes had no means of being reloaded unless a ramrod, ball, powder and caps were carried, which many pistol owners appeared disinclined to do. Most men who carried a revolver had a spare, loaded cylinder in a pocket, but apparently a large number did not, and as a result many gunshops offered a reloading service for those who had foolishly emptied their weapons, which raises an interesting question of what happened in the event of an emergency. Scholl's of Marysville, California were not untypical in advertising the usual gunsmith's services as well as adding that 'Revolvers could be reloaded at short notice.' Presumably, entering into a gunfight on an early closing day could be something of a problem. For those who expected trouble, the words of that highly experienced adventurer and explorer, Sir Richard Burton, were probably best heeded:

> I carried two revolvers … the pistol should never be absent from a man's right side … nor the bowie from his left. The instinctive consent between eye and hand, combined with a little practice, will soon enable the beginner to shoot correctly from the hip, all he has to do, is to think that he is pointing at the mark, and pull [the trigger]. As a precaution … it is wise to place the cock upon a capless nipple rather than trust to the intermediate pins. In dangerous places the revolver should be discharged and reloaded every morning … a revolver is an admirable tool when properly used; those however who are too idle or careless to attend to it had better carry a pair of 'Derringers'.[8]

The reference to carrying the pistol on an uncapped chamber was sound advice. Many revolvers had safety notches set between the nipples, onto which the hammer could, theoretically, be lowered to keep it in a safe condition with the cylinder loaded. In practice, these notches wore and loose mainsprings did not hold the hammer firmly in place, and many a man spent the rest of his life with a severe limp through trusting this dubious means of mechanical safety. Until the comparatively recent advent of transfer bars and other safety devices, wise six-gun carriers always kept the hammer resting on an empty chamber.

In 1857, an event occurred that was to prove pivotal in the subsequent history of American handguns, and that was the expiry of Colt's Patent on revolving cylinder pistols. Not only did this allow a whole raft of copies and imported revolvers to be produced, but it enabled a tiny revolver to be introduced that was to be a landmark in firearms' technology.

THE CARTRIDGE REVOLVERS

Horace Smith and Daniel Baird Wesson had been involved in firearms' design and manufacture for some years. Smith became interested in repeating firearms in the late 1840s, when he worked for Robbins and Lawrence, a partnership that resulted in the production of the unusual Volcanic magazine pistol and the issue of later patents for a lever-action rifle.

The Wesson brothers, Daniel and Edwin, worked together in Edwin's shop in Northboro, Massachusetts, making the very highly sought-after Wesson target rifles, and during this time they met and undertook work for Sam Colt and Captain Walker, producing 1,000 barrels for the Walker Colt as well as limited production of their own percussion 'Dragoon' revolver. All of this, however, came to an abrupt end in 1849 when the Wesson company foundered following Edwin's sudden death, which left Daniel penniless. There, but for a chance meeting, the story of the revolver might have ended ignominiously. Daniel was forced to work for a number of manufacturers and, while helping to produce a pistol quirkily named the Leonard, he met Horace

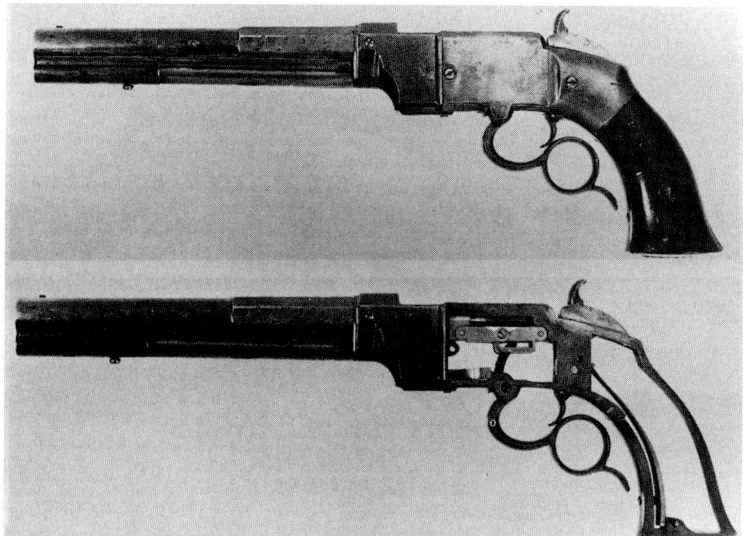

The prototype Smith and Wesson Patent model of the ring-lever pistol, later to become the Volcanic. Courtesy of Roy Jinks and The Smithsonian Institution.

Smith who was then employed by Robbins and Lawrence. This was to result in the formation of the embryonic Smith and Wesson Company in 1852, the two men working on a Hunt and Palmer design rifle, but it was the little revolver they patented in 1854 that was to make their fortunes.

The story of the company's ill-fated venture into repeating firearms with the Volcanic pistol has already been touched upon, and Smith and Wesson realized that there was little future in the lever-action design when used in a handgun, so they turned instead to an idea patented by an ex-Colt employee, Rollin White. This was simply a bored-through revolving cylinder. The problem was exactly what to do with it, as no reliable metallic cartridge ammunition was then in existence. The answer came in the shape of a tiny .22-calibre Flobert-type self-contained cartridge, subsequently known as the rimfire, whose appearance coincided almost perfectly with the expiry of Colt's Patent. In 1856, Wesson wrote to White and asked for permission to incorporate his patent in the prototype of a revolving cylinder tip-up pistol that he had constructed. This historic letter is worth reproducing as the agreement that resulted from it was to spawn a design of revolver that has remained little changed to this day.

> I notice in a patent granted to you … one claim, viz, extending the chambers of the rotating cylinder right through the rear end of said cylinder so as to enable the said chambers to be charged from the rear... Which I should like to make arrangements with you to use in the manufacture of firearms.[9]

White's affirmation enabled Smith and Wesson to open small premises in Springfield, Massachusetts, and full-scale production began of the Model 1 Tip-up revolver. A brass-framed single action .22-calibre seven-shot, it had a latch at the bottom of the frame that when released permitted the entire barrel and cylinder assembly to be swung upwards. Like all of the best ideas, it was simple and it sold like the proverbial hot cakes, but the tiny cartridge held only three grains of powder and managed to propel its 30 grain bullet with little power beyond about 20yd (18m). The No. 1 was soon improved with the introduction in 1861 of a more powerful .32 rimfire and other models of tip-up, the No. 2 and No. 1½.

Some measure of their popularity can be seen from the fact that up to the expiry of the Rollin White patent in 1869 some 272,000 had been made, and they became one of the most popular pocket pistols on the Frontier. Without a doubt, the introduction of this series of Smith and Wesson revolvers promoted a fundamental change in revolver concept and design. Of course, not everyone was enamoured of its underpowered .22 cartridge for, as Mark Twain commented:

> I was armed to the teeth with a pitiful little Smith and Wesson's seven-shooter, which carried a ball like a homeopathic pill, and it took the whole seven to make a dose for an adult. But I thought it was grand. It appeared to me to be a dangerous weapon. It had only one fault, you could not hit anything with it.[10]

Rollin White were also making copies of the 1½ but they did so with the agreement of Smith and Wesson whereas others were not so bothered by the finer points of patent law, and the company was forced into a number of lawsuits to protect their pistols. Bacon, Prescott, Cone and Manhattan all produced illegal copies, but some makers looked for rather more inventive ways of avoiding patent infringement and the resulting very expensive lawsuits. Two of the more unusual designs were those of Daniel Moore and the Plant Manufacturing Company.

Moore's idea was to produce a cylinder that was not bored through completely, so he designed and

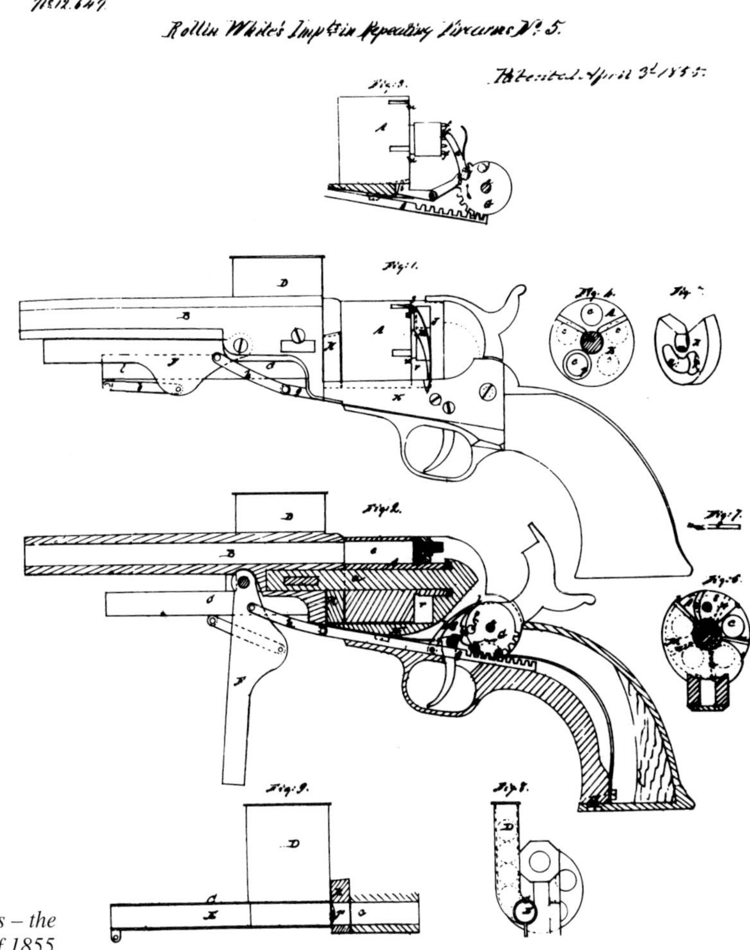

The future of revolvers – the Rollin-White Patent of 1855.

THE SEVEN SHOOTER.

SMITH & WESSON'S
PATENT REVOLVER.

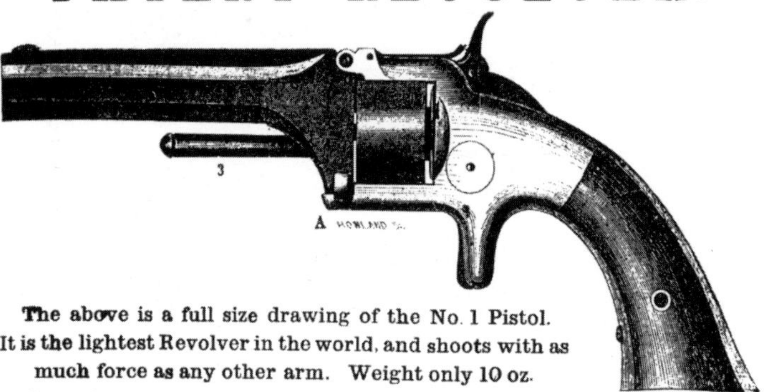

The above is a full size drawing of the No. 1 Pistol. It is the lightest Revolver in the world, and shoots with as much force as any other arm. Weight only 10 oz.

The cartridge for this arm consists of a copper cap having its closed end enlarged, which enlarged end forms a receptacle for the percussion priming. The remainder of the cap being filled with powder, the ball is firmly inserted in its open end, thus enclosing the powder and priming in a perfectly water-proof case.

Some of the advantages of an arm constructed on this plan are :—

The convenience and safety with which both the arm and ammunition may be carried ;
The facility with which it may be charged, (it requiring no ramrod, powder-flask, or percussion-caps) ;
Certainty of fire in damp weather ;
That no injury is caused to the arm or ammunition by allowing it to remain charged any length of time

DIRECTIONS FOR USE.

By pressing the knobs, A, towards the top of the pistol, the barrel will be allowed to turn back to a right angle with its present position. Place the thumb lightly upon the hammer, and with the other hand remove the cylinder. Place your charges in the chamber of the cylinder, at the *rear end.* Replace the cylinder, turning it to the left, until it becomes locked. Return the barrel to its place, (being sure it is down,) and the arm is ready for use. After having been discharged, the refuse caps are removed from the cylinder by means of the rod 3 shown in the drawing.

While carrying the arm, allow the hammer to rest between two of the caps to avoid accident.

J. W. STORRS, Sole Ag't,
121 Chambers Street, [up stairs,] New-York.

N. B.—These Cartridges are sure fire in this Pistol, but are not warranted in other kinds of Pistols.

An advertisement for Smith and Wesson's No. 1 rimfire revolver, about 1859.

patented a revolver in 1864 that used a 'teatfire' cartridge. The cylinder was, in effect, little different from that of a percussion cylinder, but the nipple was dispensed with and the flash hole was enlarged so that an elongated bell-shaped cartridge could be inserted from the front, its primer contained in a projecting 'teat' at its base. When inserted, this projected through the rear of the cylinder so that it would be struck by the nose of the hammer. These .32-calibre pistols were quite effective, but suffered from two problems. If the cartridge was not properly inserted it simply dropped out,

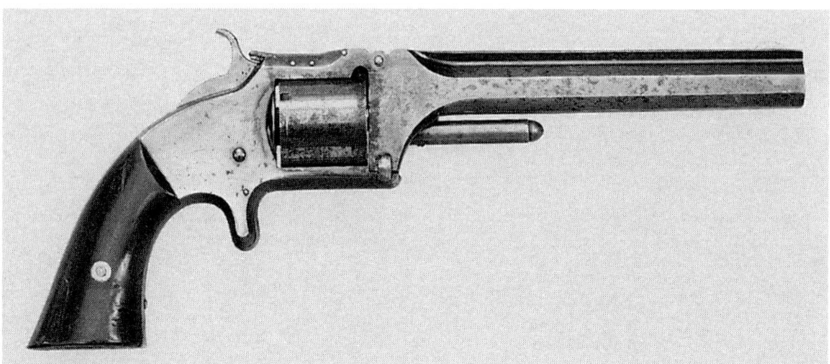

The result of the Rollin-White Patent, a 6in-barrelled Smith and Wesson Model of the 1861 Army in .32 calibre. Courtesy of the Trustees of the Royal Armouries.

Remington advert, circa *1870.*

and once fired, ejection could be difficult, if not downright impossible. One unnamed traveller commented dryly in 1866 that '… the revolvers of Smith and Wesson were much in abundance, and also a few 'titfires' [sic] which were soon traded in for something more useful'.

Aside from Colt, other manufacturers were also making good quality revolvers and one of the best was the Remington. These were initially sold as the Remington-Beals, after Fordyce Beals's 1858 Patent covering the design of axis-pin and loading lever. Two calibres of this solid-framed percussion revolver were produced in .36 and .44 calibres. Ironically the Remington, like many other revolvers of this period, did not sell in large numbers until the outbreak of the war in 1860, despite being an excellent and reliable arm.

By 1859, the demand for revolvers had once again soared in the West because of a geological quirk that had hitherto lain undiscovered in Nevada. The Comstock Lode was a vast silver deposit, possibly the largest ever to be mined, and like the Gold Rush a decade before, it attracted huge numbers of men and women. Inevitably, robbery and murder were commonplace, with miners often being killed for just a few dollars worth of silver. Anything that could fire a bullet was carried, from old single-shot flintlock pistols to the latest six-guns, and in his book George Brewerton commented on the typical weaponry of the inhabitants of the mining towns:

> … a preventative to interference … in the shape of Bowie knives, Derringers and six-shooters which latter weapons lay prepared for instant use, being loaded and capped.[11]

Colt were working on several new revolvers, and in 1855 they brought out the sidehammer Pocket Pistol, a stubby small-framed gun in .26 and .31 calibres that never proved a success due to its fragile internal mechanism. They also introduced a .36 Pocket pistol that was a small-framed Navy. However, they were well aware of the lack of power of their .36-calibre Navy revolvers and in 1860 introduced a larger-framed .44-calibre Army Holster pistol that incorporated a novel rack-and-pinion loading lever and used what Colt literature proudly described as 'Silver Steel' (high-carbon steel) in its manufacture. The Army was arguably one of the most handsome of all Colt's percussion pistols and was subsequently to prove very successful.

There were others appearing on the scene who naturally took advantage of the lapse in patent. One of the more prolific manufacturers was the Manhattan Company of New York who began in 1859 making Colt copies in .31 and five-shot .36 calibres using a complicated patent of their own that they maintained did not infringe Colt's rights. It did, but it took Colt's lawyers five years to prove it. Manhattan pistols are often confusingly and spuriously marked 'London Pistol company', but were in some respects actually better designed than Colts, many having detachable sideplates to give easy access to the lockwork, an important consideration in the days when broken springs were commonplace. Manhattans were also cheaper than Colts and some 85,000 were purchased.

Another company to take early advantage of Colt's lapsed patent was Eli Whitney, that veteran of firearms' manufacturing who had actually been making some unremarkable revolvers since 1848. Whitney's new .28-calibre pistol of 1857 was actually a better, sturdier design than the Colt with a solid

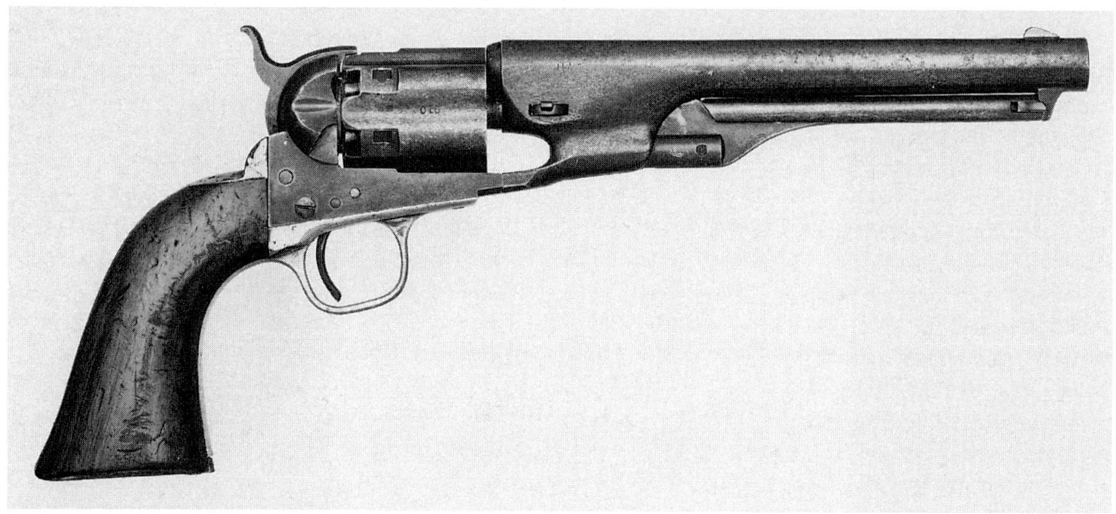

An early production 1860 Colt New Model Army pistol in .44 calibre with the fluted cylinder. Later models had a rounded cylinder. Courtesy of the Trustees of the Royal Armouries.

frame and what the company described as a 'walking beam' system for cylinder rotation. This was, in effect, a bar that operated when the hammer was retracted. Pushing the ring-trigger forward rotated the cylinder, and pulling back on it locked the cylinder and enabled the revolver to be fired. Unaccountably, Whitney did not file a patent for his design and subsequently lost a fortune in royalties. His next revolver was a solid-frame Colt Navy copy in .36 calibre, known as the Belt Revolver, that was to see much use during the Civil War and was to spawn some Confederate copies, of which more later. By the end of the 1850s, despite the steadily increasing use of rimfire and pinfire cartridges, the bulk of the pistols used in the frontier were repeating percussion types. Despite their popularity in the new towns that were springing up in the West, the majority of travellers still saw the pistol in much the same way as the early single-shot flintlocks. It was a weapon good only for hand-to-hand, last-resort fighting and all but useless for hunting or defence against Indian attack, where it was secondary to the role of the rifle.

All this was to change with the experiences that many men had of using revolvers in the Civil War, and that, allied to the subsequent opening up of the Frontier after the war, was to give the revolver far greater prominence as a potent weapon. There had been a virtual cessation of emigration West between 1861 to 1865 as the ravages of the war and nationwide conflict prevented easy or safe movement across the country.

Not everything had come to a halt because of the war, for pre-war plans for the construction of a transcontinental railway had been put forward in 1862 and were agreed by Congress, coincidentally in the same year that Sam Colt died. President Lincoln had signed an act allowing the building of a railroad from the Missouri River to the Pacific Ocean. The railroad was to prove something of a double-edged sword for the Frontier, for it was both to open and eventually help to destroy it. In 1830, there had been some thirty miles of track in the whole country but by 1861 there were over 31,000 miles. The huge numbers of emigrants who began to flock West after the war provided the raw material for the years celebrated in books and films as the 'Wild West', although in reality this period only lasted for around two decades, from the late 1860s to late 1880s. These new 'Westerners' were also to bring about a fundamental and permanent change in the landscape, bringing with them farming, cattle and at the same time civilizing the West with law and order. They succeeded also in destroying forever the culture of the native peoples.

After 1865, the threat from the Indian tribes who had long waged a desultory war against the encroaching whites began to escalate. Almost none of the Western tribes had been subdued despite the presence of the army, but over the years atrocities had been committed on all sides, by civilians, Indians and military alike. Those heading into Indian territory took great care to arm themselves, and while there were hundreds of surplus military cap and ball revolvers and single-shot pistols available, many men with war experience of the rapid-fire, easy-loading cartridge longarms that had appeared were keen to obtain similar revolvers. A number of primitive cartridge revolvers had begun to appear late in the 1860s, mostly conversions from percussion to rimfire, and both Colt and Remington were obvious candidates for this.

The Remingtons were New Model Army pistols, factory-converted from .44 to .46 rimfire using a replacement 5-shot cylinder and modified hammer, the conversions being sent to Smith and Wesson for inspection. The cost of the work was modest, about $3.50, and over 4,000 New Models were altered. Colt marketed their own conversion, the Thuer, that had been patented by Alexander Thuer in 1868. It was an awkward system that required the percussion cylinder to be shortened by machining off a length of its rear section and the fitting of a ring behind it that contained a rebounding firing pin. The cylinder was loaded from the front with a slightly tapered copper cartridge, and as the cylinder rotated, the cartridge was fired by the hammer striking the firing pin set into the ring. Pistols of .31, .36 and .44 calibre were modified to use the new rimfire cartridges, but one major design flaw of the Thuer was its ejection system that included an ejector arm which struck the side of the case. This was no problem if the case was empty, but a loaded rimfire cartridge could be, and often was, ignited by a sharp blow on the ejector. It did not endear the revolver to the buying public and Colt wisely abandoned it in 1871 after less than 5,000 had been made.

A far better conversion proved to be the 1871 Richards. The initial Richards' conversion of the Model 1860 Army was not dissimilar to the Thuer, using a circular disc about ⅜in thick that locked into place on the rear of the slightly shortened cylinder, being held in position by the cylinder axis pin and a projection that engaged into the machined channel in which the rebounding

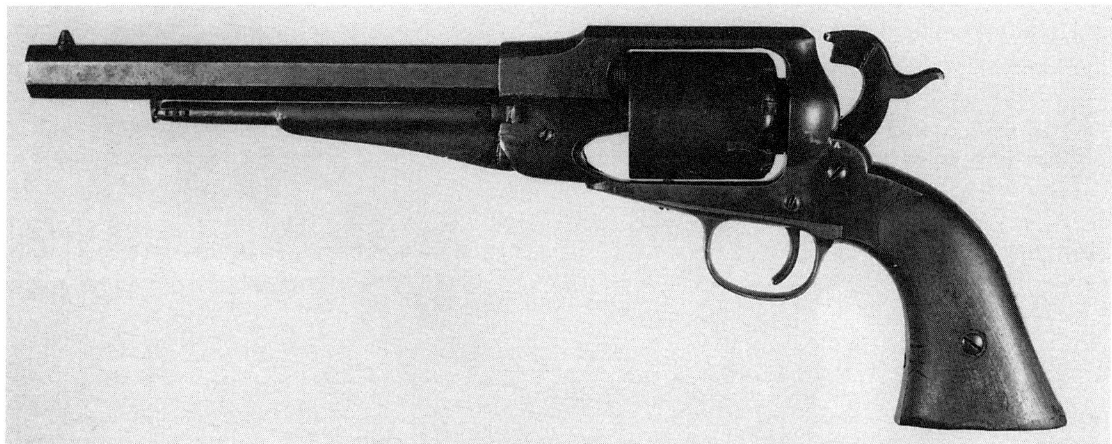

(Top) A .44 Remington New Model used by W.L. McKenzie to kill two of Quantrill's guerrillas at Baxter Springs, Kansas in October 1863. Photo courtesy of Kansas State Historical Society.
(Above) The Colt Richards cartridge conversion of 1871. Courtesy of the Trustees of the Royal Armouries.

hammer sat. The rammer was replaced by an ejector attached to the right side of the barrel and it worked quite well, pushing the spent case backwards out of the cylinder through a loading gate. A later Richards-Mason Patent improved on the system, doing away with the rebounding hammer by using an improved hammer with lengthened nose, and newly forged barrels with a sprung-loaded ejector rod in a tube on the right side of the barrel, soon to become a standard feature on many six-guns. Converted Colt revolvers were inexpensive, being sold for around $13 each, and sometimes for less, and Richards-Mason conversions were undertaken on over 39,000 Colts. The factory also played with producing their own large-framed rimfire revolver, using surplus parts left over from wartime military contracts and they came up with a hybrid pistol, the .44 New Model Holster Revolver, or more simply the Model 1872. This was to all intents a Navy pistol with round barrel and an ejector-rod housing with a sprung loading gate in the right recoil shield. The design was to be the direct ancestor of the incredibly successful 'Peacemaker' revolvers.

Meanwhile, Smith and Wesson were confidently leading the field in cartridge revolvers. Although they had purchased the vital Rollin-White Patent in 1855 it had finally expired in 1869, opening the way for every other maker to use it as they saw fit. Aware of the limitations of the tip-up revolvers, they had

A little fun on the Denver and Rio Grande railroad as employees stage a mock holdup. They have Winchester Model 1873 rifles and Model 1887 lever-action shotguns, plus a couple of Smith and Wessons – a New Model No. 3 and .32 hammerless. Courtesy Denver Public Library, Western History Dept.

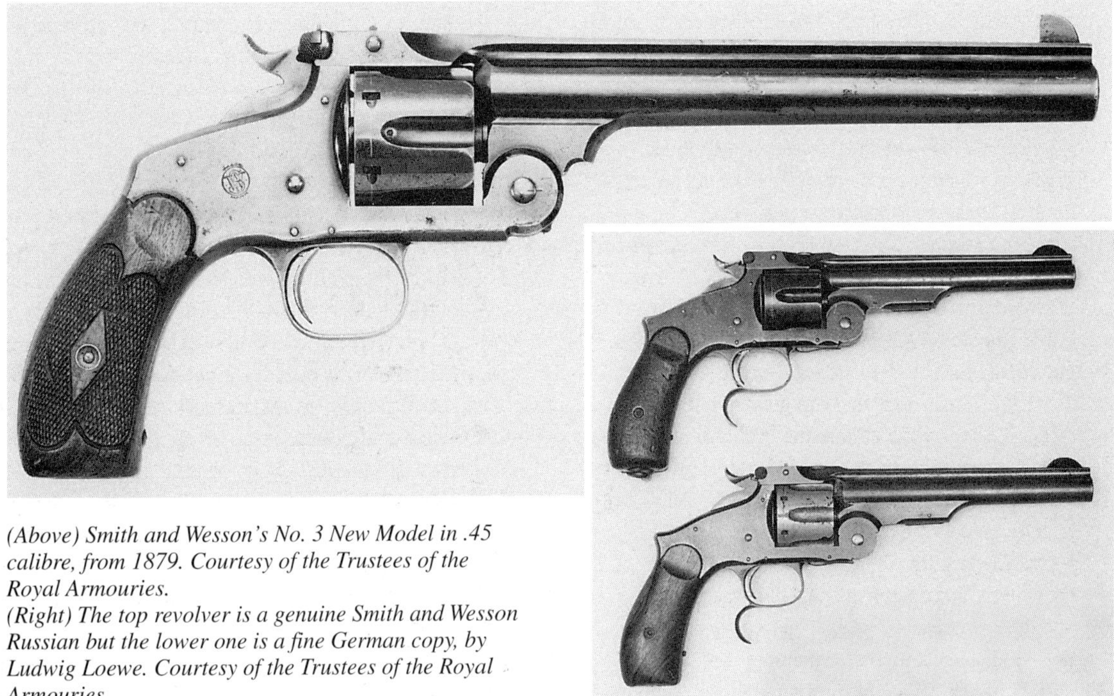

(Above) Smith and Wesson's No. 3 New Model in .45 calibre, from 1879. Courtesy of the Trustees of the Royal Armouries.
(Right) The top revolver is a genuine Smith and Wesson Russian but the lower one is a fine German copy, by Ludwig Loewe. Courtesy of the Trustees of the Royal Armouries.

designed a top-break revolver with a very strong frame that latched just in front of the hammer. When unlocked, the entire frame and cylinder pivoted downwards. They had also tackled the problem of the slow loading and ejection that plagued Colt and other conversions. They placed the cylinder on a hollow tube inside which was a rack mechanism. The rear face of the cylinder had a star-shaped plate that lifted up as the barrel and cylinder lowered, enabling the cartridges to simply be dropped clear by inverting the revolver. The new pistol, with its distinctive frame and 8in barrel was called the Model No. 3, later the First Model American and by 1871 it was already making an appearance in the west. Chambered for a copper-cased .44 centrefire cartridge it was the first in a very long and successful line of revolvers, the basic design of which has remained little changed today. It became immensely popular, and was quickly followed by the Second Model in .44/100 and .44 Russian, so called because of a large contract of some 70,000 revolvers initially supplied to the Russian government by Smith and Wesson between 1871 and 1877. Many more were later sold as military contracts to Turkey and Japan, where the big revolver proved enormously popular. These revolvers, understandably, became known as 'Model 3 Russians', and were to be produced in three different models.

Oddly, the Russian cartridge proved to be more accurate and harder hitting than the original .44 and it was to become a popular American calibre. Many Westerners took immediately to the technologically advanced new revolvers that were available in blued finish for $15 and nickel-plated for $17, and it proved particularly popular on the Frontier, for no other maker could match it for speed of loading or reliability. Smith and Wesson received hundreds of letters on the subject, many of whose writers hoped that a little flattery would go a long way. One fine example was from the picturesquely named Sumner 'Cimmaron' Beach, who worked as an army scout.

Ellsworth Kansas Jan 23rd 1876. Gentlemen, I have just come up from Camp Cantonement, Texas you will doubtless remember me when you look at my name at the bottom of this page, or you may know me by what I am called out west, vise Cimmarron Beach, you may remember that I got one of your latest style Russian Models two years ago with 500 rounds of ammunition, that has been a companion to me since. I also carried a Gov Colts 45 Cal, Given me by Major Bankhead at Post Cantonement, but I did not like it, it takes more time to punch the shells out and to load it than one of your six shooter's does, then the Gov cartridge is not as good as citizen cartridges are, and did not have the quality of powder in as your Russian model cartridges do. I gave my Colts to a friend of mine … he has plenty of time to pick shells out of the gun. I have been scouting … for the Government for the last two years. I know all the country and am relied on by old Maj. Bankhead and the Lieutenants. I wish to get one of the Russian Models square butted handles not the saw shaped handle I wish it for a mate to my Russian Model that I have now. If you will send it to me … send me a Six Shooter to Great Bend and I will make it all right with you, I am a little short of money now, I can do you as much good as the worth of a Revolver even if I don't pay you for it … I will be over to Great Bend for a week or two more maybe, there was 11 head of good mules stole down on the Cimmarron River and run up in the Sand Hills South of Great Bend. I will have to hunt them up. I am respectfully, Sumner Beach.[12]

Although Colt were certainly trying hard to produce a comparable revolver, their hybrid .44 proved to be a mechanically weak pistol; so in 1873 they introduced a new design, called the Model P, or Single Action Army, more universally to become known as the 'Peacemaker'. The Colt was initially chambered for .44in rimfire ammunition, which was still a widely available cartridge in the west, and some 2,000 were produced, but in 1875 it was rechambered for the new .45 Long Colt cartridge that had a heavier bullet and was a far more powerful proposition. Contemporary tests showed the Colt could group at just under 4in at 50yd (46m) and its .45-calibre bullet would penetrate over 4in of timber. Its solid and simple construction made it almost unbreakable; although it did have a tendency to snap mainsprings, the pistol could still be fired in an emergency by whacking the hammer with a stone. The smooth grip contour and balance meant that its tactile qualities were far better than those of its contemporary rivals, and it lent itself easily to

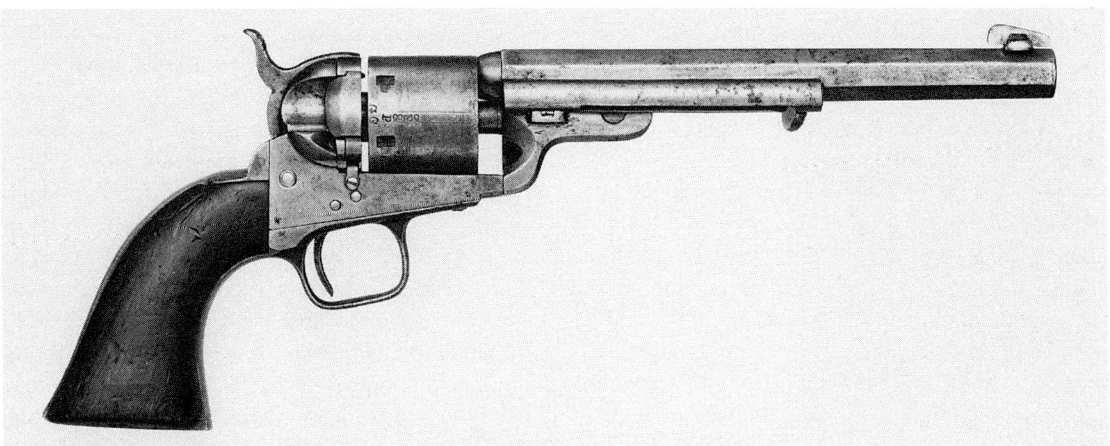

The later 1872 Mason conversion, the pistol being almost identical to the Model 1872 Open Frame. Courtesy of the Trustees of the Royal Armouries.

quick handling, not always with success. A.C. Gould, commenting on displays of trick handling in 1897 noted of these 'pistoleers' that:

> ... they never did any good shooting by twirling the revolver around ... shooting it upside down, or any other of the absurd ways which stage shots sometimes attempt. I have seen several narrow escapes from death by attempts to handle in such a ridiculous manner, and have known of several deaths from such cause.[13]

The new revolver was available in standard 4¾, 5½ and 7½in barrel lengths although 8, 9, 12 or 16in could be specified. The appeal of the Single-Action was further increased by a chambering in 1878 for the .44-40 cartridge that was also chambered in many Winchester rifles, giving the option of two firearms but with the necessity of only carrying one type of ammunition. While it was fine in a revolver, the .44-40 cartridge was underpowered for use in a rifle. The Peacemaker was carried by many Western characters from Wyatt Earp, who used a 7½in Colt that he cut down to 5in, to Jesse James, who had (among many other types) at least two, and who was killed by Bob Ford using a Single-Action. Innumerable cowboys, prospectors and shopkeepers also used them. In fact if Hollywood is to be believed, virtually everybody west of the Missouri carried a Colt to the exclusion of absolutely anything else.

The reality was different of course, and Remington in particular were trying hard to bridge the gap. In 1872, they had introduced the 'Improved Army' revolver, which was a modified .44 Army with ejector and loading gate, but they did also sell the powerful .50-calibre 'Rolling Block' single shot, which used a 32 grain charge and potent 320 grain bullet. While it was capable of felling a buffalo at 50yd (46m), it was still only a single-shot pistol, so Remington looked to producing a better, purpose-designed revolver, which they did in the shape of the No. 3, New Model of 1875. This handsome and much under-rated revolver was manufactured with a 7½in barrel and chambered for Remington's own .44 centrefire cartridge. It was superficially similar to the Colt, but had a distinctive strengthening web underneath the ejector housing. Wisely, Remington also offered the Model 1875 in .44-40, and this became the favourite pistol of Jesse James' brother Frank, who explained his preference:

The .45-calibre Colt Model 1873. This example has had target front and rear sights added. Courtesy of the Trustees of the Royal Armouries.

COLT'S

New Model Army Metallic Cartridge Revolving Pistol.

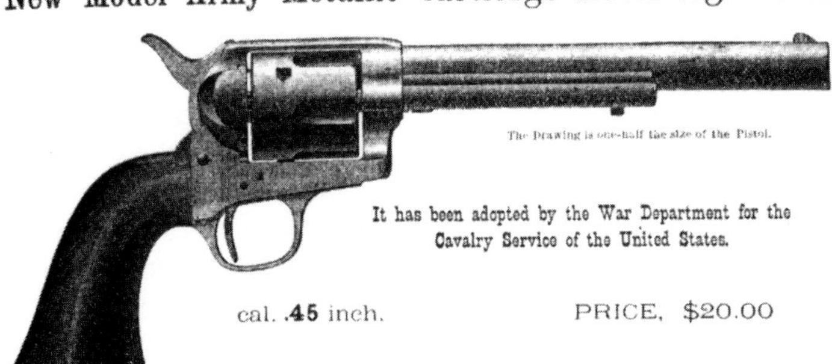

The length of the pistol is 12½ inches; length of barrel, 7½ inches; its bore or calibre, .45 inch. Weight, 2 lbs. 5 oz. Rifling, six grooves, one revolution in 16 inches; depth of groove, .005 inch. Number of chambers in cylinder, six. *It has a solid frame, case hardened.*

CARTRIDGE. Weight of powder, 30 grains; weight of lead, 250 grains. Central fire, external priming.

IT DIFFERS FROM OTHER REVOLVERS IN THE FOLLOWING POINTS, VIZ :

The hand, or finger, or pawl, which revolves the cylinder has two points, one above the other. The upper engages the ratchet of the cylinder when the revolution begins. But before the necessary sixth of a revolution could be made, as the pawl moves in a plane, and the ratchet tooth in the arc of a circle whose plane is perpendicular to the pawl's plane of motion, the pawl would lose its hold on the tooth, and the revolution of the cylinder would stop. To prevent this, the second point is added, and just as the first point will disengage from the ratchet, the second or lower point engages another tooth of the ratchet and completes the revolution. By this arrangement the pawl actuates a larger ratchet than it could otherwise, and therefore exerts more force upon the cylinder, by acting upon a longer lever arm. This permits a smaller sized cylinder for the same diameter of ratchet.

The cylinder has a bushing, which projects in front of it, and gives three surfaces upon which the cylinder revolves, thus diminishing the chance of sticking from dirt or rust, and also giving a very small axis upon which to revolve, decreasing the moment of friction.

When the ejector is used it springs back to its place and is ready for use again, avoiding the necessity of putting it back.

TO TAKE APART THE PISTOL. Half-cock the pistol, loosen the catch screw which holds the centre-pin, draw out the centre-pin, open the gate, and the cylinder can then be withdrawn.

To remove the ejector, turn out the ejector tube screw, then push the front end away from the barrel and pull it towards the muzzle. The barrel can then be unscrewed.

The stock can be removed by turning out the two screws just behind the hammer and that at the bottom of the strap. All the parts of the lock are then displayed and can be readily separated.

The cylinder bushing should be pushed out for cleaning.

To remove the gate, turn out a screw in the lower side of the frame, (hidden by the trigger guard,) then the gate spring and catch can be withdrawn, and the gate can be pushed out. The best sperm oil should be used for oiling the parts.

TO LOAD THE PISTOL. 1st motion: holding the pistol in the left hand, muzzle downwards, half cock it with the right hand and open the gate. 2d motion: insert the cartridges in succession, with the right hand, close the gate, cock and fire it, (taking it in the right hand,) or bring the hammer to the safety notch, as may be desired.

TO EJECT THE CARTRIDGE SHELLS. 1st motion: holding the pistol in the left hand, half cock with the right hand and open the gate. 2d motion: eject the shells in succession with the ejector pushed by the right hand, moving the cylinder with the thumb and forefinger of the left hand. When the shells have been ejected, the pistol is ready for the 2d motion of loading.

N. B. There are three notches in the hammer of this pistol. The first is the safety notch, the second is the half-cock notch, and the third is the cock notch. The pistol cannot be fired when the hammer rests in the safety notch or half-cock notch, and can be fired by pulling the trigger when the hammer rests in the cock notch. The pistol should be carried habitually with the hammer resting in the safety notch.

COLT'S NEW .22 PISTOL, SEVEN SHOT.

TERMS CASH.

All Communications must be addressed to

Colt's Patent Fire-Arms Manufacturing Company,

HARTFORD, CONN., U. S. A.

Calhoun Printing Works, Hartford, Conn.

An advert for Colt's new single-action '.45' and the New Line .22, about 1876.

> The Remington is the hardest and surest shooting pistol made and because it carries exactly the same cartridge that the Winchester rifle does. My armament was two Remingtons and a Winchester rifle. You can now see why I prefer the Remington. There is no confusion of ammunition … when a man get into a close, hot fight, with a dozen men shooting at him all at once, he must have ammunition all of the same kind.[14]

Despite selling some 25,000 model 1875s, Remington were to go bankrupt in 1886 and, although reformed as the Remington Arms Company in 1888, they never again pursued the revolver market, though they did produce one last revolver, the Model 1890, that was to all intents the 1875 with the distinctive web removed from underneath the ejector housing; but it was too late and was not a commercial success. Smith and Wesson had not rested on their laurels either, producing the New Model Russian in 1874. But the established makers certainly did not have the field to themselves, for there were literally dozens of new revolvers being produced throughout the 1870s by manufacturers trying to establish themselves in a very competitive market.

There were some forty companies producing a wide range of pistols, ranging in quality from the truly dire to the equivalence of anything offered by Colt or Smith and Wesson. Attempting to cover the whole range would require a book in itself, but a selection of the better known marques were Iver Johnson, Merwin and Hulbert, Forehand and Wadsworth, Harrington and Richardson, Hopkins and Allen, and others. Their offerings covered the whole gamut of prices, types and quality. At one end of the scale, Norwegian-born Iver Johnson had begun to produce very cheap, very basic revolvers in 1871, of less than stunning quality in a variety of calibres from .22 to .44, that sold through hardware shops across the country. They were as cheap as $3 each and were virtually disposable, but they fulfilled a need and sold in quite large numbers. At the other end of the scale were the beautifully manufactured pistols of Merwin and Hulbert, which were actually made under contract by Hopkins and Allen. In production from 1876, they were mostly medium-frame revolvers in .38, .41 or .44 calibres selling at a modest $12 to $18, depending on the model. Originally open-top frames, they had an unusual rotating and sliding cylinder mechanism, but by 1880 had gained top-straps as well as such mechanical refinements as folding hammer spurs on some models, to prevent snagging on clothing. Others had a useful projecting spur on the butt that could prove deadly if used in a fist fight. The Merwins had sufficient reputation for a cased .38 example with nickel finish to be presented to Sheriff Pat Garrett after he rid Lincoln County of Billy the Kid.

Among the many other makers, Forehand and Wadsworth produced a competent, very well-made .44 single-action Army revolver that was not dissimilar to a cross between the Remington and Smith and Wesson. By the late 1870s, imported pistols were finding the crowded American market difficult

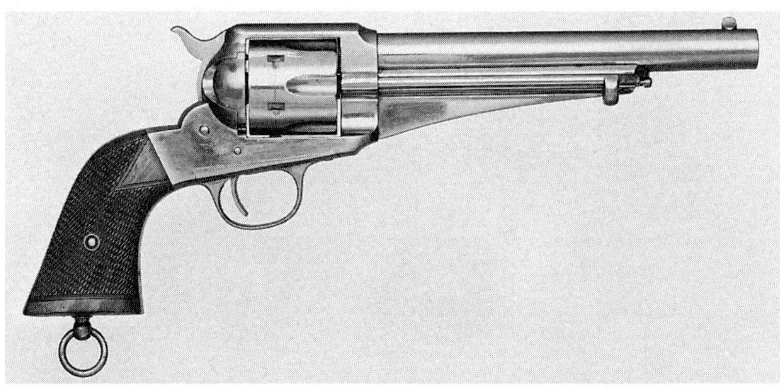

The fine Remington 1875 Army revolver, in nickel finish. Courtesy of the Trustees of the Royal Armouries.

to penetrate, home competition being so fierce. Some French and Belgian revolvers had a measure of popularity, but the Webley 'Bulldog' or the very similar Royal Irish Constabulary revolvers were hard-hitting, handy and reliable self-extracting double-action pistols that were actually one of the better selling imported handguns, proving to be one of the most successful non-American designs ever. Naturally, US makers were not slow to copy them and the majority used on the frontier were made by companies such as Forehand and Wadsworth, who manufactured their own very successful version. One of the selling features of the Bulldog was that the Webley ammunition was brass-cased, and in the harsh conditions of the West they proved more durable and more reliable than the softer copper cases still in use in American handguns. However, this does not entirely explain the extraordinarily broad appeal of these little English pistols.

The popularity of their double-action trigger mechanism had not gone unnoticed and by 1872 Smith and Wesson had built a double-action revolver, although it was to be another eight years before the design went into production, as the .38 Double-Action. This was a top break of standard Smith and Wesson type that initially suffered from a weak frame causing some breakages. This was soon rectified, and the Double Action proved highly popular, selling over 554,000 during its production life. Colt had meanwhile produced an excellent single-action target revolver in 1894, in the shape of the Bisley model, with a specially designed butt to facilitate target shooting, but it was based on the design of the now ageing Peacemaker, and they had little option but to look to manufacturing a double-action revolver, which resulted in 1878 in the 'Lightning' revolver. It, too, had a striking resemblance to the Peacemaker, albeit with a bird's-head grip, and unusually it bore no patent marks, as the design of the self-cocking revolver action was considered, in legal terms at least, to be in the Public Domain (although the prolific William Mason was later to be granted three patents relating to the Colt's internals in 1881). It was not the most robust of designs and mechanical failures were common. In fact the Lightning soon gained a reputation as a poorly made firearm, and sales were very slow.

Colt persevered with a range of heavier-framed Army and Frontier double-actions introduced in 1878 in a wide range of calibres, though most people preferred them in .45 Colt and .44-40. These were certainly an improvement on the Lightning, although 150 sent to England for Government testing were rejected as being 'too unreliable for service use'. One of the problems inherent in the Colts was the slowness in ejecting and reloading

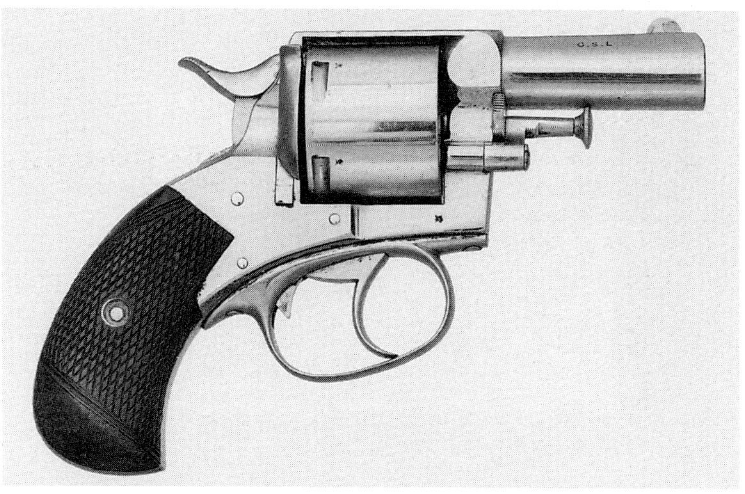

A 'British Bulldog' .44 in nickel finish. There is no maker's name on this example. Courtesy of the Trustees of the Royal Armouries.

the cartridges through the loading gate. So in 1889, Colt totally revised their revolver design, coming up with a Double-Action pistol that for the first time incorporated a cylinder hinged at the lower front edge of the frame that when unlatched swung out to the left. This was to prove the basis for all of the later Colt revolvers plus many imitators, and was to take the company into the twentieth century and beyond, although Colt had one final trick up their corporate sleeve.

Smith and Wesson, despite the popularity of their top-break revolvers, were also facing a dilemma. They had been going from strength to strength producing double-action top-breaks – first a .32, then a .44 as well as the very handy Hammerless Safety revolver, that incorporated a novel grip safety in the backstrap. But they too realized that the design that had served them so well was not well suited to the more powerful smokeless cartridges being introduced, and the automatic ejection system was not always ideal. Their response was to come up with the .32 Hand Ejector Model of 1894, with a system similar to the Colt, but using a locking latch operated by pulling the head of the extractor rod forward. This enabled the cylinder to be swung out to the right, and ejection was then done manually by pushing the ejector rod towards the cylinder. The advantage of this system over the earlier auto-eject was the ability of the shooter to simply pull out a couple of used cases and replace them, as well as making a revolver with a far stronger frame than it had previously. This design was to prove the most important in handgun history, and has subsequently been copied more than any other. Smith and Wesson were to remain with these new 'I' and 'K' Frame

(Above) The first swing-out cylinder revolver, Colt's .38-calibre double-action. Photo courtesy of B. Lees.

(Left) Colt's double-action .38-40-calibre Lightning revolver of 1878. Photo courtesy of B. Lees

COLT'S PATENT REVOLVING BREECH

PISTOLS, RIFLES, CARBINES AND SHOT-GUNS,

AND

Patent Combustible Envelope Cartridges,

PUT UP IN WATER-PROOF CASES.

MANUFACTURED BY

COLT'S PATENT FIRE ARMS MANUFACTURING COMPANY,

HARTFORD, CONN.

1872 **1872**

LIST OF PRICES:

PISTOLS.

OLD MODEL POCKET PISTOLS. Plated Mountings, Calibre or size of Bore 31-100ths of an inch diameter, carrying 92 Elongated or 140 Round Bullets to the pound.

4 inch Barrel, Lever Ramrod, Weight 24 oz., 6 Shots,	$8 50	5 Shots,	$8 00
5 " " " " " 26 oz., 6 "	8 90	5 "	8 40
6 " " " " " 27 oz., 6 "	9 25	5 "	8 75

OLD MODEL NAVY OR BELT PISTOL. Plated Mountings, 6 Shots, 7½ inch Barrel, Calibre or size of Bore 36-100ths of an inch diameter, carrying 50 Elongated or 86 Round Bullets to the pound, Weight 2 lbs. 10 oz. 14 00

NEW POCKET PISTOLS. ***Navy Size Calibre.*** Calibre or Size of Bore 36-100ths of an inch in diameter, carrying 50 Elongated or 86 Round Bullets to the pound.

4½ inch Barrel, 5 Shots, Plated or Blued Mountings, Weight 25 oz., 9 25
5½ " " 5 " " " " " 26½ oz., 9 65
6½ " " 5 " " " " " 28 oz., 10 00

PISTOLS WITH PATENT CREEPING LEVER RAMROD ATTACHED.

NEW MODEL POCKET PISTOLS. Calibre or Size of Bore 31-100ths of an inch diameter, carrying 92 Elongated or 140 Round Bullets to the lb.

3½ inch Barrel, 5 Shots, Steel Mountings, Weight 16 oz., - - - - 11 50
4½ " " 5 " " " " 16½ oz., - - - - 12 00

NEW MODEL POLICE PISTOLS. Calibre or Size of Bore 36-100ths of an inch diameter, carrying 50 Elongated or 86 Round Bullets to the lb.

4½ inch Barrel, 5 Shots, Plated or Blued Mountings, Weight 24½ oz., 11 75
5½ " " 5 " " " " " 25½ oz., 12 15
6½ " " 5 " " " " " 26 oz., 12 50

NEW MODEL NAVY OR BELT PISTOL. Pattern now used by the U. S. Navy. Calibre or Size of Bore 36-100ths of an inch diameter, carrying 50 Elongated or 86 Round Bullets to the lb.

7½ in. Barrel, 6 Shots, Brass, Plated or Blued Mountings, Weight 2 lbs. 10 oz. 15 00

NEW MODEL HOLSTER PISTOL. Recently approved by a board of U. S. Army Officers, and adopted for the use of the U. S. Regular Military Service. Calibre or Size of Bore 44-100ths of an inch diameter, carrying 33 Elongated or 48 Round Bullets to the pound.

8 inch Barrel, 6 Shots, Steel Handle Strap, Brass, Plated or Blued Trigger Guard, Weight 2 lbs. 11 oz. - - - - - - - - - - - 16 00

"Attachable Carbine Breech," for Navy and Army Pistols, plain, extra, - - 7 50
" " " with Canteen, extra, - - - - - - - - 9 00
Ornamental Engraving on Pocket Pistols, extra, - - - - - - - - - - 4 00
" " Belt and Holster Pistols, extra, - - - - - - - 5 00
" " Attachable Carbine Breech, extra, - - - - - - 3 00
IVORY STOCK, for Pocket Pistols, extra, - - - - - - - - - - - - 5 00
" " Belt or Holster Pistols, extra, - - - - - - - - - 6 00
POWDER FLASKS, for Holster Pistols, extra, - - - - - - - - - - 70
" " Belt Pistols, extra, - - - - - - - - - - 60
" " Pocket and New Model Police Pistol, extra, - - 40

All Pistols are furnished with a Bullet Mould, Screw Driver and Nipple Wrench, free of charge. Pistols are put up, assorted or otherwise, in packages of 10, 20, 25, 50 and 100 each.

CARTRIDGES.—Pistols.

Old Model	Pocket,*	31-100ths	in. Calibre, p'ckges of	1,200,	per thousand,	$10 00
" "	Navy or Belt,	36-100ths	" " "	1,200,	"	12 00
" "	Army or Holster,	44-100ths	" " "	1,200,	"	14 00
New "	Pocket,	265-1000ths	" " "	1,000,	"	8 00
" "	"	31-100ths	" " "	1,000,	"	14 00
" "	Police,	36-100ths	" " "	1,000,	"	12 00
" "	Navy or Belt,	36-100ths	" " "	1,200,	"	12 00
" "	Army or Holster,	44-100ths	" " "	1,200,	"	14 50

*Orders for Cartridges for "Old Model Pocket Pistol," should specify the number of Shots.

RIFLES, CARBINES and SHOT GUNS.

RIFLES. New Model Steel Mountings, 6 Shots, Calibre or Size of Bore, 36-100ths of an inch diameter, carrying 42 Elongated or 86 Round Bullets to the pound

24 inch Barrel, Weight 8 lbs. 14 oz., - - - - - - - - - - $30 75
27 " " " 9 lbs. 4 oz., - - - - - - - - - - 32 25
30 " " " 9 lbs. 14 oz., - - - - - - - - - - 33 75

RIFLES. Same Style, 6 Shot. Calibre or Size of Bore, 44-100ths of an inch diameter, carrying 28 Elongated or 48 Round Bullets to the pound.

24 inch Barrel, Weight 8 lbs 8 oz., - - - - - - - - - - 34 00
27 " " " 8 lbs. 12 oz., - - - - - - - - - - 35 50
31 5-16 " " 9 lbs. 8 oz., - - - - - - - - - - 37 00

RIFLES. Same Style, 5 Shots, Calibre or Size of Bore, 56-100ths of an inch diameter, carrying 14 Elongated or 24 Round Bullets to the pound.

24 inch Barrel, Weight 8 lbs. 14 oz. - - - - - - - - - - 35 50
27 " " " 9 lbs. 11 oz. - - - - - - - - - - 37 00
31 5-16 inch Barrel, (Pattern used by U. S. Army,) Weight 9 lbs. 15 oz., 38 50
37½ " " " " " " same length as U. S. Rifle Musket, Springfield Pattern, - - - - - - - - - - 42 00

CARBINES. New Model, Steel Mountings, Rifled Barrels, 18 or 21 inches long.

6 Shots, Calibre or Size of Bore 36-100ths of an inch diameter, carrying 42 Elongated or 86 Round Bullets to the pound, Weight 8 lbs. 8 oz., 28 50
6 Shots, Calibre or Size of Bore 44-100ths of an inch diameter, carrying 28 Elongated or 48 Round Bullets to the pound, Weight 8 lbs. 12 oz., 31.00
5 Shots, Calibre or Size of Bore 56-100ths of an inch diameter, carrying 14 Elongated or 24 Round Bullets to the pound, Weight 9 lbs. 8 oz., 33 00

SHOT GUNS.* Calibre or Size of Bore 75-100ths of an inch diameter.

27 inch Barrel, 5 Shots, Weight 9 lbs. 9 oz., - - - - - - - - - 47 25
30 " " 5 " " 9 lbs. 13 oz., - - - - - - - - - 48 75
33 " " 5 " " 10 lbs., - - - - - - - - - - 50 25
36 " " 5 " " 10 lbs. 4 oz., - - - - - - - - - 51 75

Powder Flasks, for Carbines and Rifles, - - - - - - - - $1 60 and 1 75
Globe Sights, for Sporting Rifles, - - - - - - - - - - - - 60
Adjustable Target Back Sight, - - - - - - - - - - - - 2 40
Telescope Sights, with new and improved adjustment, adapted to any Rifle. 30 00

All Rifles and Carbines are furnished with a Bullet Mould, Screw Driver and Nipple-Wrench, free of charge. All Shot-Guns are furnished with Wad-Cutter, Screw Driver and Nipple-Wrench, free of charge.

*Shot-Guns of 60 Calibre are also made. Lengths of Barrels 27, 30 and 33 inches. Prices $9 less than corresponding lengths of 75 calibre.

CARTRIDGES.—Rifles and Carbines.

36-100ths	of an inch Calibre, in packages of	1,200,	per thousand,	$15 00
44-100ths	" " "	1,200,	"	18 00
56-100ths	" "	1,000,	"	20 00

Shot Guns.

60-100ths	of an inch Calibre, in packages of	1,000,	per thousand,	$20 00
75-100ths	" " "	1,000,	"	25 00

TERMS CASH.

ALL COMMUNICATIONS MUST BE ADDRESSED TO

COLT'S PATENT FIRE-ARMS MAN'FG COMPANY,

Hartford, Conn.

UNITED STATES OF AMERICA.

A price list for Colt firearms, dated 1872.

revolvers into the twenty-first century – a proud testimony to the solidity of their original design.

But the era of the handgun was not to end here, for in 1897 Colt were to patent a pistol that would create an entirely new handgun industry, and it was a semi-automatic. Colt's design was not the first, of course, for many European designers had been making efficient semi-autos for some years. Hugo Borchardt had produced a rather ungainly but efficient pistol, and Mauser's C96 'Broomhandle' with its awesomely powerful 7.63mm cartridge had first been produced in 1896. Some had appeared in the West shortly afterwards, for some reason becoming a particularly popular pistol in Mexico. One of the problems with these imported semi-automatics was the need for special ammunition that was not widely available, making it almost impossible to reload, which limited their appeal quite drastically. The advantages of the automatic over the revolver will probably be argued until doomsday, but few could disagree that for sheer speed of reloading and fire, as well as the greatly increased power of their ammunition, the semi-auto was hard to beat. Colt adopted a design by John Browning who had created a simple recoil operated blow-back system that fired a .38-calibre bullet at a hitherto unimaginable velocity, 1,200fps, with penetration at 50yd (46m) of 11in (28cm) of pine. Bearing in mind the generally dismal power of the average .38in revolver bullet, this was indeed a revelation. The first of these pistols rolled off the production line in 1900 just at a time when, ironically, the Frontier was declared officially to be history.

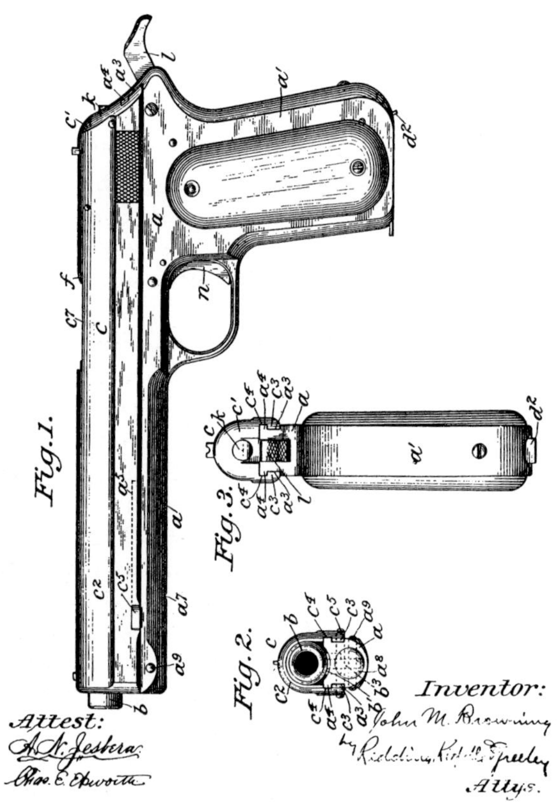

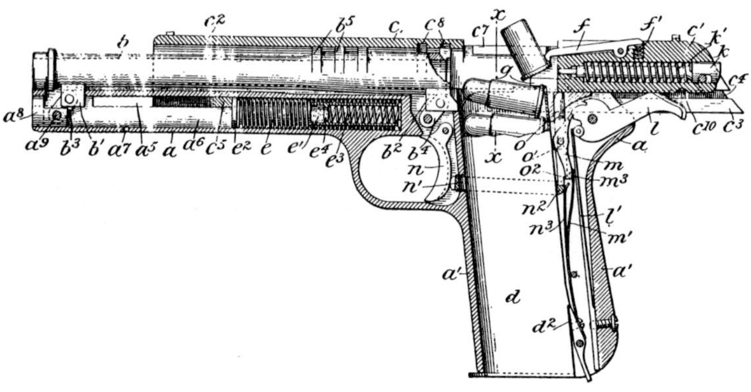

John Browning's simple but efficient semi-automatic pistol.

8 Military Pistols

As with most armies of the eighteenth century, pistols for general issue were not a consideration. Tactically there was no point and they were generally scorned by the American military who regarded their weight as an encumbrance, their practical range limited to virtually point blank and their requirement for special cartridges with smaller charges than the muskets as a logistical drawback. True, some officers were armed with braces of holster pistols, privately purchased and frequently of very high quality, but for the most part, certainly until the Revolutionary War, the pistol was not regarded as a useful item of military hardware. The war that broke out in 1776 against Britain began to change that, for mounted units carried carbines or musketoons that, while practical enough, were almost impossible to reload during combat once fired. As a result, pistols became increasingly common amongst mounted units, braces of simple flintlocks being carried in leather holsters on the saddle. Many were purchased abroad, from France or England, and small numbers were manufactured in the workshops of American gunsmiths, but as with earlier muskets, it was the French influence that was initially to affect US design and manufacture, their Model 1777 pistol providing the basic design for the US Government's first regulation pistol, the Model 1799.

Manufactured by Simeon North of Berlin, Connecticut it was a substantial pistol, 14½in long, weighing 3½lb (1.59kg), with a round tapering 8½in barrel, 1in longer than the French 1777, and in .69 calibre. It had a distinctive rounded lock-plate and walnut grip but no fore-end. They were sold to the Government at \$6 a piece and some 2,000 were manufactured, but it was soon superseded by an improved model that was made at Harper's Ferry, the first martial handgun to be made at a Government armoury. Variously referred to as the Model 1805, 1806 or 1807, the first eight pattern guns were actually manufactured at the Armoury in 1806,[1] although production did not start until the following year. It was of more conventional design than the North, having a heavy, round 10in barrel of .54 or 'rifle' calibre,

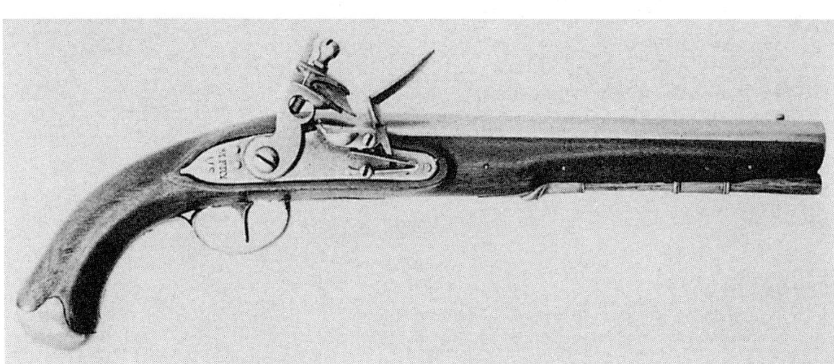

A model 1807 military contract pistol by M. Fry.

brass buttcap and being half-stocked, the barrel retained by wedges. Around 4,000 were manufactured, and although regarded as rather fragile for military use, many were retained in Government arsenals, and some even converted to percussion post-1848.

As manufacturing momentum gathered, a number of other models of flintlock pistol were produced, being known as 'contract pistols', and these were mostly variations on the same theme, with models of 1807, 1808, 1809 and 1811, all manufactured under the same arrangements as the muskets, with commercial contractors supplying the Ordnance with pistols of a set pattern. These were made by various contractors such as Simeon North, as well as established Pennsylvania makers such as William Calderwood, J. Guest, J. Henry, Jacob Cooke, Martin Frye, Henry Deringer and others.

Of all of these makers, it was North who was to become established as the premier designer and supplier, producing no less than four models, the 1811, 1813, 1816 and 1819. They were all of .69 or 'musket' calibre with 9in smoothbore barrels, but the most important feature of the Model 1813 was that for the first time all of the lock parts were interchangeable. The problem with all of these pistols was that in use they proved to be heavy, inaccurate and kicked like the proverbial mule when fired. Even Ordnance officials were in agreement that the .54 rifle calibre was far more easy to handle than the .69 and of the 20,000 ordered only 1,100 were actually produced in .69, presumably much to the relief of the long-suffering troopers to whom they were issued. By 1822, North had supplied some 20,000 pistols under contract at $7 each. In 1826 he received another contract for a shorter-barrelled pistol with the same 'stirrup' ramrod swivel, as fitted to the Model 1819, that prevented the loss of the vital ramrod, a common occurrence for mounted troops.

In 1833, demand for military pistols grew with the formation of the US Dragoons but, as with the percussion military musket, the US Ordnance hesitated, being in something of a quandary about what sort of pistol they wanted. They certainly needed a new pistol but opted for the devil they knew and approved the manufacture of yet another flintlock, the Model 1836 which was of the now standard configuration with an 8½in smoothbore barrel of .54 calibre weighing 2¼lb (1.02kg). In fairness, it was a tough and well-made sidearm, that was to see hard use in the Indian wars on the Frontier and in the Mexican wars. Indeed, many were still to be seen in the hands of soldiers on both sides during the early months of the Civil War. But time had run out for the flintlock mechanism and it was only logical, in the wake of the adoption by the army of the percussion musket, that percussion was also to become the primary means of ignition for military pistols. As a result of tests, the Ordnance Department contracted with Nathan Ames of Massachusetts for a new pistol:

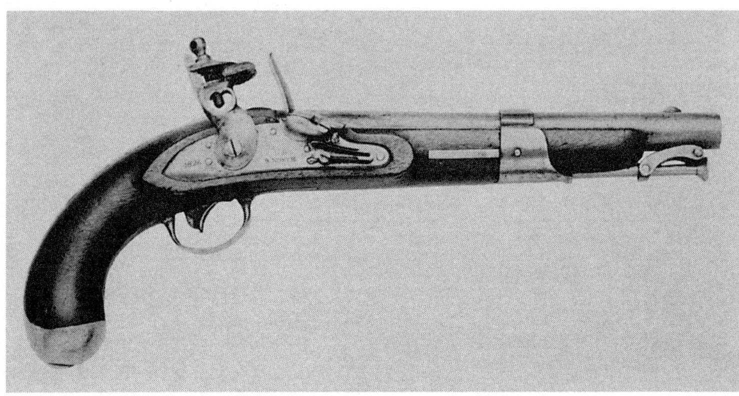

A Model 1826 pistol by Simeon North with stirrup-ramrod. Courtesy of the Tøjhus Museum, Copenhagen.

> … to be made of the same form and dimensions as the present [1836] model … A percussion lock on the same principle as for the other US arms is to be adopted to it. The bands and sideplate, the butt plate, the guard bow and plate and the sight are to be of brass.[2]

Several contractors were used to make the new Model 1842, Aston and Johnson and A.H. Waters being the two primary manufacturers of what was essentially the Model 1836 with a percussion lock. The Ordnance did not believe that there was any requirement for repeating pistols to be supplied to the cavalry or dragoon regiments, one officer voicing the commonly held opinion that the men would only waste powder given repeating pistols. He had clearly never been armed with an empty single-shot pistol while facing a determined tomahawk-wielding Indian. This belief persisted in the upper echelons of the Army until the Mexican War when attitudes were to undergo something of a transformation.

Revolvers of several types had been available for some years prior to the adoption of the 1842 pistol, the most prominent being Colt's Paterson pistol that coincidentally was patented in the same year that the last contract for flintlock pistols was awarded by the Ordnance Department. It was regarded with suspicion by the military, partly because of its complexity, apparent fragility and, of course, greater cost. Some purchased privately saw use in the Mexican War, but it was their success in the hands of the soldiers of the new Republic of Texas, who had ordered some 460 revolvers and revolving carbines in 1839, that was to bring the revolver to the notice of the military and the public in general. In 1844, some fifteen Texas Rangers under the command of Col John Coffee Hays had fought a running battle with about eighty Comanches. The normal outcome of such an encounter would have resulted in the Indians returning home with fifteen new scalps, but Hays's men were armed with Patersons. Samuel Walker, subsequently to have considerable influence on the design of Colt revolvers, recounted in a letter to Colt, how the influence of the revolver in the battle changed its outcome:

> In the summer of 1844 … 15 men fought about 80 Comanche Indians … killing and wounding about half their number. Up to this time these daring Indians had always supposed themselves superior to us, man to man on horse, – the result of this engagement was such as to intimidate them … and I can safely say that … without your pistols we would not have had the confidence to have undertaken such daring adventures.[3]

The publicity surrounding this event, doubtless music to Sam Colt's ears, was widespread and the net result was the production of the Walker Colt that was mechanically more efficient and robust than the Paterson, and infinitely more powerful. Each chamber of the Walker could take 57 grains of powder, producing a muzzle velocity for the .44 bullet of some 1,400fps. Naturally, the soldiers, working on the basis of 'most is best', crammed as much powder in the chambers as possible, which resulted in a number of cylinder failures that oddly did little to dent the popularity of this big new revolver.

In January 1847 an initial Ordnance contract was issued for the improved new 'Dragoon' revolver, followed by another in July of that year. They were supplied at $25 each, exclusive of such accessories as a shoulder stock and powder flask. The manufacture of the Dragoon rectified many of the faults of the earlier Walker, and by 1850 out of 2,082 revolvers, only one barrel and cylinder failed testing. The Ordnance went on purchasing Colt's Dragoons, including some 1,000 with detachable shoulder stocks being supplied up to 1860. If the age of the revolver was about to dawn for the US army, it was going to happen slowly, for the single-shot percussion pistol was still the most widely issued handgun. An audit of army stores in 1853 showed that 2,600 single-shot percussion and 'other' pistols were on hand of which only 847 were Colts.

This situation would not remain for long. In 1855, there was a wholesale reorganization of the US military and some 2,150 of the new smaller-framed .36-calibre Colt Navy revolvers were

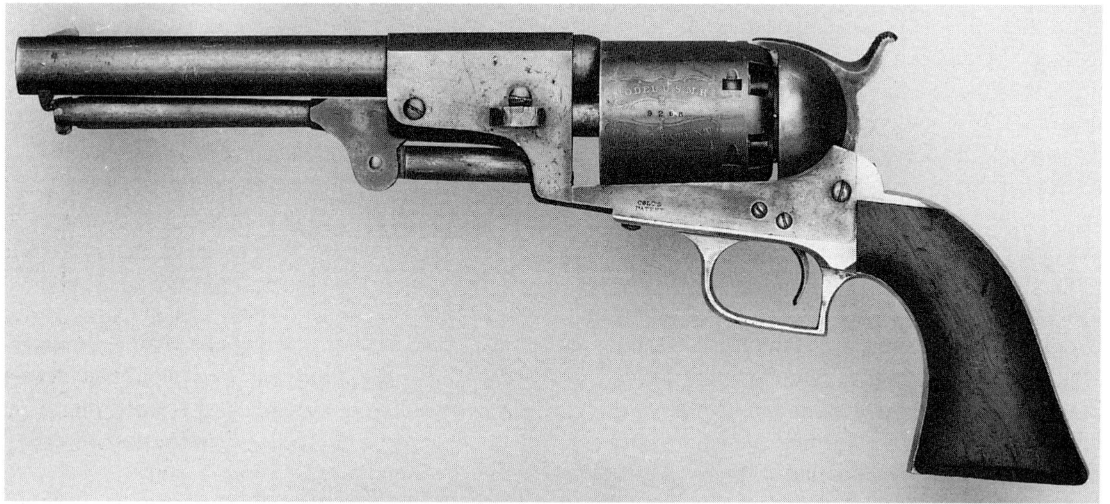

A Colt Dragoon, one of eight purchased by the British Board of Ordnance for testing in 1851 but, apparently, never fired. Courtesy of the Trustees of the Royal Armouries.

ordered, these being more manageable and 1½lb lighter than the Dragoon. This was an important point, for one of the problems with the Dragoon was simply carrying it. While portable enough when in a holster hung on a pommel, it was too big to tuck into a belt and when in a flap-secured holster worn at the waist was simply too heavy and unwieldy for comfort and ease of use when on horseback. When Indian attacks could occur almost from nowhere, speed of response was of the essence and soldiers modified their equipment to their own preference. As one cavalry officer wrote:

> The flap of the holster, placed to protect the pistol from the rain, had long before been cut off; it was preferable to suffer a little rust on the weapon rather than run the risk of losing a fraction of a second in drawing it.[4]

PISTOLS IN THE CIVIL WAR

The modernization of the army required the purchase of more revolvers than Colt could supply, so after 1857 the Ordnance Department purchased dozens of other makes and models of revolver, most of which were subsequently to see service throughout the Civil War years, and beyond. One of the largest orders was for Massachusetts Arms-manufactured .36 and .44-calibre Beaumont-Adams revolvers, an improved version of the double-action-only Adams' design, that had both a single- and double-action trigger mechanism. In practice, the Adams was a better combat pistol than the Colt, being solid-framed and, unlike the Colt, it did not rely on a weak spring to lock the cylinder in position but used a trigger-operated pawl pressing against a ratchet tooth that positively locked the cylinder in place and provided a far more durable mechanism. It also had a patented pre-manufactured combustible cartridge, that in 1851 was something of a novelty for a revolver.

The early design of these used a simple, skin-bodied, paper-covered cartridge, with ball and wad. Tearing a small strip of paper at the rear of the cartridge exposed the charge that was then loaded in its entirety into a chamber. It was a system soon commonly adopted for many percussion revolvers and was undoubtedly quicker than using the normal method of powder in a flask and separate ball, but the bulk of the casing limited the charge that could be carried, and reduced the performance of the pistol. Early Colts used a similar paper and foil cartridge but by the Civil War his revolvers were supplied with skin cartridges with a ball glued at one end, although throughout the war soldiers continually complained of the fragility of these pre-prepared cartridges that broke apart in their cartridge pouches and absorbed moisture, resulting in misfires. Many simply preferred to carry two or three spare loaded cylinders, and loose powder and ball to recharge the empty chambers with as large a charge as the chambers could hold. In practical terms, as most revolvers were used at less than 20yd (18m), range was not really an issue but reliability was, and a capped and loaded cylinder, with the chamber mouth well covered with grease, was to all purposes immune to the vagaries of the climate.

Not all military pistols were issue sidearms, for many officers and men opted to purchase their own, officers frequently opting for the Adams or the small-framed .31 Colt, but for a Frontier soldier earning $10 a month, a new Colt was nearly 2½ months' wages, so many looked for cheaper alternatives. As a result, at the outbreak of war in 1861 almost any type of commercially produced revolver could be found in the hands of the soldiers, and this situation was compounded as the demands of war placed a greater strain on the manufacturers supplying the US and Confederate armies, and both sides cast desperately around for sufficient handguns to supply the huge numbers of men swelling the ranks of their armies.

Meanwhile, back at the Colt factory, development work was still continuing to improve the model 1851 Navy, and the result was the New Model Navy, or Model 1861. This was a clever modification, using the same barrel forging as the

Robert Adams's solid-frame design manufactured by William Tranter in 1853. It has a distinctive double-trigger, the lower of which cocked the revolver. The rammer lies alongside the barrel. Courtesy of the Trustees of the Royal Armouries.

.44 Army, albeit with different machined dimensions. It was really just a smoother version of the '51 Navy, incorporating the Army's rounded barrel and shrouded loading mechanism, and it was to remain in production until the introduction of the first cartridge revolvers in 1874, almost 39,000 being sold. It was the New Model Army that still proved the most popular in combat, however, its .44 ball having greater range and penetrative power and some 1,600 were even smuggled into the Confederacy at the start of the war.

There was certainly no shortage of pistols available and one of the best alternatives to the ubiquitous Colt was the Remington. Originally produced as the Remington-Beals, it was improved in 1861 and 1863, becoming the New Model .44 revolver. With its distinctive octagonal 7½in barrel, solid top-strap and shrouded loading lever, it was to become the most popular pistol of the war, some 130,000 being purchased by the Federal government, although their popularity with the Ordnance may have had something to do with their modest price of $13. Remington were able to undercut Colt's not by using inferior materials, but by much improved and simplified construction methods, such as casting the frame and backstrap as one piece, although many of the early pistols suffered as a result of poor quality control and some cavalry units refused to use them because of their poor reliability. Nevertheless, they saw considerable service throughout and beyond the war, as did the Starr, which accounted for nearly 13 per cent of all the revolvers supplied to the US Army. This hinged-frame .36- or .44-calibre revolver was patented by the Starr Arms Company of Yonkers, New York, and was well designed with a semi-solid hinged-frame six-shot. It had an unusual feature in having a quick-release screw on the right side of the frame, next to the hammer; when undone, this allowed the frame and top strap to drop down for access to the cylinder. It had a fitted loading lever and was manufactured in single or double-action, the former proving more popular with the Union cavalry to whom the majority were issued, despite the fact it was 2in longer and ½lb heavier than the double action.

After the war, many hundreds of Starrs were sent to the German states and saw use in the Franco-Prussian war, many subsequently finding their way to England, where they proved very popular.

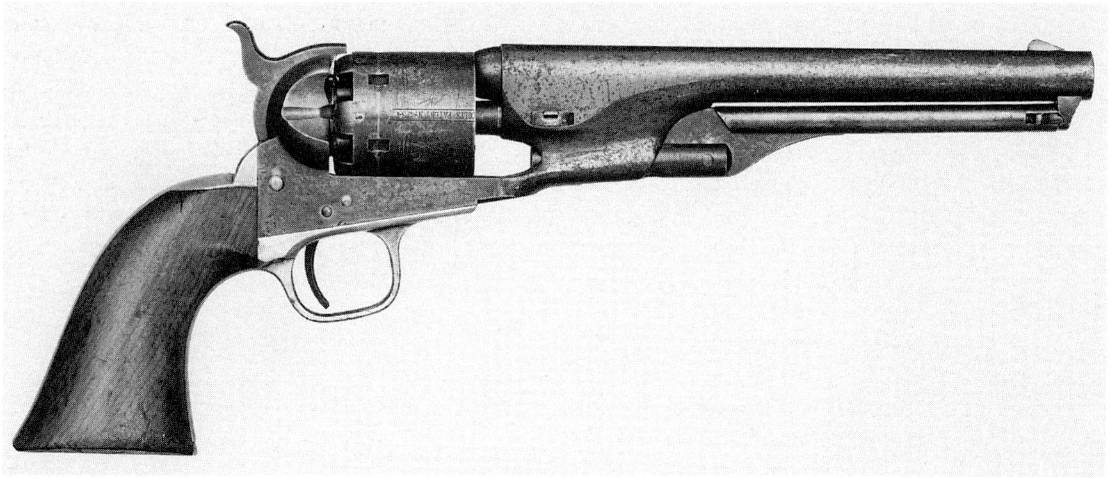

The improved Navy of 1861 with round barrel and shrouded rammer. Courtesy of the Trustees of the Royal Armouries.

A Starr double-action in .44 calibre with 6½in (16.5cm) barrel. Courtesy of the Trustees of the Royal Armouries.

The sidehammer Kerr was also purchased in some numbers, and was considered a good, solidly made pistol, the majority being used by the Confederacy, whose manufacturing ability was severely limited. It was patented in late 1858 by James Kerr, who was the superintendent of the London Armoury Company in England, who were to manufacture them. It was a five-shot .44-calibre sidehammer double-action with the useful facility of having the lock mechanism enclosed within a removable sideplate. If needed, the entire mechanism could be removed as a unit making it particularly easy to field-repair. It also benefited from having a fitted loading lever, something that the Adams did not, making reloading a faster task.

The only home-produced revolver used in any real quantity in the Confederacy was the Spiller and Burr, initially manufactured in Atlanta, Georgia, that was in fact almost a clone of the US Whitney revolver. It used a cheap cast brass frame, but it was a stronger design than the Colt, and a steel .36in barrel was screwed into it. They were never issued in large numbers, most Confederate soldiers arming themselves with captured revolvers, and it is thought less than 1,500 were made.

There were other Confederate revolvers being made by a number of companies, most being Colt Model 1851 'Navy' copies and although their numbers were small, probably a combined total of under 7,000 revolvers, they are worth mentioning as they formed an important part of the Confederate arsenal. The most prolific were the brass-framed Griswold and Gunnerson from Griswoldville, Georgia who made some 3,700 'Colt' revolvers. Other makes, in order of manufacturing quantities, were the Leech and Rigdon (1,500), Rigdon Ainsley and Co (1,000), Dance Brothers (500) and the August Machine Works, Columbus Firearms Company and Schneider and Glassick, none of whom produced more than 100 revolvers each. If the South could not make enough of its own pistols, it certainly adopted other makes with a will, and one revolver in particular has become synonymous with Confederate use – the LeMat. This unusual revolver had the advantage not only of a nine-shot .40-calibre cylinder, but also a 16-gauge smoothbore barrel that could be loaded with buckshot and fired separately. It was single-action, 14in long, weighing 4lb (1.8kg) and had a pivoting head on its hammer that could be flipped down to enable the smoothbore barrel to be fired. At $30 they were expensive, but they found favour with many Confederate officers, including J.E.B. Stuart, and over 1,500 were imported.

Not all of the Confederacy's pistols were purchased by direct routes for many, like the North and Savage, ended up in Southern hands by being smuggled across through the West. The .36-calibre revolver with its 7½in barrel had a complicated double-trigger system, the lower ring of which cocked the hammer, rotating the cylinder and forcing it against the rear of the barrel, while the upper trigger fired it. It was too muzzle-heavy to give good balance and proved awkward to use, but was improved in 1860 and some 12,000 were bought. Most of these odd-looking revolvers were purchased by the Federal Government to supply soldiers stationed in the West and Texas, and an unknown number were to find their way back East, into the hands of Confederate cavalrymen.

Another good revolver to emerge from the war years was the Whitney, also much copied by the South. Whitney had also collaborated with Beals, and had been producing commercial percussion revolvers since the early 1850s. His best-selling pistol was to emerge after 1857 and this was the Navy, a .36-calibre six-shooter that bore a close resemblance to the Remington. Whitney had examined both Remington and Colts, and adopted the best features of both, so he used the Colt action, Remington frame and his own cylinder pin and rammer, retained by a quick-release screw. Most had 7½ barrels and iron frames. A useful feature was that its cartridges were interchangeable with the Colt, which made it popular among the Army Quartermasters who were faced with all sorts of logistical complexities when it came to the supply of ammunition. As if this was not enough of a problem, some of the percussion revolvers were even found to be inoperable with standard issue of percussion caps, Ordnance tests showing that:

> A cap suitable for Colt's pistol does not suit either Savage or Starr's because the main spring is too weak to explode it. Second, a cap suitable for Savage's or Starr's pistols does not suit Colt's because the hammer drives it in pieces, a fragment often lodges in front of the cock and renders the arm useless … therefore I am compelled to have two qualities made … one for Colt's … one for Savage and Starr's.[5]

Evidence of the confusion created by such a broad range of calibres and pistol types can be seen in the story of the first Lefaucheux pinfire revolvers to be issued to the Federal cavalry. The Lefaucheux were French-made 12mm (.47in) pistols and the company were the largest foreign suppliers of revolvers to the Federal army, although most were not issued to front-line troops, being given to militia, Western-based units or volunteer units. Its self-contained copper cartridge was a mystery to most quartermasters and when it was issued to the 5th Kansas Volunteer Cavalry they were accompanied with .44-calibre skin percussion cartridges, but no pinfire ammunition. This was the least of the worries of the troopers issued with them, one Sergeant writing 'The Lefaucheux were worthless, and would not carry a ball over fifteen steps.'[6]

This is doubtless an exaggeration but it was true that the weak open-frame design of the revolver was poor and its cylinder locking system relied simply on a flat spring to keep the cylinder in alignment with the bore. This meant that they frequently misaligned upon cocking and, like the Colt, the barrel could be knocked out of true very easily. Trooper Vincent Osborne of the Second Kansas Cavalry commented in 1862:

> We drew our revolvers on the 20th … but no cartridges at that time had been procured. The 2nd Kansas were inspected by an officer of the regular army who condemned … our revolvers and we turned them in and drew sabres.[7]

Regardless of their performance, these pinfires were technically significant, being the first metallic cartridge revolvers adopted into US service. Pinfire obviated the problems with percussion caps, and, assuming ammunition was actually supplied for them, they were faster by far to reload than any comparable percussion revolver. Their introduction was a precursor to the wholesale adoption, after the war, of metallic cartridge handguns. Other manufacturers still relied on percussion and produced variations of the solid-frame design of the Remington Army. Freeman, Joslyn and the fine Rogers and Spencer all used basically the same design, although the Joslyn utilized a sidehammer. Few were supplied in time for the war, the order of 5,000 Rogers not being finished until after hostilities had ceased. Some found their way to England, where they could be purchased for the modest sum of seven shillings and sixpence, but the bulk were sold off for scrap.

By the cessation of hostilities in 1865, the percussion revolver had been perfected to the point that little more could be done to improve it, and in the immediate postwar years the country was awash with surplus revolvers that one would have thought could have more than satisfied the demands of the buying public. But the opening of the West by the railroad during the war years had conspired to make the new frontier not only more desirable to thousands of the war-weary ex-soldiers, but also much more accessible. This was to lead to the short but tumultuous years of the Indian Wars, where the military handgun became not an accessory but a vital weapon of war.

THE MILITARY CARTRIDGE REVOLVERS

In the late 1860s, most regular army soldiers garrisoned in the far-flung Western forts were carrying a .44-calibre percussion revolver, primarily Colt's, or New Model Remingtons with a smattering of the Model 1865 single-shot Remington Rolling Block chambered for the big .50-calibre rimfire cartridge, as well as some Starrs. Many soldiers found a lucrative market for their pistols in the shape of settlers passing through, who would purchase good quality revolvers for four or five times the replacement cost to the soldier, a practice that stopped only when the Government upped the cost to the soldiers to $50 dollars for a lost pistol. Whilst the cavalry were issued with a pistol, most infantrymen were not and so a motley selection of revolvers, single-shot pistols and pepperboxes were carried. The Ordnance were certainly interested in the benefits of the new rimfire cartridge revolvers, but the problem was the strict control that Smith and Wesson kept on their Rollin White patent. Strangely, Smith and Wesson did not

Revolver: .22 S & W, .41 Colt, .44 Colt, early .45 copper-cased Colt, .45 S & W, .45 Long Colt. Photo courtesy of B. Lees.

produce a revolver suitable for military use, and there was no way for the Ordnance to avoid patent infringements by designing their own.

Many of the guns in the hands of the army were long in the tooth, and most of the revolvers were arsenal refinished Civil War vintage weapons. However, in 1869, the Rollin White patent expired and wisely perhaps, the Government refused to allow Smith and Wesson to renew it. This meant that the Ordnance could at last now tender for a new metallic cartridge revolver to replace their ageing percussion pistols. They were looking at the newly developed centrefire cartridge in the tried and tested .44 calibre that had served so well during the war.

In 1870, Smith and Wesson offered a self-ejecting top-break revolver, the No. 3 (later called the American) for trials, and it acquitted itself well, the Board liking its solid top-strap, ejection mechanism and handling characteristics. It had an 8in barrel and at 25yd (23m) the 205 grain .44-calibre bullet proved capable of penetrating 3½in (9cm) of board with a 25 grain charge behind it, and it would group at just over 4in (10cm). An initial Government contract was placed for 1,000 revolvers, that by 1871 were being issued to cavalry units on the Frontier at a cost of $14.75 each in blued finish. Some 1,200 Model 1860 Colt-Richards cartridge conversions were also supplied the same year and proved fairly satisfactory, although a problem was that their longer, fatter .44 cartridge was not interchangeable with the No. 3. A surprise acceptance was the Ordnance's order to Remington, not for converted .44 revolvers as one would expect, but for 6,500 of the Rolling Block single-shot pistols. They chambered the potent 320 grain .50-calibre bullet with a 30 grain charge, and their immensely tough construction made them a popular, if slow-shooting sidearm. About 1,500 were actually to reach the western outposts and see active service.

But all of these pistols were an interim measure, for what the army really needed was a revolver with a standardized calibre that was reliable, easy to repair and hard hitting, so trials were organized in 1872 to find such a gun. The Colt's new 7½in barrelled, solid-framed single-action proved, in the words of one Ordnance officer '... superior in most respects and much better adapted to the wants of the army than the Smith and Wesson'. It therefore seemed a foregone conclusion about which pistol would be adopted, but this apparent *fait accompli* did not deter Smith and Wesson, for they had been approached by a Cavalry Major named George W. Schofield, who had seen much service with the Tenth Cavalry. He liked the American model, to the extent that in 1870–71 he acted as agent for Smith and Wesson, purchasing over 100 revolvers. He understood the problems experienced by mounted soldiers trying to reload a revolver whilst on the move, and he sent details to the company of improvements he had made to the latching system on his Russian model:

> January 3, 1875. Being just returned from my second expedition against hostile Indians in which I was again successful, having captured 52, making 323 in all taken in by my command, my mind naturally turns to the pistol. Have heard nothing except indirectly from your establishment since I left Springfield. As soon as it can be done I would like six of them sent to me by express to Fort Sill ... Indian Territory. The one I have (altered from your Russian model) has stood every test. I have killed almost everything – but an Indian – with it and used it in all kinds of weather and in the roughest sort of a way. On the last trip I loaded twice with my horse at a run and killed a buffalo each time. Let me hear from you at once, in a month I may be off on another scout. Yours truly G. Schofield.[8]

The result was two improvements patented in 1871 and 1873; a barrel catch that was frame mounted and a simplified ejection system. This enabled single-handed reloading of the revolver by a mounted man and the eventual result was the production of the Model 3 Schofield, First Model. The Army was impressed and undertook tests with the three revolvers, Colt, Remington and Schofield. In comparative tests, the Schofield could load, fire, and eject

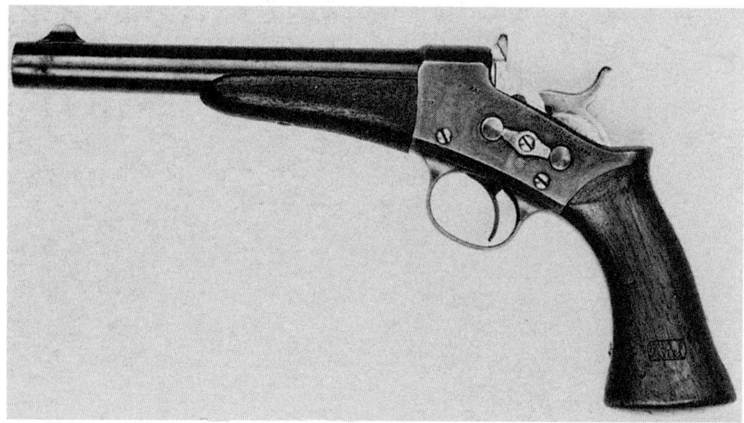

A Remington Model 1871 Army .50-calibre single-shot pistol.

eighteen cartridges in 59 seconds, while the Colt and Model 1875 Remington revolver took 1 min 54 sec. The real problem lay in the mechanisms of the pistols, for while the Colt was almost unaffected by dust and dirt, the Smith and Wesson became hard to load, and the Remington hard to eject. Stripping took 5, 7½ and 7min respectively, while re-assembly, always trickier, was 17min for the Colt, 19 for the Schofield and an extraordinary 24min for the Remington. By 1874, after Smith and Wesson had made modifications, the Board concluded that:

> Major Schofield's revolver is well suited to the military service, and we recommend that a limited number of these pistols be placed in the hands of troops for comparative trials with the Colt … and that as far as possible the different pistols be tried side by side.[9]

The Ordnance, meanwhile, specified that the revolvers be chambered for the more powerful .45-calibre centrefire cartridge, so all test pistols were chambered accordingly. Bizarrely, Smith and Wesson chose a cartridge of smaller dimensions than the more powerful Colt round, so while a Smith and Wesson cartridge would fit both types, the Colt cartridge could not be fired in the Schofield. This led to considerable confusion among units issued with them, but did not stop officers in some units privately purchasing Schofields in preference to their issue Colts. This led to a certain 'mine's better than yours' rivalry between units issued with the Model 1873 Colt and the Schofield as field tests continued through 1876, the Remington having been rejected, although some 25,000 were sold commercially. In practical terms, the Colt had a simpler, stronger mechanism at the expense of being slower to load and eject and not as well manufactured as the Schofield, but it was more accurate and its cartridge more powerful. Consensus of opinion among the men who used them was summed up by an anonymous contributor who signed himself 'Cavalryman', writing in the *Army and Navy Journal* of 1878, who said that 'The 'Colt's … and the … Schofield are both good, both have their advocates, and no serious complaints can be brought against either, and I think that in a fight one is as good as the other.'

It was the Colt, in the now classic form of the model 1873 Single Action Army, that was to dominate the West as a military sidearm, some 35,000 being issued, as opposed to 8,000 Schofields, but they were by no means the only revolvers in military use. As always, the products of the British firearms' industry found a niche in the hearts and holsters of many soldiers, and Webley's .450in Bulldog and Royal Irish Constabulary revolvers were much in demand, particularly as the R.I.C. had a lanyard ring fitted on the butt, an item that curiously no US Service revolver had, apart from some Remingtons. Possibly the most famous R.I.C. type were the pair of revolvers, carried by General George Custer during his ill-fated stand at The Little Big Horn

A Schofield Smith and Wesson, Second Model. Courtesy of the Trustees of the Royal Armouries.

in 1876, and that he apparently used with some effect. After the battle, among the litter of empty cases, soldiers noticed:

> Government and Winchester shells, and one peculiar brass shell was found that nobody knew anything about, but which was supposed to belong to General Custer's pistol.[10]

Two other English service revolvers, the Tranter and Adams, both large-framed, double-action revolvers of extremely solid construction, were to be found in service, although at least one owner complained of a problem he had as the service issue flapped holster couldn't accommodate the English pistols. Many soldiers on the frontier, well aware of the slow and lingering death they could expect if captured by

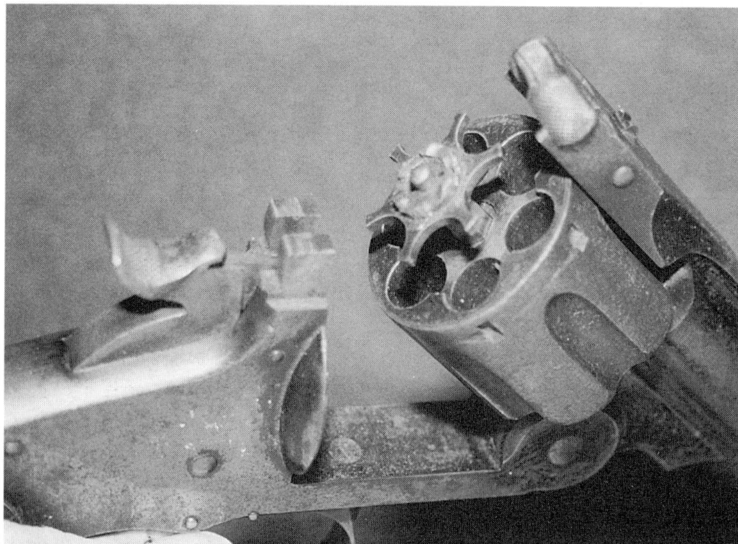

The open cylinder of a Smith and Wesson showing the ejector star. Photo courtesy of B. Lees.

The open loading gate of a .45 Colt. Photo courtesy of B. Lees.

Indians, carried derringers of one type or another, and it was a little prophetic that Custer, of all people, should have written of the derringer he was given.

> [It] may not impress the reader with being a very formidable weapon to use in Indian warfare... [but] It was given to me under the firm conviction that the Indians would overwhelm and massacre my entire party; and to prevent my being captured … and reserved for torture, that little pistol was given to me in order that at the last moment I might become my own executioner – an office I was not seeking.[11]

Although the Ordnance had tested and rejected both the Forehand and Wadsworth 'Army' and a Merwin and Hulbert open-frame, they had their own followers, as did Hopkins and Allen. In fact, the very positive extraction system on the Merwin was an advantage over most other revolvers, in that the cartridge rims engaged on a fixed ring on the face of the breech. A latch on the bottom strap of the frame enabled the barrel to be manually rotated, and as it did, screw threads on the cylinder axis pin pushed the barrel and cylinder forwards a short distance, freeing the fired case from the chamber. Pulling the barrel forward then allowed the cases to drop free. It was considered too complex for military use, but Merwin owners seldom had a problem with jammed cases. The .45-calibre cartridge did sterling service and remained in service until 1890 when a number of trials' revolvers chambered in .38-calibre were sent to the Ordnance. The popularity of this calibre had been growing among civilian target shooters, and there was no doubt that it was less punishing to shoot and more accurate. In addition, the smaller frame of a .38 revolver could also be made lighter.

Once again the Board of Ordnance embarked on the search for the perfect revolver, taking ninety-four samples each from Colt in the shape of the Model 1889, a double-action revolver with swing-out cylinder and Smith and Wesson, who provided a 6in barrelled .38 Hammerless, with grip safety but with the traditional top-break action. In trials, neither proved perfect. Criticisms of the Colt centred on weak rebound springs and poor pawl design that led to premature wear and insecure cylinder locking. This led to the introduction of the Model 1892 with a positive cylinder lock and stronger spring. The grip safety on the Smith and Wesson was much admired, but it too had problems, for the rust test totally disabled it, its finer machine tolerances causing it to jam, whereas the Colt would continue to function. Another practical problem was that of loading. The Smith and Wesson could be held in either hand to be reloaded, whereas the cylinder of the Colt swung open to the left. On horseback, troopers were taught to hold the reins in their left hand, which meant that they had to open the revolver with their right. To load

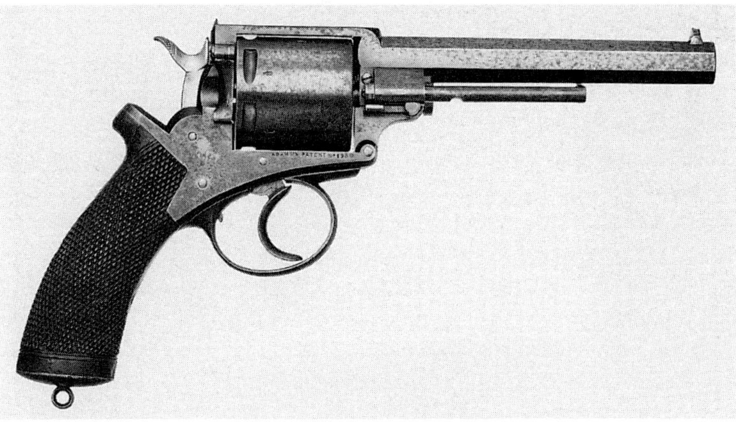

.450 Adams of 1875, showing its solid frame construction. Courtesy of the Trustees of the Royal Armouries.

Colt's first semi-automatic pistol. This a Model .38 Pocket of 1903. Courtesy of the Trustees of the Royal Armouries.

the Colt, this necessitated also holding the revolver in the left hand, so as to use the right to load the cartridges. Officers lobbied the Ordnance Department hard for a revolver with a right-side opening cylinder, but their pleas were ignored. So in 1892 the Board ordered 5,000 Colts, chambered for the .38 Long Colt cartridge. This choice of ammunition seems a curious decision to have made in view of the known lack of power of the .38 bullet, which weighed only 150 grains and had a paltry 18 grain powder charge. Yet despite years of combat evidence showing .44 and .45 were the most effective bullets, the Board appeared unaware of this, noting: 'Whether these arms have the necessary stopping power, the board has no means of knowing.'

However, they persevered with their belief that the Army really needed a .38 and left it to the hapless soldiers to discover whether a .38 really could stop a charging native. It couldn't, as was clearly demonstrated during the vicious war in the Philippines in 1898. Spanish-supported Moro tribesmen were tough, fanatical and utterly deadly at close-range fighting and they inflicted heavy casualties on the well-armed but inexperienced American soldiers. The uselessness of the .38 against such adversaries was illustrated by an incident when a US landing party disembarked on a beach and began to head into the thick jungle fringing the shore. Unexpectedly, a large party of tribesmen burst out of hiding and swarmed down on the soldiers. Most opened fire with their Trapdoor Springfield rifles, but one officer, a very competent target shot, drew his Colt and waited for the leading tribesman to come within range. He then fired six shots in quick succession, but the charging Moro, with spear raised, didn't falter. With seconds to spare, a soldier behind the officer fired with his rifle, sending the man crashing down. Later examination showed that all six shots had struck the tribesman in the chest, the bullets simply being too light to inflict mortal injury. By the end of the campaign, the .45 Single Action Army was again being widely issued and the experience of the army in the Phillipines settled beyond doubt the question of .45 versus .38.

Colt did try to improve the reliability and performance of their double-action revolver, with the introduction in 1897 of the .45 New Service, which was a robust and ultimately reliable design, but the model 1897 was to prove the swansong of the revolver in military use, for by then the Ordnance Board were hard at work testing automatic pistols by Borchardt, Mannlicher, Bergmann, Mauser and a new .38 Automatic Colt. Testing was exhaustive, with many designs proving mechanically fragile, but the Browning-inspired Colt triumphed, one pistol being fired 6,000 times with no jams or mechanical failures, and inevitably the Board adopted it, but chambered for the .45 ACP cartridge.

By the time they had done so, there were no more Indians to fight, no pioneers or miners to protect and no buffalo left to shoot. As the Frontier ended, so the myths began and ultimately the Wild West was born.

Notes

Chapter 1

1 Biggar, H.P. (ed.), *The Works of Samuel de Champlain* (Toronto, 1922–36).
2 Brackenridge, H.M., *Views of Lousiana, 1814*. Reprint (Ann Arbor [edn], Michigan, 1966).
3 Russell, C.P., *Guns of the Early Frontiers* (Los Angeles, 1962).
4 *The Henry Papers*. Order from the Office of Indian Affairs, 11 April 1853. Library of Congress.
5 Kurtz, Rudolph Friederich, 'His Journal, being an Account of his Experiences Among the Fur Trader's and American Indians on the Missouri and Mississippi and the Upper Missouri, 1846–1852'. *Bureau of American Ethnology Bulletin* 1937, 15, ix 382.
6 Hamilton, W.T., *My 60 Years on the Plains* (Norman, Oklahoma, 1960).
7 Palliser, John, *Solitary Rambles and Adventures of a Hunter in the Prairies* (London, 1853).
8 Stratton, Joanna L., *Pioneer Women* (Touchstone, New York, 1981).
9 *The San Antonio Herald* (June 1856).
10 Parkman, Francis, *The Oregon Trail*, E.N. Feltskog (ed.) (Madison, Wisconsin, 1969).
11 Garvaglia, L.A. and C.G. Worman, *Firearms of the American West 1803–1865* (New Mexico, 1984).
12 Holliday, J.S., *The World Rushed In* (New York, 1981).
13 Burton, Sir Richard Francis, *The City of the Saints*, Fawn Brodie (ed.) (New York, 1963).
14 Dimsdale, T., *The Vigilantes of Montana* (Norman, Oklahoma, 1953).
15 Chisholm, James, *The South Pass* (rep) Lincoln Nebraska, 1960).
16 Bellesiles, Michael, 'Guns in America', *The Economist,* 3 July 1999; 'The Origins of Gun Culture in the United States', the *Journal of American History*, Sept 1966; 'Gun Laws in Early America', *Law and History Review,* Autumn 1998; *Lethal Imagination* (New York University Press, 1999).
17 *The Missouri Republican*, St Louis, October 1868.
18 Stuart, Granville, *Diary and Sketchbook of a Journey to America* ([rep] Los Angeles, 1962).
19 Wyatt Earp. *The Untold Story 1848–1880* (Frontier Books, 1963).
20 Roosevelt, Theodore, *Hunting Trips of a Ranchman* (New York, 1927).
21 Letter from Simmons Hardware Company, St Louis to the Colt Company, 1878. Quoted in Garvaglia and Worman, *Firearms of the American West, 1866–1894* (New Mexico, 1985).
22 *Scientific American*, October 1893.
23 Winchester sales brochure dated 1888. Private collection.

Chapter 2

1 Sage, Rufus B., *Rocky Mountain Life* (Chicago, 1859).
2 Ross, Alexander, *Adventures of the First Settlers on the Oregon or Columbia Rivers* (Ann Arbor [edn], Michigan, 1967).
3 Ruxton, George, *Adventures in Mexico and the Rocky Mountains* (New Mexico, 1973).
4 Held, Robert, *The Age of Firearms* (New York, 1957).
5 Larpenteur, Charles, *Forty Years a Fur Trader on the Upper Missouri* (Chicago, 1933).
6 Burton, Sir Richard, *The City of the Saints and across the Rocky Mountains* (London, 1862).
7 Bidwell, John, quoted in Garvaglia and Worman, *Firearms of the American West 1805–1863* (New Mexico, 1984).
8 Ibid.
9 Webb, James J., *Adventures in the Santa Fe Trade*, Ralph Bieber (ed.) (California, 1931).

10 Stuart, Granville, *Forty Years on the Frontier* (California, 1957).
11 Clark, Alvan, *Essay from The American Repertory of the Arts, Sciences and Useful Manufactures*, April 1841, undated reprint.
12 Palliser, John, *Solitary Rambles and Adventures of a Hunter in the Prairies* (London, 1855).
13 Gould, A.C., *Modern American Rifles* (Reprint, South Carolina, no date given).
14 Parkman, Francis, *The Oregon Trail*, (ed.) E.N. Feltskog (Wisconsin, 1969).

Chapter 3

1 Marcy, Randolph P., *Thirty Years of Army Life on the Border* (New York, 1963).
2 *Minutes of The Board of Ordnance*, September, 1776.
3 Sellers, Frank M., *Sharps Firearms* (California, 1978).
4 Olmstead, F., *A Journey through Texas* (London, 1857).
5 Garvaglia and Worman, *Firearms of the American West, 1866–1894* (New Mexico, 1985).
6 Cody W.F., *The Life of Buffalo Bill* (Reprint, London, 1991).
7 War Department General Order Number 9, issued February 1874.
8 Murphy J. Mortimer, *Sporting Adventures in the Far West* (London, 1878).
9 Cook, John R., *The Border and the Buffalo* (Chicago, 1938).
10 Gould A.C., *Modern American Pistols and Revolvers* (Reprint, South Carolina, 1946).

Chapter 4

1 Gregg, Josiah, *Commerce of the Prairies*, (ed.) Max Moorhead (Oklahoma, 1954).
2 Howbert, Irving, *Memories of a Life in the Pikes Peake Region* (London, 1925).
3 Colt Firearms Company advertising broadsheet, circa 1856. Private collection.
4 Breakenridge, William M., *Helldorado* (New Mexico, 1971).
5 Garavaglia and Worman, *Firearms of the American West, 1866–1894* (New Mexico, 1984).
6 Cook, James H., *Fifty Years on the Old Frontier* (New York, 1967).
7 Catalogue of the New Haven Arms Company. Reproduced in 'Ten Old Gun Catalogs' (New York, 1965).
8 Parsons, John E., T*he First Winchesters* (New York, 1955).
9 Winchester Repeating Arms sales brochure, circa 1868. Private collection.
10 Cody, W.F., *The Life of Buffalo Bill* (London, 1991).
11 Report of the Chief of Ordnance to the Secretary of War, 1880. Library of Congress Doc 1, Pt 2, 46th Congress, serial no. 1956.

Chapter 5

1 Reno Court of Enquiry. Ordnance Notes, 1 Oct 1879.
2 Craig, Col H.K., Report to the Secretary of State, 1852 State Papers, Washington 1832–61. Quoted in Scott A. Duff, *Arms for the Nation* (Massachusetts, 1994).
3 Annual Report of the Chief of Ordnance, 1842. National Archives, Washington. Record group no. 156.
4 Inspector's Report of the Eighth Military Department, 1853. National Archives, Washington. Record group 94.
5 Annual Report of the Chief of Ordnance, 1845. National Archives, Washington. Record group 156.
6 Hanger, Maj George, *Advice to Shooters* (London, 1815).
7 Lewis, Meriwether, *The Lewis and Clark Expedition* (Reprint, New York, 1976).
8 Pike, Maj Zebulon, *An account of Expeditions to the Sources of the Mississippi* (Reprint, Michigan,1966).
9 'Civil War Smallarms'. *American Rifleman* supplement (Washington, no date given).
10 Garvaglia and Worman, *Firearms of the American West, 1803–1865* (New Mexico, 1984).
11 Ibid.
12 Petersen, Harold L., *The Book of the Gun* (London, 1963).
13 Annual Report of the Chief of Ordnance, 1856. National Archives, Washington. Record group 156.
14 Crook, Gen George, *My Autobiography* (Reprint, Oklahoma, 1960).
15 Meyers, Augustus, *Ten Years In the Ranks of the U.S. Army* (New York, 1922).
16 *Gettysburg, the Confederate High Tide* (Time-Life publishing, 1985).
17 Annual Report of the Chief of Ordnance, 1862. National Archives, Washington. Record group 156.

18 *Minnesota in the Indian and Civil Wars*. No author cited (Reprint, Minnesota, 1972).
19 Official Records of the Union and Confederate Armies, National Archives, Washington. Series 1, 15; 649.
20 Garvaglia and Worman, *Firearms of the American West, 1803–1865* (New Mexico, 1984).

Chapter 6

1 Ibid.
2 Senate Ordnance Document No. 99, 40th Congress. National Archives, Washington.
3 Austerman, Wayne, *Virginia Cavalcade* (Arms Gazette, Winter 1985).
4 Merrill, Sam H., *Memoirs of the First Maine and Ist District Cavalry in the Civil War* (Reprint, New York, 1937).
5 Annual Report of the Chief of Ordnance, 1864. National Archives, Washington. Record group 156,
6 Garvaglia and Worman, *Firearms of the American West, 1866–1894* (New Mexico, 1985).
7 Annual Report of the Chief of Ordnance, 1873. National Archives, Washington. Record group 156.
8 'Description and Rules for the Management of the Springfield Rifle, Carbine and Army Revolvers' (Springfield National Armory, Massachusetts, 1874).
9 DuMont, John S., *Custer Battle Guns* (New Hampshire, 1988).
10 Annual Report of the Chief of Ordnance, 1880. National Archives, Washington. Record group 156.

Chapter 7

1 Irving, W., *The Adventures of Captain Bonneville* (Oklahoma, 1962).
2 Ibid.
3 Haven, Charles and Frank Belden, *A History of the Colt Revolver* (New York, 1946).
4 Garvaglia and Worman, *Firearms of the American West, 1803–1865* (New Mexico, 1984).
5 *The Alta California Newspaper*, San Francisco, 1859.
6 Canton, Frank M., *Frontier Trails* (Oklahoma, 1966).
7 Olmstead, Frederick Law, *A Journey through Texas* (London, 1858).
8 Burton, Sir Richard, *The City of the Saints and across the Rocky Mountains* (London, 1862).
9 Jinks, Roy, *The History of Smith and Wesson* (California, 1992).
10 Twain, Mark, *Roughing It* (Reprint, London, 1972).
11 Brewerton, George Douglas, *Overland with Kit Carson* (Reprint, New York, 1930).
12 Smith and Wesson correspondence records. Courtesy of Roy Jinks.
13 Gould, A.C., *Modern American Pistols and Revolvers* (Reprint, South Carolina, 1946).
14 'Conversations with H.H.Crittenden', 1882. Published as a facsimile of the Crittenden Memoirs. No date given.

Chapter 8

1 Report on the Expenses of the Ordnance Department 1817–1821. Library of Congress, record No. 1823a.
2 Hicks, Maj James E., *Notes on U.S. Ordnance* (New York, 1940).
3 Correspondence of Samuel Walker to Colt Firearms, November 1846. Quoted in W.B. Edwards, *The Story of Colt's Revolver* (Pennsylvania, 1953).
4 Ferguson, Lt Samuel, Kansas Historical Society Collection (Reprint, no date given).
5 Annual Report of the Chief of Ordnance, 1862. Official Records of the Union and Confederate Armies. National Archives, Washington. Group 165.
6 Bondi, Sgt Augustus, quoted in J.G. Rosa, *Guns of the American West* (Dorset, 1988).
7 Quoted in Garavaglia and Worman, *Firearms of the American West, 1803–1865* (New Mexico, 1984).
8 Smith and Wesson correspondence records. Courtesy of Roy Jinks.
9 Records of the Chief of Ordnance, 1874, National Archives, Document no. 156.
10 Official Record of the Court of Enquiry, Chicago 1879. Records by Col W.A. Graham (ed.) (California, 1951).
11 Custer, Gen George A., *My Life on the Plains* (Reprint, New York, 1968).

Index